Europe on 5 Wrong Turns a Day

Europe on 5 Wrong Turns a Day

One Man, Eight Countries, One Vintage Travel Guide

Doug Mack

A Perigee Book

A PERIGEE BOOK
Published by the Penguin Group
Penguin Group (USA) Inc.
375 Hudson Street, New York, New York 10014, USA

Penguin Group (Canada), 90 Eglinton Avenue East, Suite 700, Toronto, Ontario M4P 2Y3, Canada
(a division of Pearson Penguin Canada Inc.)
Penguin Books Ltd., 80 Strand, London WC2R 0RL, England
Penguin Group Ireland, 25 St. Stephen's Green, Dublin 2, Ireland (a division of Penguin Books Ltd.)
Penguin Group (Australia), 250 Camberwell Road, Camberwell, Victoria 3124, Australia
(a division of Pearson Australia Group Pty. Ltd.)
Penguin Books India Pvt. Ltd., 11 Community Centre, Panchsheel Park, New Delhi—110 017, India
Penguin Group (NZ), 67 Apollo Drive, Rosedale, Auckland 0632, New Zealand
(a division of Pearson New Zealand Ltd.)
Penguin Books (South Africa) (Pty.) Ltd., 24 Sturdee Avenue, Rosebank, Johannesburg 2196,
South Africa

Penguin Books Ltd., Registered Offices: 80 Strand, London WC2R 0RL, England

While the author has made every effort to provide accurate telephone numbers and Internet addresses at
the time of publication, neither the publisher nor the author assumes any responsibility for errors or for
changes that occur after publication. Further, the publisher does not have any control over and does not
assume any responsibility for author or third-party websites or their content.

EUROPE ON 5 WRONG TURNS A DAY

First edition: April 2012

Library of Congress Cataloging-in-Publication Data

Mack, Doug.
   Europe on 5 wrong turns a day : one man, eight countries, one vintage travel guide / Doug Mack.
      p. cm.
   ISBN 978-0-399-53732-5
   1. Tourism—Europe—History.   2. Mack, Doug—Travel—Europe.   I. Title.   II. Title: Europe on
five wrong turns a day.
   G155.E8M298 2012
   914.04'5612—dc23

                                                                                  2011042234

PRINTED IN THE UNITED STATES OF AMERICA

10   9   8   7   6   5   4   3   2   1

This book describes the real experiences of real people. The author has disguised the identities of some,
and in some instances created composite characters, but none of these changes has affected the truth-
fulness and accuracy of his story. Penguin is committed to publishing works of quality and integrity. In
that spirit, we are proud to offer this book to our readers; however, the story, the experiences, and the
words are the author's alone.

Most Perigee books are available at special quantity discounts for bulk purchases for sales promotions,
premiums, fund-raising, or educational use. Special books, or book excerpts, can also be created to fit
specific needs. For details, write: Special Markets, Penguin Group (USA) Inc., 375 Hudson Street, New
York, New York 10014.

For my parents,
who taught me to love travel and
books and travel books. Here's one
more for your collection.

ACKNOWLEDGMENTS

Writing is a solitary endeavor, except that it's not—especially not a travel memoir, since the basic nature of the task involves dropping in on unfamiliar cultures and basically spying on strangers' lives. So thank you, first of all, to all the people I met on my journey, locals and tourists alike, who made my Not-So-Grand Tour come alarmingly close to being genuinely grand. (Even you, Drunk Girl in Amsterdam.) I've changed many of their names and identifying characteristics throughout the book, for purposes of privacy, but they're all very much real people. Also, because I wasn't always taking notes, some conversations are re-created from memory, to the best of my ability—although all of the best lines are 100 percent verbatim.

My literary agent, Elizabeth Evans at the Jean V. Naggar Literary Agency, understood what I was trying to do with this book before even I did and was unfailingly supportive and a delight to work with. Writing this book was, of course, a journey in itself, and in Marian Lizzi, my editor, I had the ideal guide, showing me the way with patience and aplomb, and steering me back on course when my path started to meander (as it has a tendency to do). My deepest thanks also to Christina Lundy and the entire team at Perigee.

Several smart, patient friends read the manuscript at various stages, and their comments and guidance helped whip it into shape: Hannah Kaplan, Sebastian Celis, Rosalyn Claret, Alex Starace, James Lloyd, and most of all, Twin Cities travel-writing all-stars Frank Bures, Jason Albert, Leif Pettersen, and Maggie Ryan Sandford. And then there is Dennis Cass, guru and mentor and patient explainer of the publishing process, without whose initial push this would—truly—still be merely an idea kicking around in the back of my head.

I also would have been completely, panic-inducingly lost in the publishing world without the assistance of David Farley and the ongoing support of Michael Yessis and Jim Benning at WorldHum.com and the whole crew at the Key West Literary Seminar, who kindly keep letting me crash their party.

A multitude of other friends and colleagues provided more general but much-needed encouragement and advice plus soul-soothing pastries and beer, although now that I think about it, perhaps they were just trying to silence my incessant rambling on the history of tourism. In any case, thank you, Shirley Sailors, Amanda Nadelberg, John Neely, Rebecca Celis, David Brusie, Elizabeth Olson, Andrew Owen, Becky Fritz Owen, Maren Stoddard, John and Karly Case, Alexis Grant, Joseph Quintela, Rajan and Sunayana Vatassery, Vaughn Kelly, Chris Christofferson, Diane Sass, Michael Crull, and David Heide.

At various points in the writing process, I found myself pounding my head against the wall as I tried to track down assorted figures and pieces of background information. I avoided major brain (and drywall) damage thanks to the generous assistance of Sherry Ott, Steffen Horak, Jessalyn Pinneo, Arijit Guha, and others who pointed me toward the necessary information and insights. Feel free to blame them for any errors . . . just kidding, of course.

As will become evident in the following pages, I owe an unpayable debt to my parents, Bob and Patricia, and my sister, Elisabeth—my early enablers in writing, reading, and traveling, and unyielding in their support as I've chased my dreams, even the crazy ones. Thanks also to James Munger, brother-in-law and miracle worker, who restored my corrupted manuscript file two days before deadline. (Yeah. That happened.)

Mille grazie to Ann Schaefer (née Dynes), Mom's traveling companion—both in 1967 and to this day—for allowing me to peek in on her life, too. *Merci beaucoup* to Paula Hirschoff, another traveler of their era, for sharing her stories and scrapbook with me.

My friend Lee turns out to be not just a talented writer and editor (and was another key manuscript reader) but also, of course, a fantastic sidekick. Lee, man, I owe you a beer or ten. In Brussels. Also, I will note that Lee's real name is Michael Lee Cook (he asked me to use his middle name as his *nom de sidekick*), and you really ought to check out his own writing at his splendidly named website, www.LiteratureIsNotDead .com.

And Arthur Frommer. Though we've never met or spoken, I'm profoundly grateful to you for spurring me—and my mother, and millions of others—on to one of my life's grand adventures. I hope this book is a testament to your legacy—both that of your seminal guidebook and, more important, your continual exhortation to the masses to go out there and see the world. It's an amazing place. Go see it sometime.

CONTENTS

Nobody goes there anymore. It's too crowded.

—YOGI BERRA

INTRODUCTION

The Book That Started It All

I say that Europe can today be traveled,
comfortably and well, for living costs per person (that
is, room and board) of no more than $5 a day.

—Europe on Five Dollars a Day

I t began as most things in my life do: awkwardly.

It was an October morning and I was at a book festival in downtown Minneapolis, killing time before meeting my mother, Patricia, with whom I was going to attend one of the readings. As I browsed through a table of musty secondhand volumes, I chuckled at all the ridiculous titles, things like *The Tao of Tea Cozies* and *How to Get Rich in 2,451 Easy Steps*. My eyes landed on one called *Europe on Five Dollars a Day*. Right, I thought. Good luck with that.

I'd heard of the book before, of course, and I knew, in the abstract, that the promise of its title was once feasible. Now, though? Now it seemed about as laughably outdated as those medieval maps with the areas outside of Europe unmarked but for the warning "here be dragons." I thought of its potential as a conversation piece on my coffee table. I'd show it to friends, and we'd share a good laugh before resuming our usual conversation about how much our jobs sucked and how we never did anything cool anymore—too old for college shenanigans but, in our midtwenties, far too young for midlife crises. The book would sit unopened, like most coffee table tomes, its brightly colored cover serving as a piece of found art, a cheesy relic of retro design and the long-lost innocence of a bygone era. At ten cents, it was a cheap punch line. So I bought it.

A few minutes later, I spotted Mom.

"Look what I found," I said, waving the book and snickering. *"Europe on Five Dollars a Day*! Pretty funny, huh?"

But she didn't get the joke. She didn't laugh. She didn't even roll her eyes, which is her usual response when I try a bit too hard to be a hip, ironic smart aleck.

Instead, her face lit up with manic glee—you'd think I was showing her a winning lottery ticket. She danced, she hugged me, she squealed, she shrieked, "Is that for *me*? Where did you find it?!"

As I struggled to make sense of her giddiness, my face cycled through a Grand Canyon's worth of reds. I mean, far be it from me to confess to being one of those horrible people who's still embarrassed by his mother even when he's an adult. But the excited babbling, the jumping up and down, the frantic hugging: these were not the signs of a sane person. Heads turned to gawk at us. The late-morning sun slanted through the windows and sought us out across the cavernous room, spreading past the aisles of book vendors, past the literary magazine booths with their hip young staffers, past the book-signing tables where melancholy authors sat fidgeting with their uncapped pens, and casting a spotlight on us, the Weirdo Duo disrupting the literary quietude. A bookseller cast us an irritated glare and let out a sigh that threatened to progress to a full-on librarian shush.

I laughed nervously and scanned the table for *Invisibility for Dummies*. I waited for Mom to calm down a bit, then stammered, "No, I . . . What?! It's for *me*."

"Bob didn't put you up to this?" she asked, still out of breath. Bob's my father; her husband; the man with whom she had just spent a year in Scotland, the culmination of a lifelong dream and the logical result of their shared incurable wanderlust, which turns out to be a hereditary trait.

"Um, no."

"I've been looking for that," she said. "It's the book I used with Ann."

Ah. Finally things were starting to make sense.

Mom was one of the original hippie travelers, touring Europe with her friend Ann for ten weeks in 1967, when she was twenty-one, shortly before my parents got married. That much I already knew, because she still talks about it—rather a lot, actually, and often with a wistful tone and a slight smirk on her face, as though remembering details that she never intends to tell. It was a seminal event in her life, the catalyst for her peripatetic ways and the underlying reason why my childhood story times were heavy on the travel writing, as likely to include Steinbeck's *Travels with Charley* or a Calvin Trillin essay on street food as any of the classics of the children's lit canon.

So this was her guide, the key to that famous trip, the corner-stone of her life as a traveler. The book seemed to acquire new weight in my hand. I looked down at its cover, somehow expecting that, as happens when Indiana Jones finds such relics, it would

suddenly begin exhibiting supernatural powers—glowing or hum-
ming or conjuring spirits.

Mom took the book from my hand and gazed at it admiringly.
"I've been *looking* for this," she repeated.

"Yeah, apparently," I said.

"I still have all my postcards to Bob, you know."

"Seriously?"

"All the postcards, all the letters—they're still around somewhere. I'm sure they're very romantic. Or boring." She paused,
then added, brightly, "I think there's even a letter I wrote on toilet
paper! We were really on a budget."

The fact that she still had them wasn't particularly surprising,
given that my parents seem averse to throwing out anything with
words on it. This, I suppose, is the dream of all pack rats: that
someday, your children will want to examine some aspect of your
past, and you will be able to crow triumphantly that this—*this!*—is
precisely why you have spent the last forty-plus years saving every
scrap of paper that has come into your possession, and which you
have sort-of-kind-of archived in assorted Leaning Towers of Clutter that fill your house, creating both a sense of sprawling
intellectualism—so much to read, so little time!—and a more tangible feeling of *fire hazard*.

Actually *finding* a particular piece of paper was, of course, an
entirely different matter. Unlikely, probably impossible.

But somehow she did it—almost immediately. I went over to my
parents' house to observe this miracle and discovered that, sure
enough, she and my father—who had been back home in Minneapolis, in architecture school—had kept every last letter, postcard,
and aerogram (remember those?) to each other. Most had been
in the living room all along, throughout my entire childhood,

crammed into shoeboxes and stashed under a coffee table along with stray kindling for the fireplace, a creepy antique duck decoy, and an impressive collection of spider webs (which is why I'd never looked under there before).

I sat on their living room floor and sifted through the contents of the boxes, taking care not to get them mixed in with the rest of the clutter scattered about the room.

From one-sentence postcards to meandering, multipage letters, they were treasure troves of observations on the profound joy of travel, the disappointing nature of certain "must-see" destinations (Louvre, this means you), the constant torments of French plumbing and lecherous Italian men, and, of course, gooshy comments about how much they missed each other. They evoked, as images of the past often do, a sense of innocence and wonder, a free-spirited peace with the world that was far removed from my own existence.

Every few minutes, after reading Mom's description of an exotic place or thrilling adventure, I paused and ruminated in frustration, wondering once again why I'd never done anything remotely this interesting, why I'd never acted on my passed-down wanderlust. I'd done a bit of travel writing, but always felt like a phony, culling from family trips abroad and a few solo excursions to the wilds of . . . Chicago, Key West, or Seattle. I'd never been anywhere more exotic on my own.

After an adolescence and college years of résumé-padding achievement, I had found myself stagnant in life and stuck in a dead-end job as a marketing assistant. I was so exhausted and frustrated at the end of each day that I didn't have the energy to do much other than lie on my futon and find comfort and escape in those travel books on which I'd been raised. It was, I'll confess, the stereotypical ennui of the overeducated, underachieving middle-class kid who suddenly finds himself, much to his confusion and dismay, in adulthood.

I also had never experienced anything like the love my parents had for each other—and still have today, I'm happy to report. Each letter bore testament to their mutual heartache of separation and ended with what is still their typical sign-off, IDLY. I Do Love You. I wanted some of that for myself. My sister had gotten married over the summer, as had my college roommate. All of my friends were pairing off, getting hitched, like normal people do. I, however, seemed to be the master of awkward dates and relationships with the life span of a fruit fly.

Well, no more, I decided. If Europe could help launch my mother's life, perhaps it could relaunch mine. And why not use this old guidebook? Even if it didn't have the supernatural powers of an Indiana Jones relic, maybe it still had some of that old magic—maybe, like a divining rod, it could lead me to Truth, Enlightenment, Bliss, my own love story, my own gooshy letters. This would be my shortcut to Happily Ever After.

Right?

I'm aware that most people don't go looking for happiness on the beaten path. "Enlightenment" is a word that conjures images of meditating in a forest or consulting a toga-attired guru on an isolated mountaintop—not tour groups and souvenir shops and overpriced, overrun landmarks. The term these conjure to many people and pretty much every single travel writer is, most likely, "godawful."

But I'll acknowledge right here that I'm no Marco Polo, no bold adventurer. I'm kind of a wimp. Trekking across Nepal holds zero appeal for me, and meditating in a forest sounds like a great way to get eaten by a bear.

And actually, if you're a travel writing addict, as I am, you may have noticed something: Himalayan odysseys, quaint towns, and "the Europe no one knows about" have, in fact, become tediously familiar destinations in modern travel literature. I'll let those other writers have their epic tales of climbing K2 or skateboarding across the Sahara or living for a year in a sun-dappled, history-steeped Mediterranean village, where, by international law, said writers must meet delightfully eccentric locals, ruminate on the importance of tradition in the modern world, and learn "what really matters in life."

My journey was going to be an arguably more treacherous one, a voyage into the heart of straight-up, cliché-ridden tourism, a path seldom taken by more bold travelers for the very fact that it is so well beaten.

Enough with the road less traveled. This would be a full immersion in the modern tourist experience.

Which is, in part, the creation of *Europe on Five Dollars a Day* or, more specifically, the man who wrote it, Arthur Frommer.

Tourism as we know it today traces its roots to the concept of the Grand Tour, beginning with seventeenth-century British aristocrats who journeyed to the Continent ostensibly as something of an informal but dignified academic exercise, but often involving a certain level of timeless tourist debauchery—heavy drinking, sexual escapades, barroom brawls. Think of it as Ye Olde Spring Break. According to Tim Moore's book *The Grand Tour*—in which Moore follows in the footsteps of the original Grand Tourist, the amusingly crass and eternally unlucky Thomas Coryate—there were some forty thousand Englishmen on the Continent in 1786. In 1851, Thomas Cook initiated the package tour, leading a group from Leicester, England, to the Paris Exhibition.

The term "tourist" dates to around 1780, according to the *Oxford English Dictionary*. The pejorative usage followed shortly, with the English diarist Francis Kilvert grousing, in 1870, "Of all noxious animals . . . the most noxious is a tourist." It's a timeless sentiment, to be sure, for those who live in tourist-attracting locales and perhaps even more so for those fellow travelers who want nothing to do with the masses of people who happen to have journeyed to the same places as they—in the immortal words of Evelyn Waugh, "The tourist is the other fellow."* Someone else, not you.

Still, in 1957, one could use the term "tourist" without shame or irony, as Frommer does in the very first line of *Europe on Five Dollars a Day*:

> This is a book for American tourists who
>
>   a) own no oil wells in Texas
>   b) are unrelated to the Aga Khan
>   c) have never struck it rich in Las Vegas
>
> and who *still* want to enjoy a wonderful European vacation.

------

*This is often misquoted as "The tourist is always the other chap." If Waugh were alive to make the edit, he might change it himself, the fake version being a snappier and more memorable summation of the point he had been making throughout "The Tourist's Manual," the 1934 *Vogue* essay from which the quote is taken.

This was one of the first things that struck me about reading *Europe on Five Dollars a Day*: its casual use of the terms "tourist" and "vacation," words that make many twenty-first-century travelers recoil in horror.

As I read through the book and pored over my mother's letters, I found myself continually amazed by—and I know how obvious this realization is going to sound, but bear with me—how super-crazy-astonishingly outdated it all seemed. It wasn't just the cost increases, although I still can't quite believe that five dollars was ever enough. It was the effort involved in booking a plane ticket—through a travel agent—back then, compared to the ease of comparison-shopping on Travelocity and Expedia now. It was the fact that Dad wrote to Mom in care of the American Express and Thomas Cook Travel Agency offices in various cities, and Frommer took care to list the addresses of these offices across the Continent, presuming that collecting mail was a daily ritual for all travelers. It was Frommer's description of the nightclub where you could ride a horse on the dance floor, his politically incorrect (and two-page-long) section on "girl-watching" in Stockholm, his recommendation that if you wish to visit East Berlin, you should "register your name with the American MP's at Checkpoint Charlie, tell them the time at which you plan to return, and if you're not there at that time, they'll take action." (Let us pause for a moment to give thanks that World War III was not accidentally started by a tardy tourist.) It was the general tone of the book, lyrical and lively in a way that modern guidebooks rarely are, with a unique personality shining through, a voice that I came to think of as a peripatetic hybrid of Ann Landers and Falstaff. It was, most of all, the breathless wonder and delight with which both Frommer and my mother described European travel on what we now call the beaten path, the tourist trail.

. . .

Journeys abroad for purposes of leisure rather than immigration were mostly an elite endeavor for Americans until the advent of affordable air travel, and it's here that the story of tourism—and, yes, let's call it that—really begins. Quick-and-dirty version: tourist-class fares started in 1952, the first jumbo jet took off three years later, and the long-haul commercial jet trip debuted with a New York–to–Paris flight on Pan Am in 1958. By then, transatlantic journeys by air already outnumbered those by boat. The following year saw the debut of the key to frugal, long-term, intracontinental travel: the Eurail pass.

The evolving postwar psyche also helped fuel what was to become a travel boom. It was the era of the Beats and *On the Road* and *The Man in the Gray Flannel Suit*, a time of prosperity but also of restlessness and discontent about boom-time conformity in an aspirational society. As Maxine Feifer points out in her book *Tourism in History*: "In the era of the 'lifestyle,' one expressed oneself more at leisure than at work; by one's hobbies, one's possessions, one's tastes. . . . The tour represented them all. Or, as the anthropologists saw it, the tour was the 'sacred journey' to a plane which gave meaning to ordinary life." The U.S. government played a large part in this, promoting tourism as an integral component of the Marshall Plan, a sort of soft-sell diplomacy and financial assistance. "Vacations, not donations," went the Eisenhower administration line. Government officials even met with the *New York Times*, *Li'l Abner* cartoonist Al Capp, and other popular-media figures to discuss subtle promotion of overseas travel to the American middle class. Going abroad was a key part of the new American Dream.

As all of these pieces were coming together to create the infra-structure and demand for affordable European travel, Arthur Frommer stepped in with the how-to manual for putting the desires into action: *Europe on Five Dollars a Day*, which he first published in 1957. At the time, most other guidebooks available in the American market, such as the Fodor's Modern Guides line and *Fielding's Travel Guide to Europe*, were light on budget-oriented tips and heavy on lyrical prose and rumination. Fodor's first effort, *1936 . . . On the Continent*, checked in at 1,200 pages and contained an extended section on French wallpaper: "it is populated either by flowers or by birds in all colours of the rainbow, so that you see them even when your eyes are shut. . . ." *Europe on Five Dollars a Day* (or *E5D*) was different. With its manageable size and straight-forward manner—twelve cities in the initial 1957 version; 124 pages; each chapter divided into sections listing hotels, restau-rants, and other items-of-note; each of these further broken down by neighborhood; the listings all bold-type recommendations and pithy descriptions—it was simply more user-friendly for the novice traveler than its predecessors. (By 1963, the year of my edition, the book had grown to include seventeen cities.)

In its egalitarian approach and tone, too, this was a book that aimed for a broad audience, one that had never traveled abroad before—like my mother. On the first page of his introduction, Frommer mocked *Fielding's*:

> *I have one of the better-known European guidebooks before me as I write. This tome states that one really can't consider staying in Paris at hotels other than the Ritz, the Crillon or the Plaza Athenee. . . . It shudders at any form of European train transpor-tation other than First Class. It maps out, in other words, the*

short, quick road to insolvency that most American tourists have
been traveling for years.

He then offered, as his alternative, the words that launched the
era of budget travel as we know it: "I say that Europe can today be
traveled, comfortably and well, for living costs per person (that is,
room and board) of no more than $5 a day." It was nothing less than
a manifesto for the common traveler, a thin volume with a cobbled-
together feel and a populist message presented in a spirited voice.

Frommer doesn't get much credit for opening tourism up to the
American masses, but this line in particular and the book's tone
and format in general seem proof positive that he was to travel as
Julia Child was to food: the public figure who arrived at just the
right cultural moment and said, with a light but nurturing tone,
"You can do this. It's not that hard. Here's how."

Just fifteen years after the first edition of *Europe on Five Dol-*
lars a Day, a 1972 profile in *Harper's* observed, "[Frommer] has
done more to change if not the face then at least the feel of Europe
than any living man. It is probable, for example, that he is indirectly responsible for the widespread use of English as a second
language on the Continent."

The mass tourism era had officially begun.

In the late 1950s, Europe welcomed (or at least tolerated) some
eight hundred thousand American visitors annually, a number
that rose to 4 million by the early 1970s. The trend was so striking,
its ramifications so profound, that the United Nations declared
1967—the year my mother set out on her own Grand Tour—the
International Tourist Year. By 2009, approximately 10.6 million
Americans traveled to Europe (down from a peak of 12.3 million in

2007), with the United Kingdom, Italy, and France topping the list of destinations.

Half a century after his first book came out, "the dean of travel," as the *Los Angeles Times* crowned him in 2009, is still going strong, even in his eighties. Each week, he pens a syndicated newspaper column and hosts a radio show with his daughter, Pauline. In a potent symbol of How Times Have Changed, he also has a blog on Frommers.com, with well over a thousand posts, and where he still preaches the gospel that spending less means enjoying more, offering tips on everything from Caribbean cruises to skiing in eastern Europe.

From that first volume of *E5D*, Frommer's publishing house has expanded to 470 different titles, including *Europe for Dummies* and *Frommer's 500 Adrenaline Adventures*; annual sales for the company's guidebooks are now more than 2.5 million copies. Frommer's also has an extensive website, which contains information on some 4,300 destinations.

The guidebook industry as a whole has seen equally astonishing growth. Lonely Planet, perhaps the best-known guidebook line today, was founded in 1973 by Tony and Maureen Wheeler and has grown to some 650 different titles; it sold its hundred-millionth book in 2010. And then there's Fodor's, Rough Guides, Let's Go, Moon Handbooks, Rick Steves, Michelin, Berlitz . . . the list is staggering.

A few days before I set off on my trip, I trekked to the mammoth Barnes & Noble in downtown Minneapolis to gape at the guidebook selection. I wondered if the experience would be like that of a recent immigrant on his or her first trip to an American grocery store, a sense of incomprehensible excess and overwhelming, almost repulsive variety.

Yes. It was. For starters, *Europe on Five Dollars a Day*'s direct descendant, *Frommer's Europe*—note the title's lack of a daily budget; that ended in 2007 with *Europe from $95 a Day*—was comparatively expansive and extravagant, with 1,088 pages plus a fold-out map. I picked it up and marveled at its weight and size, trying to reconcile this behemoth with Frommer's lengthy warnings, in my own volume, about the "burdens of baggage."

And then were the spin-offs and competitors, a breathtaking number of narrowly focused, activity-specific titles targeted to those interested in the local food, shopping, art, music, sports, history, architecture, religion, hiking, or ways to get their groove on (see *Rough Guide: World Party*). There are books for those traveling with kids, with pets, solo, or via cruise ship, rail, RV, bike, or car. There's now hardly a speck of land that doesn't have its own weighty guide or several—surely the collective amount of paper constitutes a decent-sized swath of forest that, were it still standing, would have its own competing guides. I have not yet found one titled *The Extreme Athlete's Guide to the Vatican*, but surely it exists.

Even aside from the titles, a glance at the back covers of the books demonstrated that these were not my mother's travel guides. On the back of *E5D*, there is a black-and-white photo of Arthur Frommer wearing a suit and an expression of assertive pensiveness. Above the photo, in large, bold text, is a laudatory blurb from *Travel* magazine: "The mere possession of EUROPE ON $5 A DAY must become the conspicuous mark of a traveling American from now on."

Conspicuous mark? Actually, that doesn't sound like a selling point at all. To the modern traveler, the blurb basically translates to, "Buy this book and you'll stand out like the unoriginal, stereotypical Ugly American tourist you are."

The 2011 edition of *Rick Steves' Europe Through the Back Door* offers on its back cover a similar photo-and-pithy-text formula but a vastly different overall message. At the top, there's an amiably goofy snapshot of Steves, a beatific beatnik with a wry smile. The text below the photo all but promises that under this happy wanderer's guidance, you'll immediately blend in with the locals and will probably be the only American around, anyway. "Avoid crowds and tourist scams," it pledges. Delight in Rick's "favorite off-the-beaten-path towns, trails, and natural wonders."

Such promises are, of course, effectively negated by guidebooks themselves—in an inversion of the Yogi Berra line that serves as the epigraph to this book, everyone goes to these places because they're not crowded. But by the time you get to one of these hidden gems, you'll often find dozens of other tourists already there, each one bearing the same guidebook and the same glum expression that says, "This is *not* what I was promised."

In addition to all of the dead-tree guides, there are countless websites ready with advice from the experts and the masses. Flickr and Google Earth allow you to see your destination before you even leave your house; TripAdvisor and others offer a daunting variety of information and reviews (many of them conflicting) about hotels and restaurants; Expedia and Travelocity fill your email in-box with special offers and hot deals. Type "France travel guide" into Google and you'll get more than 9 million hits; post a request for tips on Facebook or Twitter and you'll get another 9 million responses, give or take. And the rise of smartphones means you can access all of this information on the go, wherever you are; everything and everywhere has its own smartphone app. There's even cell phone service at Mount Everest base camp.

But where's the fun? Where's the adventure? It's not just "If it's Tuesday, this must be Belgium," it's "If it's seven o'clock, this must be the Café Le Petit Obsessive-Compulsive, this wine must be the pinot noir that I read about on Wines.com, the server must be Yvette, who got high marks on TripAdvisor (thank God it's not François—he sounded dreadful), and I have to be done eating by eight o'clock so that I can follow the Google Map instructions to the subway station and use the Paris Metro app to catch the train to Montmartre, where I will snap a photo *exactly* like the one I saw on WikiTravel, which I will then upload to Facebook at the Internet café recommended on the bulletin boards at Yahoo! Travel because it accepts American credit cards."

Even getting ostensibly off the beaten path can be all too effortless, all too predictable—never before has it been easier to journey to the farthest corners of the world and know exactly, down to the minute, down to the vista, what you'll see and do, to be so overloaded with information that you miss out on the wonder, serendipity, and sense of blissful disorientation that are among the most profound joys of travel.

I'm as guilty of this as anyone, my travels tethered to a strict, neurotically overplanned itinerary and freighted with highly specific expectations—and never quite as fun as I'd imagined. Well, enough of that. Time to try something else, something more adventurous (well, by my standards) and more willfully ignorant. I would do the old-fashioned Grand Tour relying solely on my old-fashioned guidebook, my mother's letters, and—*gulp*—my wits. No

Internet research. No Lonely Planet. No safety net. Wave good-bye to the ol' comfort zone.

I would go to Florence and Paris first, because Italy and France are two of the top three most-visited European countries for American tourists (behind only the United Kingdom), and Mom had especially interesting things to say about both of these cities. A very short tour for now, since my travel funds were low and my vacation time from my job was more or less nonexistent. But if I survived those first two cities, well, maybe I'd just have to figure out how to go back again later.

As much as possible, I'd stay in the same hotels as Frommer, eat in the same restaurants, take in the same sights—the same route, if not the same budget, since I knew that five dollars would probably get me a cup of coffee, a day-old pastry, and a trash-bag mattress beneath a bridge.

This, then, was my mission: to chart a different course, one firmly on the standard tourist path, but undertaken without the familiarity and knowledge of the modern information-overloaded traveler. To see if it could be done, to see what would happen, to connect the dots between the previous generation of travel and my own, and to find out if there were any stories left to tell or joy to find on that all-too-beaten path.

Florence

Authentically Overwhelmed

*[Florence's museums] contain priceless collections
of the world's greatest art, and they require slow,
unhurried, reflective visits for maximum enjoyment.*

—Europe on Five Dollars a Day

In the days before I departed for Europe, Italy was all over the news, with common themes of discord, tumult, corruption, confrontation. Rome was drowning in traffic and street crime; Naples was drowning in garbage and organized crime; Venice was just plain drowning. This was the reality of modern life. The Italy of tourist daydreams was now located somewhere between Atlantis and Oz, a lost land of wistful fantasy.

In Frommer's day, apparently, the fantasy had been a reality. "A vast number of Americans saw 'La Dolce Vita' and have ached to get here ever since. They won't be disappointed," he says of Rome, and his chapters on Venice and Florence carry the same sentiment: Hollywood was right. *Sun-dappled rolling hills! Renaissance statues in every piazza! Simple-but-wise peasants offering you wine and pasta!*

But I knew better. Those rolling hills would now be porcupined with cell phone towers, the piazzas crammed with cargo-shorted tourists pushing past buskers screeching dated pop songs, the statues usurped by fiberglass replicas (with missing limbs magically reattached), the charming peasants replaced by pickpockets and aggressive souvenir hawkers, the pasta tasting suspiciously like it had been prepared by Signor SpaghettiO.

So what the heck was going on, I wondered, as I peered out the window of the bus from the Pisa airport to Florence and saw a place that was just . . . just . . . *so freaking Italian.* The people, the landscape, the architecture: everything matched the stereotypical representations put forth by Hollywood, tourist brochures, wine bottle labels, and other purveyors of fantasies and half-truths. It was, as Frommer suggested, a "fantastic dream."

Those cute little houses in the Tuscan Villa style were actual, well, you know, Tuscan villas, in all their authentic, charmingly rustic, picturesquely crumbling glory. Outside each one, a wood-burning oven puffed quaint little plumes of smoke. Queues of handsomely gnarled olive trees marched insouciantly to the horizon. Old women with walking sticks hobbled regally by the side of the road. The famously manic Italian style of driving was on full display, with scooter drivers zigzagging through traffic like so many Prada-clad mosquitoes. Even the sky seemed art directed: a dome of piercing cerulean perfectly complementing the deep green of the rolling hills and scattered with a handful of pert cotton-ball clouds. It was postcard-perfect, as though contrived by the local tourism board—"Giovanni, here they come! Go drive past them on your Vespa! Carmela, hide the satellite dish and put your delightfully scruffy goats out in the field! Quickly! *Prego. Ciao.*"

Frommer starts the Florence chapter by claiming that "this is a city for reflection." To which I say: *nuh-uh*. At least not at first. It turns out that my initial reaction to such stunning sights is not rumination but blissed-out gaping. To wit: here and there, I spotted the expected trappings of twenty-first-century life— anti-immigrant graffiti, dreary industrial sites, goat herders talking on cell phones, ads for American corporations—but my brain had already become so thoroughly rewired, so taken with the soma of stereotypes fulfilled, that every time the trenchant, sarcastic internal monologue began, the giddy, altered-state tourist immediately drowned it out: *Holy crap, look at that adorable little old man in that absurdly lush vineyard—where's my camera?!*

When the bus rolled into Florence's historic city center, the authenticity high turned into an enrapturing overdose at the up-close sight of the winding cobblestoned passageways encroached by ineffably Old World architecture: arched doorways, elaborate cornices and corbels, massive shutters, and, on every wall, the perfect golden-hued, slightly cracking faux finish—er, wait, no, not *faux*. It brought to mind every example of fake Tuscan architecture I'd seen before at the Olive Garden and other Italian restaurants, in interior design magazines, in countless places.

Except it was better. Vastly superior to even the most carefully crafted fake.

Writing about themed environments such as Disneyland, the Italian writer Umberto Eco observes that "the pleasure of imitation, as the ancients knew, is one of the most innate in the human spirit; but here we not only enjoy a perfect imitation, we also enjoy the conviction that the imitation has reached its apex and afterwards reality will always be inferior to it." Yet I can't help but wonder if Florence provided a corollary argument, that once an imitation has seemingly established the apex of perfection, any reality that exceeds it can't help but appear fake itself. This was authentic-plus-one.

Florence somehow conformed even to expectations and archetypes I had not previously formulated in my mind but which became manifest as soon as I saw them in front of me: the history-of-a-culture tableau of runway-worthy outfits drying on ornate wrought-iron balcony railings; the specific carefree manner of the high-heeled, black-clad woman pedaling a rickety bicycle while talking on a tiny, sleek cell phone *and* smoking *and* gesturing wildly.

Booking my room in Florence had been one of the first signs that using a nearly fifty-year-old guidebook was perhaps an innately bad idea. For starters, well, most of the hotels didn't exist anymore. (A brief confession/digression: I initially planned to arrive in each city with no reservation, in the tradition of the old-fashioned traveler, but decided against it after realizing this very problem. In all likelihood, many of Frommer's picks would be closed, and I would spend many hours fruitlessly searching for a place to stay before finally finding a space in a cozy Old World Dumpster. So I opted to cheat a bit and consult the Internet to figure out which of Frommer's preferred hotels were still open, though I steered clear of reviews, looking only to confirm availability and price.)

Of the Albergo Helvetia, Frommer says, "[it] is the kind of place that would appeal to a Blanche-like character from Streetcar Named Desire—fading, shabby gentility, but clean and proud." The description is Frommer at his best, precise yet lyrical, and I had hoped that I could stay there. Nope. Closed. Several others were still in business but had gone upscale and were now far beyond the range of a budget traveler.

Finally I had some luck, if you can consider it good fortune to find a room in a hotel that didn't exactly get glowing marks even forty-five years earlier. "If you're game for a Fourth Class hotel," Frommer writes, "with doubles for 1500 lire and singles for 800 lire ($1.30 [about $9 in 2011 dollars]), even in the summer months, then try Via Panzani 5, where Varsavia stands waiting. Basic, but clean and decent."

"Buon giorno," I said to the graying, sixtyish man behind the counter as I entered the lobby. *"Vorrei una camera."*

The clerk, tall for an Italian but with a stooped, anxious posture, examined me with an expression that was both grimace and grin, a look that said, "I'm going to be as friendly as possible to you, but I'm already dreading this conversation because I know it's going to be awkward and uncomfortable for both of us, and you clearly don't speak any Italian." Which, alas, was true. The initial bliss and Old World overload began to fade—with nausea-inducing rapidity—as I realized that I was really, completely, *totally* out of my element.

Between my Italian and the clerk's English, we had a shared vocabulary of about ten words, and it took much stammering, gesturing, and blushing on both of our parts for me to establish that I had a reservation. We both breathed a sigh of relief when he found a printout with my name on it. He handed me a key and used hand gestures to pantomime walking up stairs.

"Due," he said. Two flights up.

"Grazie," I replied, grateful to have occasion to use one of the words I knew. *"Mille grazie."*

Before stepping back into the theme park outside, I rested for a few minutes in my room. It was not much bigger than my bed but did at least come outfitted with an aggressively ornate wardrobe (which I was convinced was going to topple over and crush me during the night), a bidet, and a sink whose basin, I discovered, had a special feature: it was perfectly angled to splash copious amounts of water onto my crotch every time I tried to wash my hands, as I did now. The room's small window looked straight into a wall, just a few feet away, allowing in only the paltriest swath of reflected daylight—even now, in early afternoon, I had to turn on the overhead light as I opened my bag to dig out a dry pair of pants and my folder full of letters.

It was time to start trying to unscramble my own history, my own sense of authentic self.

My mother had never left the United States until she stepped on that Icelandair flight—the cheapest transatlantic route of the day—heading to Europe, by way of Reykjavík. Patricia Chaffin, twenty-one years old. She wore glasses with a stylishly chunky, dark frame; an A-line skirt and matching sweater (she packed one ensemble in blue, one in green); acrylic stockings held up with a garter belt; and a pair of flats on her feet. "Very East Coast women's college," she says, looking back. "*Extremely* preppy." Her black hair was trimmed into a pert bob. Classic 1960s.

She was traveling with her best friend, Ann Dynes, whom she had known since high school. They spent one night in Reykjavík and were awakened the next morning by a knock on the door. A delivery: a dozen roses from my father. An astonishing trick in Iceland, from such a distance—"Boy am I ever engaged to a romanticist!" she wrote a few days later. After a brief stay in Scotland and

London (where their boardinghouse consisted of "a room with a dozen mattresses on the floor"), they took a boat in rough seas to Amsterdam.

The Continent. A world of unknown languages and cultures. And two young, free-spirited women eager to soak it all up. They had arrived.

Unlike me, my mother is gregarious. Today, certainly, but especially back then, if her letters are any indication. At the moment, I was content to experience that sociability vicariously, as I paged through her accounts of the various other travelers she and Ann had befriended, plus—what was this?—some very charming-sounding men with whom she'd gone sightseeing *without* Ann. My eyebrows arched, my interest exquisitely piqued. I wasn't the only one with this reaction, it turned out—I opened a letter my father sent to my mother in Florence, dated October 19, 1967, and found this:

Did you know that it is easy for me to become jealous of these guys with whom you've apparently been doing all these really neat things? Oh, yes, most definitely. There's nothing wrong with it, and I'd rather hear about it than not, but still, when "we (Guy and I) went to . . ." it is sort of bothering. Just for the record. . . . Anyway, fiancée, continue having a good time, but do come home.

Whoa! Scandal! Did my mother have any old flames in Florence? Just how fancy-free had she been?

As I kept reading, it became clear that my romanticist father had nothing to worry about, if only because the Italian men did themselves no favors—Mom's feelings were primarily limited to contempt and amused pity for their overly aggressive advances of the type that today we'd call straight-up sexual harassment.

"We're too busy to flirt and we wouldn't anyway, and you're awful to suggest it," she wrote on November 4. "We avoid the d.o.m. [dirty old men] but the prob. is when the young ones decide that they are going to communicate."

A few days later, she offered an example:

Dear Bob,

Do you know why Italian men are so awful? Because they start very young. Tonight we had a hysterically funny experience. We walked to the train station to find out what time our train leaves tomorrow. On the way back we were "blessed" with the escort of 4 young men—whose ages we estimate to have averaged 15 (at the very oldest) . . . Bob, these kids ended up walking us home from the station—which is about a mile—all the way Ann and I spoke French to each other and these little boys were trying to address us in various languages—French, Italian, English, and German. Poor kids—we really frustrated their attempts to communicate. Ever been told "I love you" in 3 diff. languages by a 14-year-old? I hope you appreciate the humor of the situation, for Ann and I are still laughing.

In another letter from Florence, she said, "In Italy it has really hit me that you aren't here. It is such a romantic country and I want you to be here so much."

In other words, no scandal. Reassuring—one less thing to worry about, I supposed, although the moment that particular fear evaporated, a hundred others flooded my mind, most of them having to do with the realization that, holy crap, *here I was*, abroad, ill prepared. The world was my oyster, but then, I don't trust oysters—all they've ever given me is food poisoning.

. . .

As I stepped back outside, the letters lingered on my mind and I felt a rush of loneliness to compound the all-purpose anxiety. Mom was right: in spite of the hordes of tourists and the din of traffic, Florence was romantic beyond belief. The Italians themselves fit the oh-so-authentic tableau: with their tight black clothes, show-stopping shoes, sculpted hair, slightly pinched smiles, and overall air of effortless sophistication, they all, male and female, looked like runway models. I desperately wanted to talk to one of the countless captivatingly lovely *signorine* striding through the piazza—gracefully, confidently, somehow never catching their achingly chic high heels on the cobblestones. But the odds of any of them taking the slightest interest in me were approximately nil, even if I had known any Italian pickup lines. (There were none in Frommer's phrasebook section. I checked. Twice.) I knew how the scene would play out:

ME: Buon gio—

CAPTIVATINGLY LOVELY SIGNORINA: *(She cuts me off with a condescending stare, which is all too apparent even though she is wearing enormous Prada sunglasses; in fact, they seem to magnify her disdain.)*

Despite my relatively plain, ostensibly nontouristy attire, I was pretty clearly an awkward, anxious American totally out of his element. There's just nothing sexy about being a tourist.

Let's put it this way: I'd heard that Italy's birth rate had dropped significantly in the last generation, and a *New York Times Magazine* article shortly after my trip confirmed this, noting that the mayor of one town where the decline had been notably precipitous had offered parents ten thousand euros for each new baby. It's a Europe-wide problem—in the early 1960s, according to that same article, 12.5 percent of the world's population lived in Europe; by 2008, the figure was about 7 percent—but perhaps most reflective of the national psyche in Italy. Paired with a simultaneous rise in immigration, it has stirred much collective soul-searching on questions of cultural identity: What does it mean to be Italian now? Are the traditions fading, the history being forgotten? *Is the culture dying?*

As I strolled through Florence, surrounded by beautiful buildings and beautiful people, the set and the actors perfectly crafted, I couldn't help but wonder: How the heck is that possible? How do people who live in a place like this and look—and dress—like fashion models not spend, like, *all day* procreating? And also: Do they need volunteers to help get the birth rate back up? Because, not to sound like a "d.o.m." or anything, but I am willing to assist in remedying this problem. Where do I sign up? Call me heroic if you must; I just want to do my part to help.

Wandering toward the center of town, I checked *Europe on Five Dollars a Day* for some dinner options. Near the Uffizi Gallery, Frommer had several recommendations, of which he wrote, "For the value received, these can scarcely be equalled throughout the rest of Europe." Only one, Da Buzzino, was still open for business, but one was all I needed. With a posted menu in both Italian and English, it seemed like precisely the sort of place I was looking for: tolerant of tourists, but not explicitly targeted to them. My optimism grew when a man appeared in the doorway and asked me, with a raised eyebrow, if I wanted to eat. He had an earnest face and looked old enough to have been around during Frommer's visits. I wondered, as I entered the restaurant, if this was going to be almost too easy.

As he handed me a menu, I dug in my bag for the book, hoping it would provoke a quick laugh and a long conversation, maybe an excited yell to the chef to come see this charming American with the old guidebook by their long-lost pal, Signor Frommer, and a plea for me to sign a menu (*"Mille grazie!"* I'd write), which he would post with all the letters and accolades on the wall.

My host, Joseph, turned away before I could show him the book. He wandered off to check in on the only other customers, a British couple in the opposite corner of the room, below a TV screen broadcasting a news program. I scanned the handwritten menu. And scanned. And read slowly, carefully trying to figure it out. It was all in Italian, unlike the menu posted by the door, and had no food terms I recognized immediately—no fettuccine, no prosciutto, no pizza.

Joseph walked back toward the kitchen, and I feebly raised my hand to catch his eye.

"Um, *mi scusi*?" I squeaked.

"Sì?" He tilted his head expectantly.

"Um . . ." Crap, I really didn't want to say it. "English?"

He sighed, pulled the sheaf of laminated pages from my grasp, and flipped it to the back cover, where the heading read, "Tourist Menu."

"Grazie," I said.

Joseph smiled weakly.

I consulted my predecessors for guidance in ordering—roast chicken, per Frommer's advice, and lasagne, which my mother had at an unknown restaurant in Florence, breathlessly reporting, in a postcard to her brother, that "they use orange cheese, not yellow." Both dishes were deliciously robust and sublimely tender, especially the chicken. *Good call, Frommer. Forty-five years later, you've still got your touch.*

Before waddling out the door, I again tried to strike up conversation with Joseph.

"Scusi?" I said. "Restaurant is in my old guide." I opened to the listing and showed him.

"Da Buzzino!" He chuckled as he saw the bold-faced type.

"Yes, and it's an *old book*," I emphasized, drawing my hand across the cover. "Nineteen sixty-three! *Europe on Five Dollars a Day*! I found Da Buzzino in here!"

"In the book?"

"Yes. An *old book*!"

"Thank you," he offered and walked away.

"There's little decent night life in Florence," Frommer warns. "Best thing to do is simply relax with a drink at an outdoor cafe in the Piazza della Repubblica, and listen to the open-air bands."

As promised, a jazz quartet played in the middle of the piazza, against the backdrop of a carousel, the imposing Pensione Pendini, and, in the distance, the final fiery brushstrokes of sunset. Outdoor cafés sprawled across large expanses of two sides of the square, with happy diners raising wineglasses and laughing boisterously. Couples walked by holding hands; some paused to dance to the music. These were not the spastic nightclub moves that most Americans mistakenly believe is the epitome of graceful locomotion, but polished, Fred-and-Ginger dancing, the kind that makes the observer mesmerized with delight and, if he is by himself, miles from anyone he knows, soul-crushingly lonely. My parents' letters rushed back into my mind, their happiness making me distinctly unhappy.

I wandered over to the loggia along the Pensione Pendini, hoping to clear my head. Big mistake—just my luck that at the precise moment I wanted to find something dreary or at least mundane, a counterpoint to an oppressively sublime evening, I happened across an unspeakably beautiful busker singing an aria. Her voice was delicate yet confident, utterly captivating, and my heart broke just a bit more with each note of her song, which was titled, I believe, "Dear Lonely Backpacker, Just Kill Yourself Now."

A small crowd surrounded her, including a very drunk Italian man who swayed with the music and gently implored every nearby woman to dance with him. They all politely rebuffed his advances, though if he'd turned to me, I just might have taken his hand. It struck me that I could very easily end up like this guy, drunkenly wandering the streets of Florence, eyes at half-mast, a melancholy smile affixed to my face, besotted by the city and forever in search of love.

I glanced back across the piazza and noticed a commotion. Something less-than-beautiful was going down. Finally. I took it as my cue to leave, pausing momentarily to toss a few coins in the singer's bucket and silently profess my undying love to her.

A group of men had appeared from the shadows, each with a bulging sack slung over his shoulder. With furtive glances, they checked their surroundings, then dropped the sacks, which turned out to be bedsheets holding an array of chic handbags bearing the names of Italian fashion houses. As they set about arranging their wares, I noticed that they were standing just a few feet from a mas-

*Synchronized touristing
at the Duomo.*

sive sign bearing a message in English, Italian, and French: "Buy-
ing counterfeit goods is a crime."

Each man was no more than twenty-five years old and lean,
with a weary posture that seemed at odds with the determined
look in his eyes. They were all West African; based on Italian immigration trends and the fact that they spoke French with each other,
I'd guess they were from Senegal.

Few tourists were interested in purchasing a handbag, but now
and then an American—always, alas, one of the stereotypically loud

and boorish ones—would stop to haggle. It was an amusing sight, both for the juxtaposition of red-faced, argumentative tourists and poised, smirking vendors, and for the circumstances of the transaction: in this oh-so-authentic place, here was a scene involving a knockoff product (probably not even made in Italy), an American tourist, and an African immigrant. A tableau of modern Italy, definitely not something that appeared in my mother's letters.

In fact, such scenes would become commonplace—they are the new authenticity of our globalized age. I was quickly discovering that, just as in the United States, the tourist industry in Italy—and much of western Europe—seemed to depend on immigrants, at least to outward appearances. Statistics back this up: more than half of Italy's immigrant population works in the service industry, including restaurants, hotels, museums, gift shops, and other tourist-oriented businesses.

Shortly after I had arrived in Florence, I had stopped in a café for some gelato, and it was served to me by a woman who, before I could open my mouth, greeted me in English inflected with a thick Russian accent. My last conversation in Florence would be with a chipper Indian man named Sathivel, who sold me my bus ticket back to the airport. In between those interactions, I saw Southeast Asian women selling brightly colored silk scarves on the Piazza Santa Croce, Rom men hawking remote-controlled cars and other toys along the Arno, a dapper West African maître d' at a fancy outdoor café, a veritable United Nations of vendors—but seemingly no native-born Italians—at the various street markets.

Many Italians seem not to have gotten the memo about changing times, changing notions of authenticity. Just a month before my trip, Silvio Berlusconi had been elected prime minister, for the third time, based in part on a campaign promise to crack down on immigration. He had also aligned himself with the explicitly anti-immigrant Northern League political party, whose campaign tactics had included a poster of an American Indian in full feather headdress with the ominous caption, "They were not able to regulate immigration—now they live on reservations—think about them." By 2010, some 4.2 million resident foreigners lived in Italy, comprising roughly 7 percent of the nation's total population, about one percentage point above the European Union average. (Interestingly, the Italian government's official "resident foreigner" figures include children born in Italy to foreign parents.) By comparison, the 2010 U.S. Census documented 36.7 million foreign-born residents, or 12 percent of the total population.

One of the ironies of Italy's burgeoning anti-immigrant sentiment is that until recently, the flow went the other way: outward. The nation's departures outnumbered arrivals until 1972, with nearly 26 million Italians emigrating to other countries between 1876 and 1976.

What's even more jarring, though, is Italy's response to the twin influxes of immigrants and tourists. The basic message appears to be: "You foreigners, the ones who don't stay, the ones who only want to examine our culture and not become a part of our social fabric, the ones who condescend to us and overrun our most cherished historic sites: we want you. You other foreigners, the ones who actually desire to live here, the ones who, in fact, fill the menial hospitality industry jobs that keep tourism afloat and ensure that the culture-dabbling Good Foreigners keep coming in droves: go away."

As I watched the vendors in the piazza, I wanted to know their stories: Where, exactly, were they from? Were they here legally? Had they faced the discrimination I'd been hearing so much about? But implicit in the question "Where are you from?" is the accusation "You don't belong here." You'd never ask it of someone who looks Italian, after all. More than wanting to know their stories, to scratch the alluring patina of this place and understand what was beyond the surface, I loathed the idea of being an obnoxious, prying American.

In any case, as I worked up the nerve to approach them, they suddenly started tossing their handbags into hasty piles in the centers of their sheets, pulled the four corners together, hefted their bundles to their shoulders, and briskly walked back into the shadows. A few moments later, a car marked "Polizia Finanza" glided by.

Thursday was my day for art. Arthur Frommer advocates a leisurely, contemplative pace for taking in Florence's museums and galleries, but I opted for a different strategy: art overload, cramming all of my museum-going into one day.

The weather was a spastic mix of drizzle and full-fledged downpour, so the line to get into the Uffizi Gallery was wedged into the narrow loggia outside the museum, tight as a rush-hour subway. Vendors worked the crowd, hawking umbrellas, but apparently someone else had beaten them to the punch, because many of the tourists wore flimsy ponchos that could only have been purchased in a moment of utter desperation and which bore a striking resemblance to enormous condoms.

Once inside the museum, my first view was not of some strategically placed masterpiece, as one might expect, but of that defining ritual of modern tourism, the Incompetent Security Check, at which the sullen guards continually scolded tourists to drop empty water bottles into a trash bin but paid no attention to the constantly beeping metal detector or the screen on the X-ray machine.

Then, finally, into the gallery, where I immediately understood what my mother said when she wrote, in a postcard, that she and her friend Ann were "drowning in art."

Goodness. As Frommer puts it on the first page of the Florence chapter, "the treasures here [at the Uffizi] are so thick that Raphael's priceless Madonna of the Chair is casually stuck away in a little nook." I couldn't find that particular nook (possibly because it turns out the painting is now at the Pitti Palace), but just after entering the museum, I took a wrong turn and ended up in a dingy, fluorescent-lit elevator lobby, where there were four works by Giovanni da San Giovanni, a Baroque-era painter. In any museum back home, they likely would have been the center of attention; here they're just, yawn, some more seventeenth-century masterpieces.

Now, I would like the record to show that I genuinely wanted to appreciate every last one of the beyond-copious works of art in the Uffizi—I honestly hoped to improve my sadly minimal knowledge of art history. So, following Frommer's advice, I began my tour of the museum with the best of intentions to take an unhurried, reflective stroll through the halls.

The thing is, though, it's hard to appreciate fine art when there are so many other people trying to do the same, especially if half of them are either (a) listening intently to their audio guide, oblivious to their surroundings and prone to walking about zombielike, crashing into benches, walls, or you; (b) students or quasi-artistic types who sprawl on the floor in front of every remotely interesting work and attempt to replicate said works on their own notepads, although passersby can't help but notice that the vast majority of these sketches are rather exquisitely crappy; or (c) checklist tourist types who carry books with titles like *The Manic Traveler's Ten*

Things to See in Ten Minutes in the Uffizi, typically peacocked with Post-its, which they pluck off one by one as they blink at each "must-see" work before sprinting to the next.

A small, cruel part of me began to hope that, just to liven things up, I would witness some of the literal swooning and panic attacks that you hear about every now and then, when the beauty of Florence's artistic and historic riches creates a potent mix of vertigo and delirium. The condition is called Stendahl Syndrome, after the French writer who wrote of experiencing its symptoms in 1817: "I was in a sort of ecstasy, from the idea of being in Florence, close to the great men whose tombs I had seen. Absorbed in the contemplation of sublime beauty . . . I had palpitations of the heart, what in Berlin they call 'nerves.' Life was drained from me. I walked with the fear of falling." I suppose I'd experienced a fleeting case the day before, on the bus, but that was born more of the Tuscany countryside's refusal to play to my jaded expectations rather than of the pure power of beauty per se.

Now, sarcastic thoughts flowing full force, I was starting to experience the Anti-Stendahl Syndrome: complete obliviousness to beauty.

I'd read Mark Twain's *Innocents Abroad* just before I left Minneapolis, and his comment about the Uffizi had stuck in my mind: "weary miles of picture galleries."

Yeah. Pretty much. I'd already seen a fatiguing number of Renaissance masterpieces, and yet, somehow, my map informed me that there were still whole floors of the museum I had not yet entered.

Maybe there was still a way for me to salvage this excursion, though. In my mother's letters, there was one painting she mentioned repeatedly, in an amused tone befitting the work's intriguingly freakish name: *Madonna with the Long Neck*. This I needed to see.

Well, let me tell you, there are more than a few Madonnas in the Uffizi. Ridiculous quantities. And allow me to further note that a lot—a *lot*—of the Madonnas have rather excessive necks. I lost count of the number of times I thought, Hmm, she has a longish neck. Is she *the* Madonna with *the* long neck?

There were Madonnas with happy baby Jesuses and Madonnas with mopey Jesuses. Jesus holding books, clutching birds, flexing his biceps, grasping Mary's breast in a frankly painful-looking way. *Madonna of the Harpies* and *Madonna of the Goldfinch* stared each other down from across one cramped room. There was bloated Jesus, colicky Jesus, Elvis-looking Jesus, and even, I noticed (though I don't know *why* I noticed), Jesus with just one testicle.

When I finally found the elusive long-necked lady, it was in the gift shop, on a postcard. I bought it and sent it to my mother with my own amused, sarcastic note.

After a quick lunch, I headed to another of the city's famous museums, the Accademia. I decided to get off the main streets and take what seemed to be a more direct route on smaller, quieter passageways. But in the labyrinth that is Florence, it's astonishingly easy to get lost, particularly if your sole navigational assistance comes from a forty-five-year-old map that lists only the most well-trafficked piazzas and streets.

It was like being stuck in quicksand: the more I struggled to get my bearings, the more disoriented I got. I became ever more removed from the tourist masses, until they disappeared completely and the only voices I heard were Italian.

In one shop window, a stooped craftsman used hand tools to fashion an elaborately detailed wooden picture frame, a scene that could have been taking place anytime in the last five hundred years. In another, a woman in a tight black dress surveyed a small but well-stocked showroom of avant-garde modern furniture, all sleek lines and neutral tones. It was wonderful and captivating and inspiring, exactly what travel is supposed to be all about.

And then I found myself surrounded by drunks.

I had wandered into a dark square filled with vacant-eyed souls and strewn with trash. I named it Piazza della Sketchiness. It seemed to have come out of nowhere, a mirage of all-too-realistic grime and grit, the first truly disconcerting and depressing sight I'd seen in Florence. It was the anti-Brigadoon, or perhaps the Ghost of Florence Yet to Come, once tourists and globalization had finally rubbed away all of the charms and sense of place. All those news stories of the horrors of modern Italy, which had been lurking in the margins of my mind since my arrival, came to the fore.

Allow me to pause here to ask a question: Is there a more perversely pleasurable travel daydream than considering all the exotic ways in which one could die while on the road? I think not. The options are endless: choking on tapas in Spain or being run over by a Porsche on the autobahn or suffering severe head trauma from falling stones at the Colosseum. A high school classmate of my mother's—this is true—crashed his bike into a canal in Amsterdam and drowned.

At this particular moment, my most likely cause of death was a wine-bottle blow to the head, courtesy of the disheveled behemoth scowling at me. I did the mental calculation: actual skinhead or just a menacing character with a shaved pate? He staggered slightly. Boozy stumble or prelude to a chase? My pulse quickened until I noticed his typically Italian footwear, all flash and no function. So at least I could outrun him. I put my head down and kept walking, stealing backward glances every few strides.

In his five-hundred-plus years, Michelangelo's *David* has had an arm broken off during a melee (1527), been attacked with a sledgehammer (1991), had his stature severely underestimated for hundreds of years (he's seventeen feet tall, not thirteen, as the *New York Times* had it in a 1991 article, or fourteen, as stated in 2008 by London's *Daily Telegraph*), and, in a replica at the Victoria and Albert Museum in London, had his manhood covered by an enormous plaster fig leaf, reportedly because Queen Victoria disapproved of such brazen nudity. He has been depicted on refrigerator magnets, replete with a wardrobe of festive magnetic outfits; as a light-switch cover, with a strategically placed cutout in the crotch forming a sort of anti–fig leaf; and on countless tacky postcards, including the ones for sale in the shop across the street from the museum, postcards that showcased *David*'s light-switch region with a pair of sunglasses balancing on the, er, "switch" itself. Let us not even speak of the boxer shorts.

In spite of these indignities, the multitudes still come, with some 1.3 million visitors to the Accademia each year. *David*'s popularity may soon get him evicted from his current home: a few months before my trip, Florence's head of culture requested governmental approval to move the statue to a new concert hall on the outskirts of town, citing "an unsustainable level of tourists" in the city center.

I joined the line outside of the museum, aware that I was doing my part to make that level incrementally more unsustainable, and again prepared myself for a letdown. With so many admirers and such déclassé associations, *David* couldn't help but feel a bit camp, even if my mother wrote that he was "magnifico"; even if Arthur Frommer says that he "may alone be worth your entire trip to Europe"; even if the ever-caustic Mark Twain was impressed, in *The Innocents Abroad.*

Well . . . it was wonderful, *magnifico*, not at all cheesy. Though tourists did indeed swarm around him like groupies to a rock star (swooning and all), I cannot offer a single snide comment about their behavior or exclamations because I was too busy staring at the Man of Marble in his perfectly lit corner.

I'll stop there for fear of sounding too awestruck, though I was (so *this* is what Stendahl was getting at!). The statue was the perfect metaphor for Florence as a whole: overwhelmed with visitors, superficially like something I had seen a thousand times before, and yet still profoundly wonderful. It transcended the tourists.

I can't say much about the rest of the museum because it all seemed so laughably small and inconsequential after *David*. The other rooms were jarringly empty of visitors, and I felt a twinge of sympathy for any obscure Renaissance artist whose only extant work was in some back corner of the Accademia, ignored by all but the most intrepid, dedicated art aficionado—I had one distant room to myself for two or three minutes and luxuriated in the sudden quietude before going back to gape at *David* again.

That evening, I had some bold and important investigations to undertake. Namely, I needed to have some pizza. Purely for journalistic purposes, understand. Solely to examine the authentic version in comparison to its American counterpart.

Here, after all, is arguably one of the greatest benefits of welcoming immigrants into one's country: it makes society more complex, richer, and tastier. Italians, of all peoples, should understand this, given that their own traditional foods have pleased countless palates across the globe.

We don't think much about the flow of culture into the United States, the effects of Fellini films, the Three Tenors, and *venti* lattes—we dwell, and not without reason, on the omnipresence of American culture and enterprise abroad. Corporations! They're taking over the world, homogenizing culture, destroying sense of place! Have you noticed?

But, really, consider the pizza. In 1944, a *New York Times* article about a just-opened pizzeria led with this description of the exotic foodstuff: "One of the most popular dishes in southern Italy, especially in the vicinity of Naples, is pizza—a pie made from a yeast dough and filled with any number of different centers, each one containing tomatoes. Cheese, mushrooms, anchovies, capers, onions and so on may be used." Gosh, sounds appetizing, doesn't it?

Twenty years after that rather detached, straightforward description appeared, pizza was so commonplace that in the menu phrasebook section of *Europe on Five Dollars a Day*, Frommer offers not a translation but a wiseacre wink: "You know this one."

Now, nearly another fifty years on, I settled myself into a corner table at one of Frommer's recommended restaurants—he claimed "no surprises; no cover," but surprise, Arthur, there was a two-euro cover—and ordered my own yeast-dough pie to see how it measured up. It was good enough, with the crust slightly charred from the wood-fired oven and the slight saltiness of the prosciutto perfectly balancing with the creamy mozzarella and the earthy depth of the *funghi*.

Here's what struck me, though: it wasn't as good as the pizza I can get at either of two different restaurants in my neighborhood back home in Minneapolis. With their imported San Marzano tomatoes, *mozzarella di bufala*, and sea salt–dusted crusts, these are marketed as paragons of authentic Italian cuisine. One restaurant is a member of Verace Pizza Napoletana, the official and famously strict arbiter of true Neapolitan pizza. Even the decor and menu design of those pizzerias back home are superficially more authentic, more Old World Italian than the restaurants I visited in Florence.

Today, some of Frommer's and my mother's comments about Italian foods sound nearly as naive and wide-eyed as that 1944 *Times* article. Frommer lists fettuccine and risotto in the vegetable section, for example; most Americans today would probably not just recategorize them but smirk at the accurate but not entirely complete translations of these as "noodles" and "rice." My mother explained the concept of a trattoria to my father in one of her letters and waxed rhapsodic about a terribly exotic dish that I recognized, having seen it on restaurant menus back home, as saltimbocca.

The fact is, in any major city in the United States today, you can easily find food that is at least as authentically Italian as that found in most cafés in tourist areas of Italy. That wasn't at all true in mid-century America, where "Italian" basically meant cheap wine and gummy spaghetti—or Chef Boyardee, whose 1950s *Life* magazine ads promised "ravioli as truly Italian as the Tower of Pisa." Most travelers of that era likely had not experienced even the watered-down version of Italian cuisine presented today by the likes of Romano's Macaroni Grill, Buca di Beppo, and the Olive Garden. (Even Fancy Feast cat food now has Florentine and Tuscany lines, "inspired by classic Italian tastes," for the citizen-of-the-world felines.)

Though Frommer and my mother undoubtedly had their own preconceptions of Europe, based on photographs, books, and previous tourists' stories, the information available to them before their trips was paltry compared to what today's information-overloaded travelers have at their disposal. My mother and Frommer and their peers couldn't presume to believe they knew exactly what to expect. They knew they didn't know anything, and that was probably for the better. They didn't expect their pizza to taste a certain way; they weren't measuring the tourist café against the better Italian food back home. Put another way, back then they were ignorant; today we're delusional.

The popularity of Italian food in the United States has also, arguably, helped fuel tourism to Italy: if the food becomes less foreign, then so, too, incrementally, do the people it represents. By importing their native foods and traditions to the countries in which they settle, immigrants provide to their new neighbors an inescapable introduction to their culture, fueling curiosity and, ultimately, familiarity (if not comprehensive appreciation). They are de facto ambassadors.

It follows that tourists arrive with distinct expectations of what "Italian" means, what images and tastes and experiences the term conjures—gelato stands, yes; kebab stands . . . probably not. Visitors' expectations help affirm the nation's already deeply ingrained traditional sense of itself and reinforce the reflexive tendency to want to essentially preserve the past under glass, which fuels nationalist tendencies and the country's aversion to immigrants and the inevitable changes they bring.

Me, I actually like the notion that I can get some pretty good falafel in Florence, pad Thai in Brussels, enchiladas in Paris, or cultural mash-ups like currywurst in Berlin.

Saturday morning I packed up my bag and headed to the bus station, resolving to come back soon but definitely not alone. In hopes of achieving that goal, I had one last task: I had to go talk to a pig.

The previous day, I'd gone to the Straw Market (Frommer's most highly recommended place for bargain shopping in all of Europe), in search of a marble chess set to buy for my father—my mother had seen one for sale and "felt sick," she wrote, that she couldn't spare the thirty dollars to purchase it. I had found one, but at 320 euros, it was out of my price range as well. As I was leaving empty-handed, I had noticed a line of tourists waiting to rub the snout of a brass boar, *Il Porcellino* (a historic and well-known landmark, I would later learn, and very much on the typical tourist itinerary, though there's no mention of it in *E5D*).

"Is for luck," I heard a guide explain as he pointed to the shiny nose, its patina worn away by countless hands. "You put a coin in the mouth, rub him, and make a wish. It will come true."

I hadn't wanted to wait in line then, but this morning it seemed important to consult the porcine talisman. The unsettled feeling in my stomach—my general trepidation about this whole trip—showed no signs of abating, and my brain buzzed with a thousand thoughts and fears, not always certain that people weren't laughing at me in various languages I didn't speak. More than that, though, I was still feeling lonely. Maybe the boar could help.

I started to give him my smallest coin, ten (euro) cents, but then figured he would somehow know—if he could make my wishes come true, he could probably tell if I were being a stingy bastard, and wouldn't appreciate it.

So I dug out a larger coin, placed it in his mouth, and asked him to ease my eternally worried mind, also to maybe throw in some enlightenment and, if it wasn't too much trouble, love. I rubbed his snout vigorously, hopefully, and gave him an affectionate pat on the head.

I adjusted the straps on my backpack and set my sights toward the bus station, then turned briefly to offer *Il Porcellino*—and Florence—one final, wistful gaze.

Paris

Life in a Movie Set

In general, go to the Left Bank for inexpensive
meals and accommodations. Go there also for a real
taste of Paris; it's the Champs Elysées which has
become commercial and hard; the Latin Quarter,
on the Left Bank, retains its honesty.

—Europe on Five Dollars a Day

Arthur Frommer was born in 1929 in Lynchburg, Virginia. He was a child of the Depression, and if you're looking for an early catalyst for his frugal ways, surely this is it. "I was probably the poorest boy in my entire public school [in Jefferson City, Missouri]," he told author Michael Shapiro in a profile for the 2004 book *A Sense of Place: Great Travel Writers Talk About Their Craft, Lives, and Inspiration.*

Frommer's father worked in the garment industry, moving from city to city, factory to factory, following the jobs. In 1944, the family headed to New York City. It proved to be auspicious: fourteen-year-old Arthur soon got a job at *Newsweek* as an office assistant. He had found his calling—he wanted to be a journalist.

After graduating from New York University, then Yale Law School, he was drafted into the army in 1953, in the waning days of the Korean War. Placed in the intelligence division and sent to Germany, he arrived on the Continent awestruck and delighted: "I had never dreamed that I would have the resources or the money to travel in Europe," he told Shapiro.

He traveled as much as he could. Stockholm, Venice, Barcelona, Majorca. In Paris, while sitting at a sidewalk café, he had an epiphany: "I looked up and saw a motor coach of forty or so American tourists passing by with everyone's noses pressed to the glass looking out at the life of Paris from the inside of the bus," he said in an interview published in 2007 on Frommers.com, marking the fiftieth anniversary of his original book. "At that moment, I realized that the difference between them and me was that they had money and I had no money—and *because* I had no money, I was having the time of my life." He decided that this knowledge—this experience— was too good to keep to himself.

Each night, he sat down in the barracks and scoured his memory—he had no notes, no specific addresses, only rough "mental pictures"—to write what would become *The G.I.'s Guide to Traveling in Europe*. In 1955 he borrowed money and had "10,000 or 12,000" copies printed in Oberammergau, Germany, then sent them to *Stars and Stripes* newsstands on army bases around Europe. It sold for fifty cents. And it sold out almost immediately.

Two years later, Frommer was working long days as a lawyer in Manhattan, but still thinking about travel and the success of his first guidebook; he was convinced that the time was right for a civilian version. He went back to Europe for a month, getting the details he'd missed in the first book, "just crisscrossing the streets until midnight, then taking a train at night to the next city," he told Michael Shapiro.

The title of this new book was *Europe on Five Dollars a Day*, with chapters on twelve cities. Frommer self-printed again, with an initial run of fifteen thousand copies.* Again, it sold out almost immediately.

Paris was perhaps the most enthralling city for Private First Class Frommer, who had minored in French at NYU and dreamed of the Left Bank café life of Ernest Hemingway and Gertrude Stein. Even today, when interviewers ask the obligatory question, "What's your favorite city?" Frommer's response never wavers: Paris. It rejuvenates him, he says.

As for me, I was not feeling rejuvenated. Pretty much the opposite. I had taken refuge in the Jardin du Luxembourg, where I sat on a bench and gave careful consideration to just staying there for the next few days, avoiding the streets, the subways, the city, the people.

Outside the fence surrounding the park was a world of gray stone and glowering gargoyles and haughty citizens with their noses permanently stuck in the air, sneers primed in the backs of their throats, waiting to be deployed the instant I walked by. Being treated horribly is a highly anticipated part of the French travel

---

* That's according to a *Time* article in 1963. Nora Ephron's 1967 *New York Times* profile of Arthur put it at twenty thousand, and in his interview for *A Sense of Place*, the man himself gives a figure of five thousand. I'm inclined to trust the *Time* number, being the middle amount and the earliest reference, but in any event, there were soon more printings.

experience—eat some escargot, be perplexed by a bidet, and get a stereotype-confirming story to share on Facebook: OMG, you won't *believe* how mean that cheese-eating surrender monkey was to me!—and I was expecting the worst. My French was only slightly better than my Italian—numbers plus the names of a few pastries—and I'd heard that if I so much as mispronounced half a syllable, I'd have a pack of feral poodles sicced on me.

Now, as it happens, the rude-Parisian stereotype is not one that either Frommer or my mother—neither of whom was typically shy about offering an opinion—mentioned at all. Both had only nice things to say. Indeed, in *Cold War Holidays: American Tourism in France,* historian Christopher Endy notes that just 5 percent of foreign visitors had "negative assessments" of the French, according to a 1958 government study. And in my half day here so far, everyone had been kind and patient with me. Disconcertingly so, actually. Maybe it was a trap.

For the moment, though, I tried to block all of that out of my mind, focusing instead on my own personal happy pill: a sackful of pastries. Chocolate croissants happen to be my addiction, and in Paris, I had found an entire city of enablers. Before I departed for Europe, I intentionally avoided any articles or advice about things to do, places to see, anything that would taint my experiment in willful ignorance—except when it came to chocolate croissants. I was going to *Paris.* They know their *pain au chocolat* there. I tracked down a Paris-based writer I'd met years earlier, Eddy Harris, and respectfully demanded patisserie tips. High on his list was Gerard Mulot, which just so happened to be near my hotel, and that was where I had stopped on my way to the *jardin.*

I opened the pastry bag and let the scent linger in the air as I watched a little boy launch a sailboat in the fountain in front of me and a pack of joggers race past, their brightly colored spandex confetti-ing the manicured parkland as they disappeared into a row of trees. An altogether charming scene. Seriously: maybe I should just stay in this spot until it was time to go to the airport.

The exterior resisted slightly as I bit into the croissant, then shattered, sending gossamer-light crumbs drifting into my open book—sorry there, Arthur—and falling to the ground. The interior was as layered and complex as a canyon wall, dense with buttery strata. I had experienced the rapture: flaky, chocolatey bliss.

Pigeons pecked the dirt around me, grateful for my messiness. The croissant was so good that I was briefly tempted to chase the birds away and scavenge the crumbs myself. One pigeon was the fattest, most hopeless one I'd ever seen. I named him Goodyear, though he (and it *must* have been male) was probably incapable of flying and was forever losing out to the other birds in the race to the crumbs. He was plucky but dopey. I felt a kinship.

I tossed a piece of croissant directly in front of him and watched him gobble it happily.

"Open your bag. Tickets downstairs. Open your bag. Tickets downstairs," the security guard repeated as a monotone mantra. I unzipped my satchel, but she waved me in without so much as a cursory glance inside.

I was back in the big, bad world, inside the Louvre's glass entrance pyramid—a bit of architectural flash, requisite in modern museums, added in 1989.

Europe on Five Dollars a Day says that the Louvre is free on Sundays. You will be shocked to learn that this is no longer true. I expected as much, of course, although I was really not yet ready to spend any more money on art—the museum overdose in Florence still had me reeling.

I had a plan B, though, which I hoped would get me either into the museum or into trouble. As I'd watched the pigeons and runners in the Jardin du Luxembourg, I'd pondered the state of my quest and realized, with a bit of disappointment, that *E5D* had not yet pushed me out of my comfort zone, aside from a few moments of sphincter-loosening panic in the Piazza della Sketchiness. It had merely created the sort of middling awkwardness that I am able to find anywhere, anytime, on my own. By the time I had finished my second croissant, I felt emboldened.

My idea was that at the Louvre, I would saunter over to one of the guards and bust out the guidebook, pointing to Frommer's claim that admission was free right now and insist that he let me in. This, ideally, would lead to one of two things. Scenario one: he'd be won over by my naïveté and bumbling charm and escort me inside, possibly for a behind-the-scenes tour and a parting gift of one of the lesser works from a back gallery. Or scenario two: hilariously haughty verbal abuse in a language I didn't speak, followed by the guard dragging me by my ear up the stairs to the plaza and tossing me into the reflecting pool outside the entrance. Awful, but potentially character building. Either result would be fine.

I flipped through my book and found the appropriate page, then picked out a guard at random, a rangy guy with a crew cut. I strode toward him with as much faux swagger as I could muster.

"Free?" I asked, poking my open book.

He looked confused; clearly he'd been expecting directions to the bathroom or the gift shop.

"In my book . . . ," I began, then paused. "It says . . . Sundays? No charge? Yes?"

More confusion. He pointed behind me. "Tickets over there."
No scorn or impatience. No smile at my scampish irreverence,
either, though I could detect a slight snicker in his otherwise stoic
command. *Keep pushing!* I told myself. *Charm and/or infuriate!*

"No, I go in . . . without ticket?" I said. "Because of the book?"

I pointed again, but my hands were shaking so much that even
if he understood what I was trying to say, and even if he could read
English, there's no way he could have made out any of the text.

My better instincts took over. I trudged to the ticket window
and opened my wallet.

By design, *Europe on Five Dollars a Day* was not an all-purpose,
everything-you-might-need-to-know sort of book like many of its
contemporaries and nearly all of its successors. For one thing, it
covered significantly less territory than its major competitors—
just twelve cities in the original 1957 edition: full chapters for London, Paris, Munich, Vienna, Venice, Florence, Rome, and Nice, plus
a page or two each for Berlin, Madrid, Athens, and Copenhagen.
Established cultural capitals all, but one can't help but wonder if
Frommer helped solidify their place in the Grand Tourist's itinerary, if he helped make *this specific path* so beaten—especially since,
by comparison, a 1957 *Fielding's Travel Guide to Europe* contained
chapters for twenty-five separate *countries*, and a 1960 *Fodor's Jet
Age Guide to Europe* had thirty-three. Both included much of eastern Europe and featured substantial information on cities and
regions that are essentially unknown to tourists even today. Both
were also rather overwhelming in the history, background, and
commentary they offered in page after page—about eight hundred
each—of tiny type.

Frommer's book was in a different spirit: just the essentials. He offered details on how to read a train table, where to shop, what exchange rates to expect (because, of course, prior to the introduction of the euro in 2002, each country had its own currency), and a brief selection of phrases in various languages, a key element that those Fielding's and Fodor's books lacked. That was about it.

There were few of the modern guidebooks' protean tips and tricks on, for example, how to use local transit systems; how to dress in various cultures; etiquette and taboos; tipping; pickup lines for captivatingly lovely *signorine* in Florence; how to call, mail, or otherwise keep in touch with the folks back home; or that eternal anxiety of travel, avoiding being scammed, mugged, or straight-up killed. Frommer intended his book to be essentially a supplement to other guides, so he intentionally limited its scope to focus on where to stay and where to eat. (By the late 1960s, the book would include sightseeing sections written by Frommer's wife, Hope, after she insisted that he had to offer more of this information.)

Frommer said nothing, for example, about what to see at the Louvre. Obviously, I could have enjoyed the museum despite the lack of guidance from Frommer about where to go and what to see. Or I could have followed the masses carrying a different variety of offbeat guidebook, one with a *Da Vinci Code* theme. But this is not the place to go if you're sick of looking at art and dealing with crowds. Really, seriously, *not the place*. I glanced through my mother's postcards, hoping for another opportunity for a scavenger hunt, but all I found were comments about being more impressed with the building than the art it housed. I had to agree. I made a quick circuit and left, opting for the vastly more entertaining spectacle a

*Thirty seconds after I savored this view and
took this photo, the skies opened up and I got
drenched by a torrential downpour.*

ways up the Champs-Élysées: the vehicular free-for-all where
twelve streets converge at the Arc de Triomphe, where the traffic
jam is every bit as eternal as the flame beneath the monument. *E5D*
won't tell you this, and modern guidebooks probably won't, either,
but this is, hands down, the best free entertainment in Paris. I
spent half an hour watching the spectacle with a family from
Madrid, trading quips on the mayhem in my mediocre Spanish.

Because my own guidebook did not always provide me with the
necessary details, I was often forced to rely on the kindness of

people who, at most other points in life, I would go to extreme measures to avoid. For the subways, this was—on multiple occasions—groups of chattering English girls, about twelve or thirteen years old, sans chaperone. One of those times was now, as I tried to find my way from the Arc de Triomphe to a Frommer-approved restaurant on the Left Bank.

I stood in front of a map on the Métro wall, trying to make sense of the tangled lines and minuscule text. I suppose I looked like a cartoon version of a clueless tourist: jaw slightly agape with befuddlement, eyes wide and panicked, hands fidgeting nervously. At my moment of maximum confusion, this group walked by, stopped their preteen prattling, and stared with amusement before one of them asked, with the sort of chipper sneer that only a tween can pull off, "You lost?"

Of course I was lost. I couldn't find my destination on the subway map, in large part because I didn't know where it was on a street map, since the only one I had was, yes, the little hand-drawn number from my 1963 guidebook. Pride, however, forced me to stammer out a reassurance: "No, no . . . I'm okay, thanks."

The girl rolled her eyes, unconvinced. After a long moment, I confessed that, well, actually, I wasn't quite *entirely* sure how to get where I was trying to go—it was a neighborhood quite a ways off, and I was new here, but that's okay, I didn't expect her to know where it was, either, thanks anyway. Cue another eye roll. Then, flashing an orthodontia-adorned pitying smirk, she took a deep breath and launched into her directions, which went something like this: "Okay, you go down these stairs, and you get on the number 1 train, toward Château de Vincennes—that's the last station on the line, not your stop. Get off at Châtelet. Then you transfer to the number 4 and take it to Saint-Michel. Follow the signs to the exit by the fountain—it'll say that, 'the fountain'—and then go down the Boulevard Saint-Michel two blocks, just past the pizza shop, which I quite like, and take a left. It should be just round the corner. Simple, really."

"Um. Okay." Her instructions turned out to be dead-on, and I soon found myself at the appointed address. Which was now a McDonald's.

One of the few areas where Frommer gave advice beyond stay-here-eat-there was what to pack, which provides an interesting insight into how his entire approach to travel differed from that of Temple Fielding and other guidebook writers of the era.

In 1968, John McPhee profiled Fielding for the *New Yorker*. This is a partial inventory of the clothes Fielding took on his five-month tours of Europe:

> *Fielding uses two suitcases, and in them he packs thirty-five handkerchiefs (all of hand-rolled Swiss linen and all bearing his signature, hand-embroidered), ten shirts, ten ties, ten pairs of undershorts, three pairs of silk pajamas, eight pairs of socks, evening clothes, three pairs of shoes, a lounging robe, a pair of sealskin slippers, and two toilet kits.... He wears one suit and carries two.*

When you dress like that, when you do everything in your power to seem like a moneyed dandy straight out of central casting, you are also required to have luggage full of absurd, nonessential items. Fielding did not disappoint. To get around baggage fees—a headache even back then—he carried a raffia basket (the airlines didn't know how to classify it, so they essentially just ignored it; try that on your next trip). Its contents included "a bottle of maraschino cherries, a bottle of Angostura bitters, a portable Philips three-speed record-player, five records (four of mood music and 'one Sinatra always'), a leather-covered RCA transistor radio, an old half-pint Heublein bottle full of vermouth, and a large nickel thermos with a wide mouth." He also had a calfskin briefcase that he designed himself and whose copious compartments held another forty-one items, including bottles of brandy and Johnnie Walker, a yodeling alarm clock, plus more standard items like toothbrushes and notebooks.

If you're keeping count, that's two suitcases, one massive raffia basket, and a briefcase. This was the classic mentality of travel: pack everything you need or want, all the comforts of home aside from your actual home itself.

What we have between Fielding and Frommer is a generation gap even more profound than the one that exists between Frommer and today's Lonely Planet–toting backpackers. Frommer's wife, Hope, wrote the packing chapter for *E5D*, and her advice was much like what you'll read in today's guides: pack as lightly as possible, the absolute essentials only. "A light suitcase means freedom." Roll—don't fold—your clothes. And don't worry about forgetting things—you can buy anything you need in Europe. They have stores there. And the food and water are safe, so don't take your own.

For men, this was Hope's recommended packing list:

3 pairs of shorts (Dacron or nylon)
3 cotton T-shirts
3 pairs of socks (at least one pair should be nylon)

2 handkerchiefs [recall that Fielding packed thirty-five]

1 sweater

2 Wash 'n' Wear Drip-Dry sport shirts

1 Drip-Dry white dress shirt

1 pair dress shoes

1 pair canvas shoes

1 light bathrobe

2 pair of nylon or Dacron pajamas

1 tweed sports jacket

1 pair of heavy slacks

1 pair of chino slacks

1 summer suit

1 raincoat

2 neckties

1 bathing suit

toilet and shaving articles (adapted for European use, if electric)

Don't take another thing!

That sounds a lot more manageable than Fielding's list. (Though, to be fair, Fielding's guidebooks did not recommend the same amount of gratuitous baggage that the man himself carried.)

Of course, to the modern reader, even Hope's list still feels a bit long (both a tweed sports jacket *and* a suit?!). Conventional wisdom among today's frugal travelers is to carry only a small daypack, to pack as though you were fleeing the country in the middle of the night and needed to escape with the barest necessities, and to make all of your attire multitask, suitable for nightclubs *and* business meetings *and* mountain climbing. (Good luck with that.) Utility trumps comfort, today's serious travelers seem to agree, and if something serves only one purpose or won't be used every minute of every day, it has no place in your backpack. Travel's better when you're kinda miserable—the road to enlightenment is paved with minimalist discomfort.

In my own packing, I had tried to find a happy medium: just one pair of shoes but five shirts, mostly cotton, which might not pack as small or dry as quickly as some other materials but *feels* a heck of a lot better. Zero suits, zero handkerchiefs.

Packing light, though, means having to do laundry all the time and makes for its own version of wretchedness if you keep putting off the task. While digging for something in the bottom of my backpack that night, I felt an unfamiliar package wrapped in plastic. I pulled it out, opened it up, and instantly wished I hadn't. It was my shirt and boxer shorts from that rain-drenched museum day in Florence, still damp and more odoriferous than the runniest, stinkiest French cheese. When you're on the road, living out of a backpack, you have to shift your hygiene standards downward a bit, but this was outside even my adjusted parameters of acceptability. I was tempted to throw them out the window, onto the Boulevard Saint-Michel, but that seemed likely to set back French-American relations at least a decade. So I filled the sink with hot water, dumped in the detergent and the clothes, and got to work.

It made me glad, once more, to be a tourist in modern times, in an era of fast-drying synthetics and, best of all, lowered expectations of formality. I like not having to pack even a single suit. Mind you, I wasn't wearing T-shirts and flip-flops—I was doing my best to blend in, with a plain but marginally classy wardrobe. (And, incidentally, I noticed my fellow Americans doing the same—the stereotypically informal, boorish Americans had given way to circumspect, well-attired ones. Good job, team.) For example, I wore only black socks, because I had heard that white ones were the classic sign of the American tourist. Black ones, though—those'll fool 'em. I suppose I hoped the European locals' conversation would go something like this:

> PIERRE: Ha! Look at that tourist with his camera and guidebook!
> JACQUES: Wait, but observe his socks! They are . . . black!
> PIERRE: *Zut alors!* You are correct! He is one of us! What a fool I am! Let us go speak to him in English and invite him to lunch!

I finished my load of sink laundry and hung my clothes up to dry on the bungee-cord clothesline I had strung across the bathroom. There were suction cups on either end, but they gave way immediately, my clothes tumbling to the tile floor with a wet, emphatic *thwump.* I put it back up more carefully, rehung the clothes, and gave a fruitless pass at pressing out the wrinkles with my hands.

I needed to look at least semipresentable the next day. I was headed to a classic Parisian bistro where no tourists ever went. Maybe I should have brought a suit along after all.

Although Frommer says it's the Left Bank where you'll find what remains of authentic Paris, he has one major find on the Right Bank, to which he devotes nearly an entire page of praise: a locals-only gem called Le Grand Colbert. It's "the cheapest restaurant of Paris," he says, and

> *It is the oddest restaurant in the world, and the only explanation I've conceived for it is that it exists primarily to serve the clerks and secretaries of the Paris "Bourse" (Stock Exchange), which is located one long avenue block away. The most amazing thing about the Colbert is that it has a huge, gilded interior, straight out of the era of Toulouse-Lautrec. . . . Paper tablecloths only, terribly crowded, get there at 1 p.m. to miss the heaviest lunch-time rush.*

As instructed, I arrived around 1 p.m. When I peeked in the window, I could see that the interior was every bit as magnificent as advertised, with high ceilings framed by elaborate crown molding and seemingly acres of wooden booths. There was a menu in the window, listing classic bistro fare plus a few nods to our globalized age, including "lamb stew curry style with basmati rice." Nearly everything was over twenty euros—so much for "cheapest restaurant of Paris." I nervously fingered the fifty-euro note in my pocket, which was supposed to last me a couple of days more.

There was something far more remarkable in one of the other windows: a movie poster for the Jack Nicholson–Diane Keaton romantic comedy *Something's Gotta Give*. An article from the *Australian* accompanied the poster. Its headline read, "Star brasserie can't stop counting its chickens." I skimmed the first paragraph and figured out the gist: a key scene of the movie was filmed at Le Grand Colbert, and tourists had been flocking there ever since—so much, too, for being a hidden, locals-only spot.

I was hungry, so I took a photo of the article, intending to peruse the rest later. I glanced at my reflection in the window and hastily combed my hair with my fingers, then took a deep breath and walked inside. I was greeted by a ferret of a maître d', who visibly recoiled at the sight of me. I silently translated what he was thinking: *Merde. Another American who saw that movie.* I was suddenly acutely aware that I was a disheveled backpacker who didn't belong here, even in spite of my clean, if rumpled, shirt and finger-combed hair. The maître d' beckoned, turned, and walked purposefully as he led me to a table away from the rest of the dwindling lunch crowd, as though quarantining me.

The waitress presented me with a menu, and I scanned it for something at least marginally in line with my budget and general culinary cowardice. *Aha*: roasted chicken. Sounds good. Serve it quick and get me out of here, *s'il vous plaît*. It arrived with a little dish of *pommes frites*, even though I didn't order them—the menu had them as a side dish, five euros. For a moment, I thought, Awesome, free food! Maybe this place wasn't so bad. Or maybe—my anxiety kicked in, full force—it was more plausible that they were going to charge me double, triple, quintuple, as part of one of those "mess with the tourists" hustles that modern guidebooks warn you about, but Frommer did not. I lightly touched the fifty-euro note again, then pulled my camera out of my bag. I scrolled through my recent photos as I chewed my chicken—which was actually quite tasty, I should note, the herb rub and tender meat perfectly balanced.

I stopped on the photo of the article in the window and zoomed in to read the text.

My jaw froze midmastication, then fell as I read. The star of the story was the maître d', outspoken in his annoyance with tourists and especially tired of those who "ring up and want to book the table Jack Nicholson and Diane Keaton ate at." No, I thought, recalling his quarantining. Surely he hadn't . . . Weeks later, at

*My last morning in Paris, I sat by the Seine, ate a
croissant, and became a tourist attraction myself,
waving to the tour boats passing by.*

home, I tracked down a copy of the movie and watched it in a panic
and found my answer: Yes. That's where he sat me. The Annoying
American Table.

I kept reading the blurry text on my camera and learned that
the staff was also sick of everyone always ordering the same meal
as the stars: roast chicken. With a side of *pommes frites.*

I wasn't just a disheveled backpacker and a stereotypical American tourist, which was bad enough. On top of that, I was a full-on
Diane Keaton groupie, a Jack Nicholson stalker, a glazed-eyed,
hard-core romantic-comedy obsessive.

The server walked by, intentionally looking away as she passed.

I strongly considered hiding under the table. Part of me wanted
to call out, "No, you don't understand! I'm not one of *them*! *Sacré*

bleu! What a misunderstanding! I am a journalist! A scholar! A tourist reenactor—not a real one." Somehow, though, I wasn't sure that pulling out my 1963 guidebook would be compelling evidence of my normalness and lack of bizarre obsessions.

"Arthur," I muttered, "what are you *doing* to me?"

My eyes darted around the room, taking in every detail, trying to distract myself from the queasiness settling into my gut. No wonder Hollywood had come calling. This place was perfect Paris, no soundstage necessary. The hydralike Beaux Arts light fixtures. The jazz concert posters behind the bar. The palm trees in massive azure urns.

Every time my gaze crossed paths with the bartender's, I noticed that he was staring at me with an unsettling mixture of confusion and contempt. I tried to focus on my food and reassure myself that I was imagining things, unfairly projecting on this guy the famous French snootiness that I still had yet to experience. He's just staring off into space, I told myself. He's bored. He's, you know, pondering Sartre or something. I glanced back at him for confirmation. *Oh, God. No.* He really was staring—*glowering*—at me. I pulled out my notebook and spent the rest of the meal doodling and jotting down random observations, my best pensive expression on my face, my eyes fixed on the page, certain that if I looked up, I'd find an entire row of Parisians leering, smirking. Maybe if I kept doing this, I told myself, my ruminative countenance would prove to him that I was, truly, not just another tourist but an incognito philosopher who had taken a stroll over from the Sorbonne for lunch. Maybe my black leather Moleskine—notebook of Hemingway and Chatwin—would win him over.

I recalled that Jack Nicholson had also played an addled writer in one of his more famous roles, in *The Shining*. My blank page, like his, was my curse; filling it was my obsession. I was running out of room in the notebook, but I vowed my pen wouldn't stop until the bill arrived. I wrote in the margins, my text running sideways, filling in gaps, becoming ever smaller.

"Just gonna keep writing and not look up," says one line. "'Cause this sucks."

This sucks. This sucks.

My mother's trip to Paris was also not going according to plan. She and Ann had a new, unexpected traveling companion: Terry, Ann's boyfriend from back in the States. He met them in Nice and proposed to Ann there; the three of them continued on to Paris together. A sign of their rock-bottom budget: even after that, they all shared a room. Awkward for everyone, for obvious reasons, and the new circumstances only made my mother miss her own fiancé even more.

Lack of time alone was not among my own problems. I had Arthur Frommer along as my imaginary traveling companion, but talking to him was getting old. The boar in Florence was really not working its magic. *E5D* wasn't helping. And I wasn't doing myself any favors, either, channeling my inner, mopey existentialist and spending inordinate amounts of time sitting in parks, eating pastries, and writing in my notebook.

A few blocks from Le Grand Colbert, I passed the open doorway of an office building. There was a young woman, about my age, leaning idly against the door frame. As I walked by, we made eye contact for a split second and the weirdest thing happened: her face absolutely lit up in a delighted, startled smile.

Wow, I thought. You'll never get *that* greeting again. If ever there were a time to strike up conversation with a random stranger, this is it.

She looked exactly like that woman from the movie *Amélie*, with short black hair and a coy sparkle in her eyes. Of course. When a young man who likes to think of himself as worldly and bookish and quirky is in Paris and falls in love at first sight, this is the natural reference point: *Amélie*.

I realize that I am not the first person with delusions of living a romantic-comedy life filled with meet-cute moments and a soundtrack of melancholy indie rock ballads. You could blame Jack and Diane and Le Grand Colbert for putting me in the mindset just now, but the truth is, these flights of fancy are fairly common for me when I'm abroad, where everything is unfamiliar and therefore unreal—like I'm the mild-mannered protagonist wandering through the set. If I keep following the script, everything will turn out just like in the movies.

I absolutely swear, though, that this was not infatuated self-deception but fact: she looked just like Amélie. I imagined our courtship: moonlit strolls along the Seine, picnics in the Jardin du Luxembourg. A brief, narrative-enhancing spat about philosophy or croissants. Our wedding in a little chapel overlooking the lavender fields of Provence. Our adorable mop-headed, bilingual children. The movie based on our story, debuting to critical accolades at Sundance—casting her role would be too easy.

I returned the smile, the gaze.

And . . .

And I kept walking. Such was my frustration and self-loathing, and my certainty that my tourist status and the language barrier would immediately kill the conversation. This is what happens when a romantic fool is also a pragmatic, coldhearted cynic: head overrules heart. Life's not a movie, I reminded myself, although I could swear I heard the Sundance audience groaning in frustration. After three minutes of wondering, "What would Arthur do?" and admonishing myself—*seriously, you're never going to get a first-glance smile like that again*—I doubled back. She was gone. I peered inside the doorway and saw not a soul.

My mother's turning point in Paris came when she hopped on a train and got out of town alone. She kept riding until something looked interesting, getting off at Saint-Pierre-des-Corps. She wandered for hours, toured a cathedral, ate crepes, enjoyed her newfound solitude. When she returned to Paris and met back up with Ann and Terry, she was refreshed. They went to a restaurant recommended by a friend, she reported in a letter on the back of a museum ticket, her paper supply and money running low but her spirits sky-high. "We got here an hour before it opens so the owner invited us in . . . and is now playing the guitar—atmosphere plus." They stayed for nearly five hours.

For me, the event that reinstilled my touristic sense of wonder was the Parade for Sex and Beer. I don't know if that was the official name, but it was definitely the theme. Champagne and wine were also involved, plus college students in diapers and baby bonnets.

It was . . . well, somewhere on the Right Bank. I was lost again. In the distance, perhaps a block away, I heard the distinctive sound of a marching band—something I associate with small-town parades in the United States, not capital cities abroad. I peered down the street and saw, sure enough, a band of perhaps thirty members. They were not especially tuneful or well organized, the rows far from precise, the marching more of a lackadaisical amble. Each musician wore a brightly colored T-shirt and a matching Afro wig.

Behind them came the floats. If the guys from *Animal House* got together with some Dadaists, this would be the result: a car with an enormous papier-mâché pretzel affixed to the top, another with a fifty-gallon wine bottle pouring into a glass on the hood, and other vehicles transformed, with sheets and paint and various accessories, into a tropical jungle, a yellow submarine, and what was either a cremation urn or a teapot. Interspersed throughout were trucks with bands and gyrating dancers.

Were they celebrating something? Advertising something? Had Frommer contrived to set this up to boost my spirits? I had no idea. When one of the diaper-wearing students tried to hand me a flyer, I declined—I didn't want to know what this was all about. Ill-informed speculation was more fun.

I had less than twenty-four hours left on this trip, and suddenly I realized how boring my life was about to become again. Constraints of budget and lack of vacation time were forcing me to return to my mundane reality, and I wasn't looking forward to it. For the past eight whirlwind days, I had been waking up each morning with no real plans and in a setting almost entirely unfamiliar to me. My brain was always on, working to keep up, confronted with new problems and puzzles at every turn—I was using it far more than I did back at the office, writing memos and cursing at the ornery printer. Even the most frustrating moments—like lunch at Le Grand Colbert—had turned out to be eye-opening or hilarious in retrospect.

At my hotel, I struck up a conversation with the desk clerk, a Parisian version of a burned-out California surfer dude. He guffawed loudly when I showed him my old guidebook. "I have not heard of this. Impossible! Maybe five *hundred* dollars a day. Is this what it should say?"

He read aloud, "Right on the Boulevard St. Michel, the big Hotel de Suez is the outstanding choice for readers who don't mind a fair amount of noise from the strollers below." Here he paused and gave the shrug-plus-head-tilt that I had come to think of as the French way of saying "Yes, it is true, and it is unfortunate. But . . . whatever, dude." He knew that I was in a street-side room and that the noise had only gotten worse.

I showed him Frommer's descriptions of other hotels and restaurants in the neighborhood, and he started rattling off details. This closed years ago; this he had not heard of; this was still around but bore little resemblance to Frommer's description. He was doing my work for me, sparing me the chore of the hunt.

"It's okay," I said, stopping him. "I want to go look for myself."

One of the few landmarks that Frommer does recommend in *Europe on Five Dollars a Day* is Montmartre. I initially skimmed past it when reading, because the listing is buried in a one-paragraph-long synopsis of some things to do. This is the entire description: "Montmartre, at dusk." Nothing about where it is or why I'd want to go there.

I should note here that my willful ignorance was not a put-on. I had made a genuine effort not to know anything about anywhere before I left home, and my general foolishness needs no embellishments. I say this because, apparently, Montmartre is a Well-Known

Thing. I'm guessing that's why Frommer felt no need to give any details aside from saying, yeah, it's worth seeing—just as his entire listing for a certain other famous landmark reads, simply, "The Eiffel Tower, of course." I'm sure I'd heard of Montmartre before, but the specifics never stuck in my mind.

But I overheard some other tourists comparing notes and mentioning plans to go there, so I figured maybe it was worth checking out. My last night, I took the train to Montmartre just before sunset, then followed the signs and the crowds trekking up the immense hill that appeared in front of me. At the summit, a sweep of stairs led up to a towering cathedral, resplendent in white travertine stone and hauntingly elegant in its symmetry and restrained detailing. The Basilique du Sacré Cœur. Another set of stairs led down to an open terrace, where a few dozen people were scattered about, in groups and alone. Some were eating a picnic supper; some were just chatting; six or seven kids played keep-away with a soccer ball. Everyone subtly nodded to the beats competing from across the plaza: a teenager's tinny boom box and a pair of drummers banging on bongos.

The real attraction, the focus of everyone's attention, was the expanse beyond and below the terrace: the city of Paris, sprawling to the horizon, as though presented on a massive platter for my own personal enjoyment.

Incroyable. I walked down the steps, not blinking, barely breathing, spellbound. I dodged a misfired pass from the soccer game and leaned against the railing at the edge of the hill.

I was glad I hadn't known about this beforehand. If I'd stuck to my usual method of overpreparation, I would have read all the details about this place, this view. I would have seen the professional photos. I would have heard the dissenting voices bemoaning the crowds and those pesky kids with their soccer ball. I would have been, I am sure, disappointed. A little knowledge can be a dangerous thing, especially in travel, where surprise and wonder and discovering the new are pretty much the entire reason for the endeavor. Never in my life have I been so grateful for being so ill informed.

Thank you, Arthur. You were right: Paris is rejuvenating.

I turned around to watch the crowd on the steps and saw a man walking toward me. I pulled my camera from my bag. *"Excusez-moi?"* I said, trying to remember the word for "photo."

He chuckled, "I was about to ask you the same thing!" He tugged his own tiny camera from his pocket.

We took each other's photos and got to chatting as the light started to fade. His name was Jay; he was a business executive from Philadelphia in town for a conference. Tall guy, athletic, confident, looked a bit like a young Colin Powell.

"I didn't know much about this place, either," he said, "but everyone said you gotta go there, gotta go there. So last night I came up here, and it's . . . amazing. I'm going home tomorrow, but I had to come back one more time."

In a few minutes, we would watch as the City of Light earned its reputation, with a scattering of far-flung flickers leading the way, followed by luminous bursts as the streetlamps switched on, coordinating with the glow spilling from cafés and apartments to make art of the sprawling grid. Jay and I would keep talking, exchange business cards, and promise to keep in touch.

But for now, it was the transition that captivated us, silencing our conversation. So this is why you go to Montmartre at dusk: to watch from above as the setting sun bathes Paris in saffron hues, then rose, seeming to spotlight only the most magnificent features and hide the rest in shadows—never mind those bits. Never mind your worries. Enjoy this moment while it lasts.

Amsterdam

Live and Let Live It Up

Amsterdam is a swinging town.

—Europe on Five Dollars a Day

A year passed. A year in which I grew ever more weary of my job and my life; a year in which my health took a major turn for the worse; a year in which, most of all, I couldn't get Montmartre out of my mind. Now and then, I revisited my parents' letters, always finding myself lingering over one of the last ones my father sent to Europe:

> *After working all day and lots of yesterday and all, I just had to get OUT, so at about 1:00 AM I just did. The night is clear, calm, and cold—so silent you can hear for miles. The crunch of snow and the sound of an occasional car blocks away only help to bring out how quiet it is. . . . And I thought about travel and decided that I would hop a freight train tonight if I did not have other responsibilities and desires which I consider—for some unknown reason— to be more __?__. But I almost did. I.e.—I'm getting itchy feet.*

One midsummer day, as I mowed my parents' lawn while they were in Scotland—yet again—my own itchy feet became unbearable.

I booked a ticket.

I would leave in a month for six weeks on the Continent. Going to all fifteen cities left in the book wasn't feasible, not unless I wanted to spend the rest of my life eating only Fancy Feast Florentine cat food. So I drew up a list using various criteria: ease of access between cities (sorry, Athens), general sense of what had changed the most in forty years (*guten Tag*, Berlin), and random whim. My itinerary: Amsterdam, Brussels, Berlin, Munich, Zurich, Vienna, Venice, Rome, and Madrid.

This time, I would have company.

Allow me to introduce my friend Lee. "Friend" might be stretching it, actually, because the truth is, I barely knew him. We had spent a grand total of perhaps three or four hours together in person, at a writers' conference in Key West, where we'd met two years earlier; since then, we'd kept in touch via email. Lee's a novelist, bartender, and freelance scribe whose beats include nightlife and the singles scene. He lives in Baltimore and looks a bit like the actor Ryan Gosling. He has a quick, broad smile and, always, a wry gleam in his eyes. From what I'd gathered from our limited interactions and the man-about-town tone of his writing, he was the very definition of dashing and rakish—in other words, an appropriately inappropriate sidekick for someone who is, as the Dutch say, *kindofaneuroticintrovert*. He would join me for the first five cities.

"If I do my job," Lee said in an email before we left the United States, "you will be fully glad to be rid of me when I leave." The words filled me with both excitement and dread in equal measure, more so the latter when we decided that we would meet in Amsterdam, a rather famously good place to get into trouble.

As Arthur Frommer puts it in his opening line about the city, "Amsterdam is a swinging town." It's a word choice that invites knowing snickers and raised eyebrows from the modern reader: *Oh, really, Arthur? What do you mean by "swinging," exactly?*

What he meant, I hasten to note, is not the sort of true debauchery that we now associate with Amsterdam. The city's famous coffee shops (meaning, wink, wink: *marijuana shops*) came to prominence only after the Dutch parliament decriminalized pot in 1976—nearly twenty years after *Europe on Five Dollars a Day* was first published—and Frommer gives the Red Light District the most cursory of mentions. It's nothing at all like the 1999 guidebook I found at my local library, *Get Lost: The Cool Guide to Amsterdam,* which features entire chapters on where to find primo weed and the best live sex shows ("I especially liked one couple who did a choreographed routine to Mozart's 'Requiem'"). No, Frommer's "swinging" was a lot more banal—burlesque and booze were as scandalous as he got.

Before we continue, let's have a quick by-the-numbers establishing of some key facts:

Total number of drinks I had consumed during the Florence-Paris part of my Not-So-Grand Tour: zero
Times in my life, ever, that I had been barhopping (as in, you know, patronizing multiple bars in a single evening): not a one

You'll understand my alarm, then, when just a few hours after Lee arrived, we were wandering the streets in search of our—count 'em—*fourth* bar of the evening. We were in the southern part of town, in a bustling commercial and entertainment district, all neon signs and blaring music. The people-watching was spectacular: tourists of all types and all nationalities staring at each other in wonder and disgust; a guy who spoke in a hilariously sinister stage whisper, offering to sell us drugs ("I got the reeeal deeal"); and a loitering group of men in their early twenties, all vacant eyed and creepily dapper in tight jeans, black sport coats, black ties, and necklaces with vaguely New Age amulets—they looked like a cult awaiting the arrival of a charismatic leader.

As we stood on the sidewalk, taking in the spectacle, trying to avoid eye contact with the cult guys, Lee said, quietly, "There."

Before I could ask for details, he finished his thought, his voice authoritative but tinged with mischievousness. "Pirate bar."

"Pirate . . . what?" I didn't like where this was going.

"Pirate bar," he repeated. He pointed toward the forest of neon. My eyes followed his gesture and, defying my brain's instructions to feign ignorance, settled on a flashing yellow sign that read, sure enough, "Pirate Bar."

"No," I said.

"Yes. We've gotta go there," Lee said, striding forward.

I composed a mental inventory of reasons why this was a bad idea, but there were so many that I didn't know where to start listing them out loud. So I followed him.

As we got closer, I noticed that it was surprisingly nonkitschy, which only made me more paranoid. It looked like the Amsterdam equivalent of the candy-offering strangers your mom always warned you about. *Come here, little backpacker,* it seemed to say. *Come inside, have a drink, pay no attention to the fact that the weird*

skeleton out front looks nothing like a pirate and everything like that
British college student who went missing last year.

"Um, I think I'm going to veto this," I said, then quickly added, to save face, "I mean, *Arthur* wouldn't approve. It's not in the book."

"We can't say no to a pirate bar," Lee said. "It's a *pirate bar.*" As if that explained everything.

The man could not be dissuaded, not even by my mumblings about roofies and canals and stories I'd heard from friends of friends. As we sipped our Heinekens, we looked around the room and noted that there really, seriously was no pirate theme whatsoever, aside from a bunch of bananas above the Coke dispenser, which I suppose could be construed as tropical and therefore pirate by association. Somehow, though, this minor detail only highlighted the overall sketchiness of the place. On one side of the room, there was a riser/ stage area that was too small for a band but would have been just about the right size to serve as an operating table for kidney removal. Behind this, there was a scratched-up mirror that appeared very likely to be one-way. We were the only patrons but for two young women dressed in Red Light District attire, if you see what I mean.

As I whimpered to myself, two more young women entered through the front door. Thank God, I thought. Strength in numbers. They were dressed for clubbing, in tight, ridiculous outfits and towering high heels. This pleased me not for the typical male reasons but because it meant that if all of my worst fears about this place were true, I could beat them to the door. Speaking in English accents, they ordered beers and Jägerbombs. A couple of minutes later, a few more women entered, same attire, same accent, same order.

And then they started coming in waves: clones or sorority sisters or something, dozens of lookalike English twenty-somethings.

Within ten minutes, the place was jammed beyond the fire marshal's worst nightmare. The music started up, then cranked to maximum volume. A fog machine belched to life. Strobes and spotlights pierced the room, frenetic, urgent, disorienting. The force of the crowd slowly pushed us off our bar stools. The party had frickin' *started*.

I looked at Lee, dumbfounded. I wanted to ask him if this was his doing, if he could just snap his fingers and conjure a mob, if it was going to be like this every night. It was too loud for conversation, though, so I just mouthed, "What . . . the heck?"

He smirked and shrugged. "Who cares?"

We ordered another round, sat back, and watched the spectacle.

Very late at night, as the room's energy peaked, we were finally treated to a bit of pirateness. The music and the strobe lights switched off, to a series of groans from the partyers, followed by an anticipatory hush as a bell started clanging. The bartenders lit torches and poured themselves shots; a couple of them put on black tricornered pirate hats.

The clanging got more frenzied; the crowd found its voice again, roaring as a single throbbing, delirious entity. The bartenders took deep breaths, downed their shots, brought their torches to their mouths, paused for a brief, dramatic beat . . . and let loose enormous, spraying, full-bodied roars, launching fireballs into the darkness.

The place erupted. A roomful of vocal cords stretched to the max and eardrums popped like champagne corks. A barrage of elbows pummeled me as every hand shot into the air in delight. Lee looked coyly triumphant, like a magician who has just pulled off a spectacular trick for the first time and can't believe it worked.

In Amsterdam, I discovered that I—and my friends, as I would later point out to them all too eagerly—had been drinking beer wrong all these years. Lee, of course, already knew this. To wit: beer should be served at cellar temperature, not cold, not warm, and it specifically *should* have a head. If you are truly sophisticated (and the pirates, for the record, were not), you will level off the head with the flick of a tool that looks much like a frosting knife.

I learned all of this at the Heineken Experience ("Meet the Beer. Share the Magic."). In the 1960s, this was just the Heineken Brewery, noted in Frommer's Readers' Suggestions section for its straightforward but convivial atmosphere:

> *The tour is very interesting and lasts about an hour and fifteen minutes. Following the tour, you return to the tap room for cheese and Heineken's beer.... Souvenir post card folders are supplied and if you address them, Heineken stamps and mails them. The tour guide sits with the guests and the conversation is interesting and international. A worthwhile tour, and with no fee of any kind.*

My mom took that free tour and got something even cooler than "post card folders": a *mailable coaster* that opened up to reveal a small booklet of photos from the brewery, along with space for a brief note.

Alas, the mailable coasters are now gone, along with the free admission. Lee and I had to settle for an e-postcard booth, at which we selected the windmill image from the various Heineken-branded background options, posed for a photo, and emailed it to my mother. Compared to the coaster postcard, it felt impersonal and sterile—awfully *modern*.

The whole experience—excuse me, *Experience*—was like that: technologically impressive but just not all that interesting. The room where visitors lingered the longest was the one filled with what looked like *Star Trek* versions of La-Z-Boys, with Heineken-green glowing sides and integrated television screens hovering above, showing the company's ads through the decades.

It wasn't until we got to the World Bar—the last room before the gift shop—that I finally started to enjoy the place. We struck up conversation with Terrance, an American in the air force. We compared notes on things to do in Amsterdam—he wanted to go to the Anne Frank House; I was concerned it would have become, by now, a cheesy, high-tech attraction like the one in which we were standing—but then moved on to other topics: travel, American politics, American culture, life. Terrance pointed around the room to the other tourists he'd already talked to, people from Spain, Germany, and Dubai. I mentioned that both Mom and Frommer had also spoken of the international multitudes here, and we toasted the power of beer to bring people together.

There was something deeper going on, though. It wasn't just the beer that created camaraderie, it was the landmark status of this place: it's in the guidebooks, it's a well-known Thing to Do in Amsterdam, so it attracts a wide range of people. This, of course, is a big reason why many of us take pains to avoid "tourist traps": they're bursting at the seams with, well, tourists. It's generally agreed that this is a problem. But is it really? Perhaps we need to take a page from Heineken and other corporations and, focusing on the positive, rebrand the beaten path as this: the crossroads of the world.

If you can find some breathing room, if you can carve out a few moments of conversation—in a bar at the end of the Heineken Experience, perhaps, or on the plaza below the Basilique du Sacré Cœur, watching the City of Light begin to twinkle and glow at dusk—you might find that your fellow beaten-path travelers are not tacky or awkward or boorish. Not Terrance, not Jay at Montmartre, not the family from Madrid I met by the Arc de Triomphe.

This is the travel platitude to end all travel platitudes: it's not about the place, it's about the people. Agreed. So let's not forget that even on the tourist trail—*especially* here, come to think of it—you can meet all kinds of people who are interesting and worldly and not at all the stereotype of the shallow sightseer. Improbable kindred spirits you would not otherwise encounter but who will be more than worth your while. And—this is important—because they are often on leave from the military or in town for a conference or just short on vacation time and planning energy, they're precisely the sort of fascinating people who you *won't* meet if you follow only the road less traveled. They're all the more interesting precisely because they're *not* jaded eternal travelers—they have full, rich lives back home, and travel serves as an icebreaker, not the entirety of the conversation. Some people mock tourists as roving bands of people who are all the same, and though there's an ounce or two of truth to that, the reality is more complex—they may not be locals, but there's actually a fair amount of diversity, especially at the big landmarks where everyone wants to go.

Granted, the beaten path will not lead you to the eccentric characters who populate the year-in-a-remote-village memoirs that have become such a cliché of travel writing. You won't encounter a lot of hobbled, grandmotherly types cloaked in oh-so-native garb. And, sure, fine: it's a shame that you won't meet those Authentic Individuals™.

Truth is, though, you're probably not going to parachute into a new culture and become fast friends with the locals. No matter how eager you are to interact with them, they probably don't want to interact with you—they just want to go about their daily lives

*Plush clog slippers: perhaps the only G-rated
souvenirs in Amsterdam.*

and not be bothered by this stranger who's come to stare at them and mangle their language and ask to see how the Authentic Local Thing is done. Looking back on my journey so far, it struck me that, unless you're truly charming and sociable (that is, unless you're more like Lee than like me), it's far easier to find conversation and camaraderie among your fellow travelers, your fellow confused outsiders, than with the quirky-authentic-traditional locals.

And, really: most tourists are pretty damn interesting.

I was proud of this insight. So proud. Until I got a reminder that, just as with any group consisting of more than two people, tourists are in no way a homogenous bunch. Some are affable and interesting, and some conform to every negative stereotype.

One evening, Lee and I took shelter from the rain in a dive bar just outside the Red Light District. There were some gaunt, sallow-eyed toughs playing pool, and I have to confess to a vision of the night ending with a broken cue stick through my chest. We took our beers to the tiny basement area, which was halfheartedly decorated with retro beer posters and broken sconces. We commiserated about our writing failures and utter lack of success and fame, then started fantasizing, in jest, about a future in which we were turning down autographs and wearing sunglasses.

A young woman gaveled a massive beer stein on the table next to Lee, then eased herself onto the adjacent stool. She had long black hair and a low-cut pink blouse.

"We heard you talking," she said in a clipped English accent frayed with tipsiness. Gesturing to four friends at a nearby table, she continued, "She says you were saying something about being famous. Are you famous?"

"Well, we will be," Lee replied, grinning. "Give us some time. A few weeks, maybe."

"Are you famous now?" the woman asked, apparently hoping we were just being modest.

"Yes, you've discovered us," I said. "I'm Brad Pitt and this is George Clooney."

She was not amused; her face became a mask of derision and disappointment. I could almost hear her thinking, "Fuck you for not being celebrities. I walked all the way over here and you can't even be some C-list reality TV stars or obscure indie rockers?"

Lee and I, however, *were* amused and willing to continue the conversation, if only to see how petulant she would become. They were from outside of London ("You wouldn't recognize the name

of the town") and had come here just for a long weekend to cele-
brate our new nonfriend's birthday.

"Wait, you flew to Amsterdam just for the weekend, for a birthday party?" Lee asked.

They gave us blank looks, apparently trying to figure out if we
really had asked such a stupid question.

"Um, *yeah*," one said, finally, tactfully leaving out the "duh."

"But . . . why Amsterdam?" Lee asked.

The five answered in gleeful, drunken unison: "To get fucked up!"

I tried to imagine my mother as part of this group. She had been
about their age. Would she have fit in with them? Would the European culture of her era have allowed women to express such a sentiment? I would have said no to both of these questions. Absolutely
not. Nice, wholesome women from Minnesota wouldn't do that sort
of thing in the '60s—even latent hippies like Mom. Her postcards to
Dad may have mentioned touring museums with other men, but
there was nothing about any late-night carousing. Her postcards to
her sister, however . . . well, they painted a different picture: "Went
to 2 student clubs last nite," she wrote from Amsterdam. "Went to
bed at 4:30 AM." She went on to offer her hangover cure, a large
glass of milk. This was information that I didn't know how to begin
processing, in its own way as jarring as it would have been to find a
photo of her dancing on a bar with a lampshade on her head. (Unfortunately, or perhaps not, all of her photos from the trip have disappeared.) Maybe things hadn't changed that much, after all.

Our inebriated interrogator's spirit dropped another notch
when we said we were writers—the lowest of the noncelebrities. I
brought out *Europe on Five Dollars a Day* and she inadvertently
tore the cover half off as she pawed through it.

"Easy there," I muttered.

"So will we be in your book?" she asked as she drained her beer.

"You haven't been interesting enough," Lee said brightly.

"Just mention the drunk girl in Amsterdam," came the slurred reply.

"Let's go see a sex show," her friend said. I'm not sure if it was a sincere suggestion or just the first excuse she could think of to ditch these noncelebrities. They headed out with half waves, leaving us once again anonymous and at peace.

Well, Drunk Girl in Amsterdam, you made it in after all. Because you—as well as your compatriots at the Pirate Bar, who we eventually figured out were all part of a group trip—are an excellent case study in this truth of modern travel: as going abroad has become easier, people do it for ever-sillier reasons and ever-shorter lengths of time. At this rate, we'll soon be teleporting around the world just to pick up sandwich ingredients.

I'd like to point out, once again, that we were in a bar, drinking beer (that is, not in a coffee shop consuming other items). Last I checked, England had bars. Rather a lot. But it was cheaper and easier, Drunk Girl said, not to mention more exotic, to come here than to spend a weekend in London or take the train up to Edinburgh. There were a variety of modern-day factors that made this possible: the European Union's open borders, the ease of booking plane tickets and hotel rooms online, and the flat-out low costs of getting here.

They'd flown over on one of the discount airlines like Ryanair and easyJet, the game changers for intra-European travel since the mid-1990s. These are "no-frills" airlines, which is a kinder way of saying, "Think of the most dismal bus on which you have ridden, and then imagine it thirty thousand feet up." (Even the airports

they serve often have a forlorn bus station vibe, far-flung and aus-
tere.) There's just one selling point, but it's the crucial one: prices
that even a 1960s backpacker would find astonishingly cheap, often
well under a hundred dollars (plus various fees, which can add up
quickly).

Once you're on the Continent today, your funds might not
stretch as far as my mother's (five dollars then would be equivalent
to nearly thirty-four dollars in 2011; good luck using that as your
daily budget), but, interestingly, it costs a lot less to get there in the
first place, even if you're traveling all the way across the Atlantic.
That's true not just in inflation-adjusted figures but often in real
dollars. According to my copy of *Europe on Five Dollars a Day*, in
1963, an economy-class round-trip airplane ticket from New York
to Rome cost $620.30 (more than $4,400 in 2011 dollars). At the
time, all the major airlines charged precisely the same price,
because they were all part of the International Air Transport Association (IATA), which set the fares. (Credit the U.S. Airline Dereg-
ulation Act of 1978 with ending this practice.) There was one
exception: Icelandair—my mother's choice—which wasn't part of
the alliance and undercut its competitors by about a hundred dollars and sold only tourist-class fares, although you did have to go
through Reykjavík.

I'm not quite ready to call today the golden age of travel, but in
many ways it's a heck of a lot easier, safer, faster, and even cheaper
to go wherever you want, on your own terms, no travel agent or
elaborate planning necessary. The world is open; the options for
escape ever-expanding. They might not always be luxurious, but
they're egalitarian, more so every day—and that's the point, the
one that Arthur Frommer was trying to make.

. . .

Lee had coined a verb: "Frommering." It was his name for the scavenger hunt I led him on all over town in search of my guidebook's recommendations. And the Frommering, as it happened, was not going well, even though we were walking six to eight miles a day, we guessed, in our search. Whenever we found ourselves frustrated and hungry at the door of a tobacco shop or row house that had once been an enchanting bistro, we relied on what Lee called "the Goddess Serendipity" and picked a restaurant or thing to do at random. I had a different, more guilt-wracked term for this: "cheating on Arthur."

One place that is definitely still around is the Red Light District, which, as I say, Frommer mentions only fleetingly, in the final entry of the Readers' Suggestions section: "A walk through Amsterdam's Red Light district is unbelievable." Like Drunk Girl's friends, Lee and I wanted to see it for ourselves, if only to check it off the list.

And it is still unbelievable—but not in the way that you'd expect. Just the opposite: the area really is not as seedy as you might think, at least during a normal person's waking hours. We went at dusk the next day, and the first thing we saw was an older couple out for an evening constitutional, licking ice cream cones, taking in the scene. Most everyone, it appeared, came here purely for the people-watching, eyeing the other tourists and, if they were anything like me and Lee, quietly making bets about who would actually enter the well-kept, neon-signed, mall-store-looking dens of iniquities around us. Few did. We peered into the offices of what appeared to be a design firm, spotting a meeting of executives in a conference room that shared a wall with a brothel. A friend of mine later told me that when he was here, he'd seen a large group of people, men and women, crowded around the picture window of one of the brothels. Curious, he peered through the scrum, expecting to see a sex show or something similarly risqué. In fact, they were watching the World Cup.

There was one place that I knew was still open but had been avoiding, particularly in light of the over-the-top cheesiness of the Heineken Experience and the fact that much of central Amsterdam seemed to have become an amusement park with a libertarian theme, all souvenir stands and head shops and museums of vice (literally: our hotel was in the same block as the Sex Museum and the Vodka Museum, and walking distance to the Marijuana Museum).

If ever there were a place that should not be turned into a proper-noun Experience or Attraction, this is it: the Anne Frank House.

It merits its own section in *Europe on Five Dollars a Day*, under the heading "The Unforgettable." Frommer calls the effect of visiting "searing, heartbreaking, infuriating beyond belief," then adds, "Let none of us ever pass through Amsterdam without making a pilgrimage to the Anne Frank House."

But Lee and I had seen the line—out the door, down the block. And we'd seen the people posing in front of the house with wide grins, casually leaning on the doorway like it was Cinderella's Castle at Disneyland. As I'd told Terrance at the Heineken Experience, no matter how serious the subject matter, this seemed to be just another overrun, tacky tourist trap—a place to visit not out of any sense of moral or historic duty, but because you saw it listed in one of those books with titles like *1,000 Things You Absolutely, Positively Must Do Before You Die, Unless You're a Total Loser*. There might even be an animatronic Anne. I shuddered at the thought.

Still, we felt obligated to visit, if only because Frommer said we must.

The young Brits in front of us in line played right into our expectations. There were four of them, all women in their early twenties, all exceptionally loud. They would have gotten along well with Drunk Girl. As they dug hungrily into a bag of potato chips, they exchanged ever-wilder stories of excess and debauchery in bars around the world and coffee shops here in Amsterdam. One woman was particularly quick with the titillating tales. She had bleached blond hair, saucer-sized sunglasses, an astonishing amount of makeup, flip-flops, and a tight black outfit that left little to the imagination. She was, I thought, the very archetype of the obnoxious, indiscreet tourist.

As we neared the entrance, Lee suppressed a snicker and said, "I bet there'll be some precious comments inside the museum, too."

Inside, though, the crowds were too hushed for eavesdropping. Oh, I tried, particularly when I could tell from my fellow visitors' amused looks that their comments were not exactly reverential. But as we moved through the lower part of the building, took in the various museum displays, and edged closer to the upstairs annex where the Frank family hid, the collective mood became more solemn and uneasy.

So did my own.

By the time I climbed the staircase beyond the famous book-shelf, all the snark had drained from my body. I felt less like a visitor in a museum and more like an inadvertent trespasser in someone's home. History had come alive in the most unsettling way.

There was one sight that literally stopped me in my tracks: a line from Anne's diary, dated December 24, 1943, and now printed on the wall: "I long to ride a bike, dance, whistle, look at the world, feel young and know that I'm free."

Reading that quote in the midst of my own six-week, transcontinental backpacking trip—a journey that was, essentially, an expression of freedom and youth—was a jarring reminder that life is not like this for everyone, not an endless stream of discoveries and delights.

For us tourists, the Anne Frank House is a destination to be checked off and posed in front of before we head on to the Heineken Experience or the Van Gogh Museum—it's a place of momentary interest in our journeys.

For Anne—and, more to the point, for way too many other nameless, forgotten individuals, then and now—travel wasn't an option, not even a dash across the street. Home was prison. It's this fact that makes the Anne Frank House so uniquely discomfiting: it is eerily familiar. We can identify with this family, this apartment. In this context, mundane details gain deeper resonance, like the section of wall with markings measuring the heights of Anne and her sister, Margot, tracking their growth and potential but also the passing and loss of their youth.

These are the details that illuminate the day-to-day existence of the Franks' lives in this hiding space—this *living* space—and their efforts to create something akin to the humdrum happiness of normalcy. Even for a cynic like me, the effect was deeply moving and chilling.

I know that some people leave uplifted and inspired by Anne's hopeful words, buoyed by their lyricism and introspection in the face of great evil. That's not how I felt. I left disconcerted and upset by the ending of the story—no matter how positive Anne's sentiments, and how admirable her ability to see the good in humanity, the fact is, she was a prisoner in her own home for years, and then she was captured and killed. This is a place that just should not exist, that should not *have* to exist, and whose very existence tugs at your soul and makes you despair in some elemental way. Life's pretty fucked up: that's my takeaway message.

Near the end of the tour, I saw the British woman who had been in line in front of us, the stereotypical tourist with the flip-flops and tales of getting plastered. Now her sunglasses were off and her makeup was streaked.

I followed her to the exit and we stepped out into the sunlight, young and free.

We didn't have much interest in bars after that. It would be overstating it to say that the Anne Frank House made us rethink our entire journey and question the wisdom and morality of trekking around Europe—in a quirky, frivolous way, no less—when we could be putting our time and energy and dollars to a more meaningful purpose. Not quite.

It did, however, lead us to seek out some calm and contemplation, a respite from Frommering and tourist multitudes. We'd heard that if we rented bikes and followed the Amstel River out of town for just a mile or so, we'd find ourselves in a pastoral wonderland with cows and tulips and windmills and clog-wearing farmers inviting us into their ramshackle canalside cottages to sample their Gouda.

We pedaled through the weekend crowds, parting them with cries of *"fiets"* ("bicycle!") or incessant dings of our bells, the going slow but the experience liberating. The pedestrian masses eventually thinned, and then the streetscape followed suit, the narrow bike lanes giving way to a wide promenade along the river. We were flying, fleeing, loving the unfamiliar sight of trees and broad expanses of sky and enjoying the transgressive European thrill of biking *without a helmet.*

This was the road less pedaled! Nary a souvenir shop or tourist-crammed landmark to be found.

We were the only outsiders around, and we had front-row seats as we watched authentic locals doing their authentic local things. Yes! Sweet! Amazing! We were travelers, not tourists! And, hark, in the distance: a bustling restaurant like the one Frommer wrote about, where "the diners are served with amazing rapidity" and the patrons are all "good-natured"!

If only ...

If only it hadn't said "McDonald's" on the sign out front. If only our surroundings hadn't been suburban wasteland, denuded of a sense of place, vacant of tourists *for a damn good reason.* No tulips here, no windmills, and certainly no cows, at least not in forms larger than a quarter pound (with cheese).

"Yeah, I don't think this is quite what I had in mind," Lee said.

Here's a little lesson for you: just because it's off the beaten path doesn't mean it's charming. Everyday local reality is not necessarily alluring or traditional.

We pedaled for nearly an hour and this is all we saw: broad highways and strip malls and industrial parks and vast swaths of land vacant but for a cover of weeds and a sign whose words I couldn't read but whose sentiment was perfectly clear: "Coming Soon: New Development." There were big-box stores and car dealerships and office parks that could have been in New Jersey or Omaha or anywhere back in the States. There was self-storage—self-storage! That quintessential icon of the too-much-stuff American lifestyle! The only canals were drainage ditches.

We biked back into town as fast as we could.

Brussels

Baffling Capital of a Baffling Continent

If you're a medievalist at heart, or have a fairly
substantial desire to study that age, then you'll love
Brussels. If not, stay far, far away, for this city is all
history, and little else. It has neither the fleshpots of
Paris, nor the grandeur of Rome, nor the
boisterousness of Munich.

—Europe on Five Dollars a Day

"Wow," I said more baffled than impressed.

"Wow," Lee echoed. "So, um, that's it?"

It's even smaller and stranger than you'd think. Not Brussels, I mean, but its most famous landmark, which we were now examining. In most countries, the national icon is a showcase of ingenuity and artistry and might: the Great Wall of China, the Eiffel Tower, the Statue of Liberty. In Belgium, it is *Manneken-Pis*. A bronze statue of a toddler boy. Urinating. He's a fountain, you see.

Frommer calls him "the statue which all the ladies from Dubuque deplore," and I suppose that even now, prudish types might find him objectionably vulgar. The prevailing sentiment, though, is surely not offense but disbelief. As in: *"Really?* That little guy is their iconic landmark? Man, what a weird place."

I snapped a photograph of the scene around the statue for a series I had begun titled "Not-So-Flattering Photos of Famous Places," showing the broader setting outside the standard postcard view. If ever there were a tourist attraction where the surrounding spectacle held far more intrigue than the object itself, this is it. This particular photo includes one of the gift shops across the street (which sells ten varieties of chocolate in the shape of the young Monsieur Pis) and a handful of our fellow gawkers, of whom four have distinctly perplexed looks on their faces and just one is actually bothering to take a photo of the bronze boy.

"Manneken-Pis doesn't interest me," I said. "What I *do* find fascinating is that so many other people find him so interesting."

Lee nodded. "He's the original tabloid star, famous for being famous. He achieves notoriety through a scandalous act, and then everyone talks about him. Forever."

The weirdness of it all is, apparently, part of the attraction for the locals. At the City Museum of Brussels, there was a large exhibit about *Manneken-Pis* featuring a substantial selection of the seven-hundred-plus costumes in which he's been adorned over the years and a video that explained his history and symbolism. I'm sure it was interesting. I wish I could repeat it. But all of this freshly acquired knowledge was instantly washed from my mind by the footage that followed, which featured a large crowd singing to and toasting the wee whizzer. They looked so proud of him. New-parent proud. College-graduation proud. Astronaut-just-back-from-space proud.

"A small and absurd symbol of a small and absurd country," said one locally produced brochure, with evident glee.

Fair enough.

If it's absurdity and confusion you're after, then this is the place for you. There's the whole Dutch-French dueling-cultures thing, for starters. Belgium is divided into two main regions, for which the term "squabbling siblings" would be too generous, given its insinuation of underlying kinship and comity. In the north is Dutch-speaking Flanders; in the south, French-speaking Wallonia. But the French-speaking Brussels-Capital Region is, in fact, located in Flanders. The city is technically bilingual, so street signs are in both languages, as are advertisements—if you should happen to arrive at a train station early one morning, still a bit bleary-eyed, you'll be forgiven for thinking that you're seeing double when you spot two identical posters side by side; it's only when you get close that you notice that the text is in different languages. And though Brussels itself is manifestly not unified, culturally, politically, or otherwise, it is the headquarters of one of the world's most ambitious efforts in cultural and political unification, the European Union (EU).

Also baffling is the city's juxtaposition of the bleakly modern and the enchantingly historic. There are medieval Gothic edifices of such splendorous detail and imposing, towering mass that you half expect to see an actual, crown-wearing king gazing upon you from the tower, issuing orders. And then, a couple of blocks away, it's a showcase of Regrettable Architecture of the Twentieth Century.

"Brussels, above all, devours itself," writes Geert Mak in his book *In Europe: Travels Through the Twentieth Century*. "The city's main artery, Boulevard Anspach, once Vienna and Paris rolled into one, is now a bare conduit, stripped of all monumentality. Brussels has always been adept at sophisticated self-mutilation. . . . No one loves this city, no one cares for her, no one takes her under his wing."

Yet Brussels may be, in fact, the very reason why the country has not split in two—neither Flanders nor Wallonia wants to relinquish it. Everyone we met seemed unreservedly proud of this city, in spite of its flaws, in spite of—or, more likely, *because of*—its weirdness. The complexity and absurdity make it feel more like a real city than many other European capitals. It is a place with no particular concern for what tourists think of it, where the split personality is on full display rather than hidden behind the bulwark of stereotypical Old World charm, where you might be bored after the first day of your visit, but where you could *live* quite happily.

It was Tuesday and we were in Belgium. We had become a cliché. That is, unfortunately, not a joke but a statement of fact. Like the Grand Tour depicted in the stereotype-solidifying 1969 film *If It's Tuesday, This Must Be Belgium*, ours was a whirlwind journey, not stopping so much as pausing in each city just long enough to give it a superficial once-over—after less than seventy-two hours here, we would move on to Berlin.

I was relieved, though (and slightly surprised), that Lee and I had ourselves broken from the Hollywood mold, with minimal melodrama or anything one might call bickering—we had few *Odd Couple* moments. There were two exceptions: First, when I dragged Lee into various bakeries in search of my chocolate croissant fix, as I was wont to do two or three times a day, and to which he would typically say, "Dude . . . *again*? You just ate!" and once added, "We need an intervention!" And, second, when we were lost. My plan of action when this happened was to keep walking, presuming that eventually we'd figure it out, or at least find another patisserie. Lee preferred the wholly unreasonable strategy of consulting a map— the current, up-to-date kind, the not-Frommer-approved kind. The desk clerk at our hostel had forced it on us, against my protestations, insisting—with a baffled, pitying look—that the hand-drawn map in my book wouldn't do us much good. Not wanting to offend our host, I took the map and shoved it in the bottom of my bag, out of sight, out of mind.

Lee humored me, but I knew it wouldn't be long before we both got desperate, meaning disoriented and hungry. In Amsterdam, we could typically rely on the concentric canals to give us a sense of where we were. Not so in Brussels. Without a logical street grid or bodies of water to orient us, our internal compasses spun aimlessly.

Now, as we searched for a Frommer-recommended restaurant, we reached an intersection that looked vaguely familiar, but this only caused further confusion: Did we recognize it because it was near our hostel, meaning that if we kept walking, we'd figure out where we were? Or was it because we'd passed it five minutes ago from the opposite direction? We were trapped in an M. C. Escher drawing.

I searched *E5D* for clues. *Help me out here, Arthur, before Lee asks for—*

"All right," he said. "Give me the map."

"The modern one?" I asked, stalling.

"The useful one."

His frustration was palpable. I handed it over.

"I'll stand over here with my accurate information so that I don't contaminate you," Lee said.

We were trying to find Restaurant Le Bigorneau, which Frommer recommended for a typical, authentic Belgian meal. Lee located the street on the map, then started laughing.

"Check this out," he said. I hesitated, so he thrust the map in my face.

"A MILLION TOURISTS," read the text. "The Beenhouwersstraat/Rue de Bouchers is a brightly lit area where only tourists come. Go there if you want to see how it works."

We couldn't find Restaurant Le Bigorneau, even with our modern map, but there were more than enough other cafés, all clones of each other, right down to the same Old World Amalgam decor: Provençal meets Tuscan meets Athenian meets 1950s Las Vegas cocktail lounge. In fact, I would have guessed that it was all the same enormous restaurant stretching for blocks if not for the different names on the neon signs above each awning and the competing hosts standing in the street, all North African men in their midthirties, who switched in an instant from glaring at each other to confronting passersby with a pitch that was more petulant than persuasive. It clearly was not an effective sales job: none of the restaurants had more than a handful of patrons. One host simply stood in the doorway, watching the scene, refreshingly indifferent to his potential customers. We rewarded his apathy. When he handed us our menus, we noted that even in the promotional photo on the cover, there were only eight patrons in this sprawling space.

The menu was also the same as all the other restaurants' and, like the decor, it covered the greatest hits of Europe: mussels, *frites*, pasta, pizza, some kind of chicken doused in some kind of sauce.

It reminded me of the snack stands we'd seen throughout

Amsterdam (including five in a single block), which all had the same display cases filled with a global tour of portable foods: hot dogs and waffles and doughnuts and croissants and pizza and kebabs—comforting munchies to satisfy stoned tourists from every culture.

I'm tempted to call the menu offerings in Brussels a typically Belgian attempt to build a collective identity from disparate cultures, a part-laudable, part-laughable stab at creating a single European identity. That would be reading too much into it. This was not fusion; it was not high-minded; it was, like Amsterdam's snack bars, lowest-common-denominator fare, following the money—if there were any to be had—rather than leading the way toward unity. It was the perfect encapsulation of the *If It's Tuesday, This Must Be Belgium* experience: a baffling mash-up of cultures, satisfactory if not thrilling or engaging, offering a reassuringly perfunctory sense of having experienced the Continent.

It didn't help that everyone spoke English. Well, it did and it didn't. It made for less confusion in the immediate experience, and I can't really complain about that. But like the contents of the menu, the prevalence of my native tongue made me pause to recall what country I was in.

The spread of English is the leading edge of culture leveling and, surely, a major cause of cultural confusion. If language is the key that unlocks culture, as the old truism has it, then this is a central question of modern tourism, perhaps the modern world in general: If we all speak the same language, at least rudimentarily, does that help or hurt our ability to understand each other on a deeper, societal level? Do we lose something by not having to struggle through in the language of our hosts, learning the nuance of the vocabulary and getting a sense of this linguistic infrastructure that defines everyday life? Or do we gain something by eliminating just enough of that struggle to communicate the essential details? (Allow me to give the obvious answer: yes to all. For an in-depth take on the matter, check out Robert McCrum's book *Globish*.)

It was something I'd been thinking about in every city since Florence, and this seems as good a place as any to offer a few notes on language:

1. Frommer writes, "The most famous last words of the American tourist are: 'They speak English everywhere.' Well, they don't. You can, with luck, be stranded in a European town among people who will simply shrug their shoulders to an English-uttered request." This was a change from Temple Fielding's approach: in decades of travel, he never learned another tongue, and the 1957 Fielding's guide offers only a thirteen-line note on language, claiming that it "is no barrier" in modern Europe. Neither Fielding's nor Fodor's standard guidebooks of the era included phrasebook sections. Frommer, for his part, listed some thirty-one phrases in each of the major languages of the countries in his book, plus numbers and an array of food terms.

2. However, Frommer tempers his caution about not relying on English with a promise that, actually, you don't need to learn very much of a language to get by:

> *In any language, a very small group of words and phrases can be shifted and rearranged to fulfill almost any need. If you can learn the foreign equivalents of such terms as "where is," "do you have,"*

"how much is this"—then you can travel comfortably in Europe
and make your wants known. Half an hour of study, packed in as
your train or plane approaches a particular country, ought to do
the job.

3. In the spirit of Frommer's reassurance and the fancy-free naïveté of the 1960s backpacker, I tried just this approach, reviewing
Frommer's phrases just before arriving in a new city, my reading
becoming decidedly more harried and anxious as we pulled into
the station and my where-am-I-what-the-heck-am-I-doing-
here-this-is-crazy panic set in once more. I can report with author-
ity that, uh, half an hour of study is not quite enough.

4. Then again, even in situations when you don't need an extensive
vocabulary, preparation doesn't help if you can't remember what
country you're in or what language they speak. Caught up in the
whirl of the Grand Tour, in one Brussels bakery, I asked for *"deux*
croissant und ein jugo de naranja, please."

5. At the EU headquarters, where we were headed the next day, we
would learn that there are twenty-three official EU languages (for
twenty-seven countries); all documents and proceedings have to
be translated into each. But they don't always go straight from A to
B—not a lot of people can speak both Greek and Finnish, or Latvian
and Irish, for example. Instead, they have "relay languages," meaning that a speech in Greek is translated into English, French, and
Spanish, and then the Finnish translator takes it from there.

6. According to the EU, 28 percent of Europeans know two other
languages in addition to their mother tongue. As a second lan-

guage, English is the most spoken, with 38 percent of non-British Europeans knowing enough to carry on a conversation.

7. English is, therefore, Europe's everyday relay language—especially on the tourist trail.

8. Go into any restaurant, museum, or souvenir shop and it's a good bet that all of the employees know enough English to communicate with you. If the employees are immigrants—and as noted earlier, many service industry workers are from other places—then they're at least trilingual: native language, language of the country they've moved to, and English. (In Brussels, they'd do well to learn a bit of Dutch, too.) At one shop in Brussels, I asked in French for six postcards. The clerk counted them out in Italian and then told me the price in English.

9. The same goes for street performers and panhandlers—anyone who has any expectation of contact with foreigners in tourist areas is likely to be at least passably bilingual.

10. In other words, it's fair to presume that nearly all tourist-area fast-food employees, and a large portion of the street performers and panhandlers, know a conversational level of more languages than do most college graduates in the United States.

11. American pop culture is a big resource for English learners abroad. Shortly after Lee and I marveled at *Manneken-Pis*, we spotted a group of teenagers conversing in French and rapping in English to a Nas song. Earlier on the trip, I had watched some big, blond Vikingesque guys play basketball in a park. For the most part

I had no idea what they were saying, but periodically there would be an outburst in English: "Shoooot!" "Three!" *"Fuck!"* "On fire!"

12. It was jarring to hear those snatches of slang out of context, but equally jarring to have a conversation with someone who didn't understand my own slang. Just about everyone you meet on the tourist trail speaks English, but perhaps not the version you're used to. The words make sense, but the meaning takes some effort to parse because there are none of the subtle shortcuts that we take for granted in everyday communication, the slang and idioms and precise cadence and intonation that are as much a part of the language as the basic nouns and verbs and grammar rules. Talking one day to a Canadian expat who had lived in Europe for a few years, I let down my linguistic guard and made a sarcastic comment. He stared at me for a moment, confused and mildly offended, before bursting into a wide grin. "Oh! Sarcasm! Haven't heard that in a while—sometimes I forget it exists. I really miss it."

Our hostel was just off the Grand Place, the central square that Arthur Frommer says is one of the most spectacular public spaces in Europe. That hasn't changed: it's certainly the most enthralling and majestic landmark in Brussels, with all due respect to *Manneken-Pis*.

This was the first time so far that I had not stayed in a hotel recommended by Frommer, but, alas, all of those accommodations in Brussels were either closed or booked solid. That's one problem with living in the Internet age, I suppose: more people make reservations in advance and conduct their due diligence with online research, leaving the procrastinators and technophobes among us with the dregs and the dungeons. Somehow, though, we lucked out and found a hostel that was dirt cheap, centrally located, and, as a bonus, decorated in a style that was part midcentury modern, part René Magritte—slick and surreal, in keeping with the baffling theme of the city.

The lobby had free Wi-Fi, that essential amenity of modern accommodations. This was a huge relief—finally, I could update my blog.

I appreciate the irony, believe me. Here I was, proud of my willful ignorance but agonizing over my inability to share it with the world. Shunning up-to-date guidebooks, doing things the old-fashioned way in an effort to prove that it was better, but carrying a laptop and documenting my experiment via the technological trend of the moment. I had started the blog only a few weeks earlier, intending merely to keep in touch with a handful of friends and family back home. But while old habits die hard, new habits are more insidious, their illicit thrills all delight and no guilt, and soon the mere thought of going without Internet access for forty-eight hours was enough to give me the shakes.

So, Tuesday evening, I sat in the lobby, updating the blog, while Lee, king of the nightlife, turned in for an early bedtime. I was halfway through my post when I heard an earth-shattering blast of opera, Wagner or something—the sort of ominous and over-the-top music played during the opening frames of a Hollywood battle scene as the army of bad guys appears on the horizon. Somewhere outside, the Four Horsemen of the Apocalypse were coming, or perhaps it was Arthur Frommer, parachuting from the clouds in his Korean War army uniform, hunting me down for having cheated on him by staying here. The music seemed to be on an endless crescendo, the intensity and volume rising with each measure. It was genuinely terrifying.

I heard someone stumbling down the stairs, and soon Lee appeared, fully dressed, groggy, and seething. "If they're not going to let me sleep," he said, "I'm going to crash their party."

"Any idea what's going on?"

"I don't know. I couldn't see anything out the window."

"You might not want to go out there unarmed."

Lee pulled a ballpoint pen from his pocket. The side of it read "Bad Boy Bail Bonds, Baltimore."

"I'm good," he said and disappeared into the night.

I quickly finished my blog post and dashed out to investigate for myself.

Town Hall, the most magnificent and imposing building in a magnificent and imposing and classically Old World square, was on fire. Okay, no, not really. Symbolically. The entire facade facing the Grand Place was covered in an ever-changing light show projected from the City Museum of Brussels, with that apocalyptic music as the soundtrack. If you've ever been to a drive-in movie, imagine that but with a screen that is, I don't know, five or six times larger and just so happens to be a fifteenth-century Gothic structure, all pointed arches and narrow windows and more statues in more places than you would have guessed was possible, an army's worth of saints and nobles. The light show spanned the width of the building and all the way to the top of the central tower, more than three hundred feet up, where yet another statue surveyed the scene below.

(We later learned that this was Saint Michael, patron saint of Brussels. "He's God's bouncer, and he uses a flaming sword to do it," Lee explained. "He's fighting Lucifer." When I asked how he knew this, he said that he was raised Catholic, then reached under his shirt and pulled out the silver chain hanging around his neck. "I used to have a Saint Michael medal on here"—he grinned—"but I lost it while hooking up with a girl.")

I cannot verify this, obviously, but I'd guess that if I had looked up at Saint Michael through a pair a binoculars, I'd have found his gilt brow furrowed and his lips frozen in a puzzled frown as he watched a light show worthy of the world's biggest rave flash below. The building and the square beneath him required no added spectacle to be spectacular. The Grand Place is a UNESCO World Heritage Site, and rightfully so—even without knowing about the history (French bombardment, 1695—look it up), you know, instantly, that epic things have happened here, that this *is* history.

The light show was entertaining, to be sure, but made me a bit melancholy for that very reason—it was incongruously razzle-dazzle, like jazz hands during a waltz. In all other respects, Brussels is like the restaurant host who won us over—charming in its lack of pretense or concern for keeping tourists delighted and amused. It's not self-confident, but it seems to be at ease with its internal confusion and dissonance, a bit neurotic but okay with that. I appreciated that. I like boring cities. I'm from Minneapolis. I like having to make some effort to find the intrigue and the spectacle and to learn for myself that a particular place isn't so boring after all.

After a restless night—there turned out to be a second light show, after which a band somewhere down the block blared "Girl from Impanema" in an unbroken loop for several hours—Lee and I woke up late but determined. We had a field trip planned.

We were headed to the European Union headquarters, most of which dates to the early 1990s or later—this is, emphatically, not the Old World part of Brussels. To walk there from the Grand Place is to see, stride by stride, the evolution of a continent.

You start with grandeur and opulence and war—the building blocks of European culture as it exists in the tourist mind. As you leave the Grand Place, the buildings are less majestic but still historic, Gothic architecture giving way to Art Nouveau, the charms more discreet and intimate but still unquestionably Continental. Here and there, a few flashes of modernity: a chic bistro in a historic building, an all-glass facade nestled between two others of worn stone topped with weary gargoyles. Old and charming gives way to old and grim gives way to modern and grim. The litter changes, too, from paper bags from the Tintin shop and Godiva store to bottles, some of them broken, and tattered plastic bags. A construction crane hovers above. The buildings are narrow postwar structures, dilapidated and dreary, some with broken windows, some with posters covering the entire first floor, some with Dumpsters out front and more cranes above. Are they destroying or renewing or . . . what? There's a Thai restaurant in the middle of the block; a woman in a hijab walks by you, chatting on a cell phone. A gust of wind drops a crumpled copy of the *Financial Times* at your feet. The buildings are nearly all glass now, with only a few remnants of the past, incongruous beauty marks of history. "TO LET / Prestigeous [*sic*] Offices / Have a look inside," says a sign on one of the glass structures. The people around you are dressed formally, corporately. Still more cranes, plus scaffolding everywhere. Then, weirdly, the landscape shifts again, as if there's a demarcation between two worlds. On this side of the street is a sports bar called Fat Boy's and a one-hour photo store (those places still exist?), both housed in what appear to be nineteenth-century buildings. And across the road is a sleek corporate campus, its design clever but placeless, a product of a time when cultures are at peace yet, you can't help but think, perhaps bereft of vigor and imagination. Because the sense that you get when viewing this campus is not "halls of power" but "big sale at the Foot Locker on the third floor next to the food court!" This is the EU.

The EU visitors' center has all manner of brochures and pamphlets for the taking, from kids' books with whimsical drawings to dense, policy-heavy publications. Most, though, are attractively designed explanations of the myriad ways that the EU helps everyone and everything: "Better off in Europe: How the EU's single market benefits you"; "From farm to fork: Safe food for Europe's consumers"; "Europe for women." Lee rolled his eyes as I helped myself, filling up my bag.

A common theme across all the booklets was the importance of being "united in diversity" while building a tangible, collective sense of identity. "The process of European integration has not smothered different ways of life, traditions and cultures of its peoples," read lesson one of a booklet titled "Europe in twelve lessons." Like the melting pot that the United States aspires to be, a united Europe, the EU says, can create a greater whole from the sum of its parts.

Sounds good, but as Lee put it, the history of Europe is the history of people being horrible to each other—and while they don't often fight literal battles anymore, true unity is elusive. As the euro struggled and the world economy tanked in 2010, the *Economist* commented on the tenuous relationship between France and Germany, two Continental powers trying to steady the EU in a storm of political turmoil. The observations were a worthy stand-in for discussions of the entire region: "Despite finding each other 'mutually unbearable,' as one European ex–foreign minister puts it, the two have found a way to get along. . . . A rival perception, however, suggests that they are more like a rival couple on the verge of divorce: they agree on little, and trust each other even less."

Since its beginnings with the Common Market in 1957 (there's that pivotal year again), the EU has ushered in a host of changes that have made travel tremendously easier: open borders, a common currency (well, for seventeen of its member states)—and with this freer flow of goods and people comes a freer flow of culture.

It's not hard to see the markers of globalization and the way that it infuses culture A with culture B, even though they are located a hemisphere apart. What's less visible, and at times more confounding to the outside observer, is the more subtle, localized version of this within Europe. We've moved away from the package tour as the main way to see Europe, but Europe has become more like a package tour itself, a moving target of cultures becoming more homogenous in some ways and more dissimilar in others. Having a front-row view of this common culture's emergence, two steps forward, one step back, and in ways intentional and accidental, is one of the most intriguing parts of the modern Grand Tour. Even those travelers who are not on a whirlwind *If It's Tuesday, This Must Be Belgium* jaunt around the Continent can be forgiven for forgetting where they are.

After we left the EU, Lee and I walked through a working-class immigrant neighborhood, which had a burned-out look but also a phoenix spirit, a renewed, remixed streetscape where I could see, without turning my head, Arabic shop signs, English posters, and street signs in Dutch and French—competing with, contradicting, and complementing each other all at once.

In this baffling era, on this baffling continent, there is no tangible, unified European identity. There never will be. Brussels is Exhibit A both for and against that statement.

Berlin

Twice the City It Was

There's a lively, electric feel to the city;
a drink-and-be-merry-for-tomorrow-we-die mood;
an urge to experience the new and different.

—Europe on Five Dollars a Day

Nineteen seventy-two. The Continent was open; the tourists were everywhere. The U.S. economy was faltering, but even this was not enough to dissuade the masses from heading abroad, although it did mean that Arthur Frommer was finally forced to adjust his titular budget for the first time, to *Europe on $5 and $10 a Day.*

The previous decade had been good to Frommer. He'd sold a lot of books, branched out to other areas of the travel industry, and become something of a pop culture phenomenon. By 1963 he was selling 150,000 copies of *E5D* annually; four years later, sales were up to 200,000, though this figure understates his true influence, because many people were lending the books to friends. Five thousand readers were *writing* to Frommer each year with feedback and tips of their own.

"This year three hundred fifty thousand Americans—one out of five who travel to Europe—will go with Arthur Frommer," observed Nora Ephron in a 1967 *New York Times* profile. "They will eat with Arthur Frommer and, as something of a witticism has it, sleep with Arthur Frommer."

E5D was the bestselling travel guide in print.

Even Temple Fielding had to concede that Frommer was on to something. Mind you, he wouldn't say so on the record. In 1968, John McPhee wrote a sprawling profile of Fielding for the *New Yorker*, in which there is just one mention of his budget-minded competitor; it read, in its entirety: "Fielding does not think much of Arthur Frommer's *Europe on $5 a Day*. 'We don't respect Frommer,' he told me in an even, sad voice." Curiously, McPhee didn't push him on this, and he even opened his profile by stating that Fielding's competitors were still "scarcely visible behind him"— though, in truth, the numbers and the zeitgeist said otherwise. Fielding's actions betrayed his unspoken concerns—in 1967, he released a new book called *Fielding's Super-Economy Guide to Europe*. I found a 1968 edition, the back cover of which says, "Let's face it—it's not realistic to expect to travel in Europe on a budget of only five dollars a day any more." Temple Fielding was on the defensive, falling behind the upstart competitor.

But a surprising obstacle had come into Frommer's—and tourism's—way: the U.S. government, the very entity that had helped promote mass tourism in the first place as a component of the Marshall Plan. The government's new message was "See America first." On New Year's Day 1968, with the U.S. economy in decline, President Johnson proposed significant new taxes on tourist expenditures overseas and called for Americans to cut back on journeys abroad. The nation's economic woes, the Johnson administration asserted, were in large part due to American tourists spending billions of dollars overseas; the nation's "balance of payments" was askew. Johnson established a Commission on the U.S. Balance of Payments and recruited Frommer to serve on it, a tacit acknowledgment of the guidebook guru's key role in creating the tourist boom.

Johnson's efforts, like Fielding's, were too little, too late. The momentum of tourism was unstoppable; the pursuit of the American Dream now led clearly across the Atlantic. In fact, Christopher Endy notes in *Cold War Holidays* that many pundits (on both the right and the left of the political spectrum) viewed Johnson's appeal as an enticement *to* travel, a way to defy an embattled president in the midst of an unpopular war in Vietnam. Some equated Johnson's entreaty with Communist travel restrictions, labeling it antiegalitarian, un-American. On balance, Endy says, Johnson's effort was doomed from the start, and in 1969 tourist spending in western Europe topped the billion-dollar mark for the first time.

Richard Nixon, ever the opportunist, spoke out against Johnson's travel stance on the campaign trail in 1968, defending tourism as a middle-class American right. When elected, though, Nixon was forced to deal with the continued economic decline, and in 1971 he devalued the dollar—which, in turn, created higher prices for Americans abroad. Nixon had inadvertently succeeded where Johnson had failed, tightening the financial reins on American travelers.

But restlessness is perhaps the most enduring of human traits. Americans didn't stay home, they just made sure that they spent less when they went abroad—and thanks to Frommer, they had the template for doing so. Airlines, too, encouraged travel by slashing prices, thanks in part to the 1970 debut of the first jumbo jet, the

Boeing 747-100, a wide-body airplane more than twice as large as its predecessor, the 707, and able to carry more than four hundred and fifty passengers. Students in particular kept traveling in droves. With job prospects drying up, "rather than spend the summer idle, they are using the meager savings they had hoped would eventually finance a future trip to travel now," wrote Paul Goldberger—a Yale undergrad who had toured Europe twice and is today the architecture critic for the *New Yorker*—in the *New York Times* in June 1971. He added that "[a]n estimated record of 750,000" students were heading to the Continent that summer, following Frommer's lead.

Arthur Frommer essentially initiated "if not the Junior Year abroad then certainly the drop-out one," Stanley Elkin wrote in a 1972 profile for *Harper's*. "Indeed, in a way, he invented abroad itself."

Elkin's kicker: "It's no accident that Arthur Frommer, the Pill, and the credit card are simultaneous phenomena. Everybody deserves everything. You only live once. Screwing for everybody and Europe for everybody too. This is the egalitarian key to a proper understanding of *Europe on Five Dollars a Day.*"

War does have a tendency to screw things up. The Continent wasn't really open in 1972, of course—all that Cold War and Iron Curtain stuff, well, it got in the way. There were few tourists in Prague, for example, one of the travel hot spots of the modern era, and not many Americans were hopping on a train from Brussels to Berlin, as Lee and I were doing now.

"Don't mention the war."

The middle-aged British men in the seats behind us thought

that this was the funniest one-liner ever and kept circling back to it as we sped through the German countryside. They paused their banter only to listen to the announcements that blared over the PA system in German, French, Dutch, and English. The messages got substantially shorter with each translation. Alarmingly shorter. I timed them: one German version was a minute and forty seconds long; the English translation was *eleven* seconds. What were they not telling us?

Eventually I pieced together a few of the tinny broadcasts. When an attendant stopped next to our seats and said several sentences in German, I was pretty sure I knew what she was saying.

"Ja," I replied.

She gave a cheery nod and went on her way.

"Did you understand that?" Lee asked, incredulously.

"Well, not the words, maybe, but the general—"

"You can't just smile and nod! That could have been vital information!"

I shrugged. "She was probably just repeating what they've been saying on the loudspeaker: the train isn't going all the way to Berlin, so we have to get off and switch in Cologne. The words were about the same."

"About the same? May I remind you, Doug: you don't speak any German."

"True. But I bet it was the train switch." A little voice in my brain, though, was agreeing with Lee: *Are you trying to get yourself killed?*

Lee shook his head and laughed. "Maybe. But still . . ."

As we disembarked in Cologne, the last words I heard came in a stage whisper that sounded like a threat: "Don't mention the war."

. . .

Our tour the next morning began on the former East Berlin side of the Brandenburg Gate. At a Starbucks. Next to the Museum Kennedys. Naturally. Frommer didn't recommend this tour, of course (though it's worth noting that it was free, so Frommer would have approved)—but then, he didn't have many suggestions for seeing the sights of East Berlin. Not much to do there, he says. He'd gone. He'd seen the bleak streets and sampled the sausages, which tasted like they were "sawdust-filled."

There were about fifty people milling around when we got to the Starbucks. In the plaza near the gate were even more tourists, plus a guy dressed as an American soldier from World War II and selling war-related knickknacks; a living statue in a form-fitting yellow outfit; and someone dressed in a sort of Winnie the Pooh knockoff costume—basically, the same scene you'll find in any tourist area in any city in the New Old World. I should have expected this, I realized: it's a tourist landmark, so of course there's a Starbucks and a living statue. But up to this point, my knowledge of East Berlin began and ended with grainy images of people clambering over and tearing down a wall on a certain night in November 1989. (I was eight years old then, watching the events unfold on a television in my third-grade classroom. My teacher told us it was important, that we should remember this forever. I duly committed it to memory, although I doubt I appreciated the full significance for another decade or so.)

Surrounding us, on the sides of this large, open square, were an array of squat buildings, mostly stone, all fairly nondescript. There was one that was a bit nicer-looking than the others, its copper mansard roof patinated to a jade hue. It was the only structure that most of our tour group photographed—upstaging even the Brandenburg Gate itself—after our guide told us its historical significance.

"Do you recall, several years ago, when Michael Jackson dangled his baby from a hotel balcony?" the guide asked, her face and voice entirely deadpan. "This is it. The MJ-baby-dangling hotel. Take your photos. I will not judge you."

We couldn't resist.

Our guide was British (as we had already discovered, tour guides might know the city better than many locals, but most of them are *not*, in fact, locals). Her name was Ines the Sixteenth. That's right: the *sixteenth*. Her family has been giving firstborn daughters that name since long before my country was even founded. Welcome to Europe. She had short, reddish hair, a checkered scarf, and a flair for the dramatic, investing each story with emotion and, when appropriate, more of that dry humor. It felt like exactly the right tone for this city.

"You are wondering why I've stopped you here," she said as we stood in the middle of a parking lot. "Mind the dog poo," she added, pointing to the ground. We all took a step back, forming an inadvertent circle around the offending pile, which only gave it added prominence.

This was the site of Hitler's bunker, she explained, the place where Der Führer died. It had been converted to its banal, utilitarian use and intentionally left landmark-free to prevent neo-Nazi nutjobs from treating it as a memorial.

"You can't make a whole city a museum," Ines XVI said. "You don't want to. The only commemoration that Hitler gets here is a small pile of dog poo. I think that's appropriate."

Lee and I struck up conversations with our fellow tourists in our group of about thirty. Most of them, like us, were in their mid-to late twenties, recent college graduates or young professionals. I'll confess to expecting, almost hoping for, some stereotypical stoner-hippie-"I'm not a tourist" types—they would add some anecdotal color as they passed around a joint and played Hacky Sack every time we stopped. I came up empty. Everyone was inquisitive and engaged, peppering our guide with questions and genuinely interested in the landmarks and history.

Sally, a law school student from the United States, was eager to discuss literature and gave me tips on books about Berlin's history. Jian, a shy recent college grad from Malaysia, was midway through a long-planned Grand Tour on his way back home after studying in England. He had put in long hours as a waiter in London to save up for this trip, and he was savoring every moment, taking a photo roughly every ten steps. A few in our group, to my surprise, were from other parts of Germany. At least ten were from Australia. Lee asked if they were all traveling together. "No," one of them said with a patient grin that suggested she must get that question a lot. "There are just a lot of Aussies in Europe."

Ines XVI stopped us again.

"This is not the Berlin Wall," she said, an inkling of a smirk showing as she pointed to a fence. "It is a wall to *protect* the Berlin Wall"—her hand shifted slightly to the tall, graffiti-covered concrete slabs behind the fence—"from tourists looking to chip off a piece for a souvenir. It's said that if you took all the pieces that have been sold to tourists since the wall came down, you could rebuild the wall three times over."

A few minutes later, we arrived at what I would come to think of as the ultimate symbol of Berlin then and now: Checkpoint Charlie.

This is perhaps the most potent of Cold War landmarks, where East literally met West. In *Europe on Five Dollars a Day*, Frommer notes that it was actually quite simple for tourists to come here—the wall was there to keep Easterners in, not others out. If you wanted to cross the border, no problem: "register your name with the American MP's at Checkpoint Charlie, tell them the time at which you plan to return, and if you're not there at that time, they'll take action."

We paused on a street corner and Ines XVI told us a few of the stories of this place. She was in her element, theatrical and lively. She told us about the West Berlin man whose fiancée had been stranded on the East Berlin side when the wall went up. As a Westerner, he was allowed to visit her, but she couldn't leave. So he bought the lowest-riding car he could find, then had a mechanic friend drop it even lower. When he returned to Checkpoint Charlie after his next visit, the guards came out to ask him about his companion.

"He pushed her head down, gunned the engine," Ines XVI said as we hung on her every word, "and they liimboooed under the gate as fast as they could. The American soldiers on the other side applauded as they sped off."

I looked over at the American soldier manning the re-created station now for our touristic benefit. He was munching a candy bar, holding an American flag, and casting a surly look at passersby. We all aimed our cameras at him.

"No photo without tip!" he growled in Russian-accented English.

He gestured to a nearby booth where another bored soldier, this one a North African dressed as an East German, stood next to a camera on a tripod. Fitting, I mused, that the symbol of the fall of Communism is now a capitalist enterprise. Freedom isn't free.

The guardhouse/Ye Olde Cold War attraction sat in the middle of Friedrichstrasse. On one side of the street was the Checkpoint Charlie Museum. We didn't have time to visit, but it looked Serious and Informative. On the other side of the street was *Snackpoint* Charlie—actual name—a food court with a Subway, a kebab stand, and a restaurant advertising "Asian Sushi Fusion Food." Surprisingly, none of these appeared to offer cheesily named foods like a Berlin Wall-dorf Salad or a U-Boat Sub. Surely, I thought, those will be here soon.

At that moment, in September 2009, unified Berlin was still a teenager; it would turn twenty later that year.

"And like a teenager," Ines XVI said, "it's still gawky and awkward," still testing new things, figuring out its identity, and growing, growing, growing. Most of all, the city seemed unsure what to make of its complicated history, which is why Checkpoint Charlie is such a striking emblem of Berlin both then and now.

A block away from Checkpoint Charlie, in East German territory, a long fence along the sidewalk bore a series of signs with a detailed history of the wall. There were photos, illustrations, and text in multiple languages; it was a moving testament to the tyranny this city and country had suffered. Right at the end of the line of historical markers was another sign, a sandwich board, blocking the sidewalk: "Ben & Jerry's Sold Here." A few steps later was a souvenir shop with tacky T-shirts.

I can't express how common this scene was—or how dizzying and jarring. The city seemingly can't decide whether it wants to dwell on the past or focus on the future. So it tries to do both, with no buffer zone between the two. (By the way, this making-sense-of-history is such a central issue in modern Germany that they have a term for it. Take a deep breath: *Vergangenheitsbewälti-gung*. Historian Gavriel D. Rosenfeld translates it as "the process of coming to terms with or mastering the past," in particular the Holocaust and the Third Reich.)

There are monuments all over: the Holocaust Memorial, with its haunting field of stone blocks of various sizes, orderly and yet chaotic; the sunken room full of empty shelves on the square where the Nazis burned books; the double rows of cobblestones that trace the line of the Berlin Wall, showing the seam where the nation was ripped apart and is slowly, even now, being sewn back together. And then, just another half stride beyond, is a billboard or a mall or a cluster of souvenir shops. The sunken room marking the book burnings is almost literally in the shadow of a three-story-tall BMW advertisement that dominates one side of the square.

You can't ignore it. The minute you start to reflect on the things that happened here, trying to make sense of the history and madness of this place, you get distracted: *T-shirts ice cream postcards coffee get your photo taken in an American GI uniform get your passport stamped at Checkpoint Charlie bus tours of the city—board here!*

I will be the first to admit that tourists are largely responsible for this. We show up wanting to get our dose of so-called *ostalgie* (nostalgia for *ost*, the East). We get our passports stamped at Checkpoint Charlie (*guilty*, though only because I wanted to talk to the Algerian vendor) or take a driving tour in a Trabant, that infamously unreliable Eastern Bloc car. *USA Today* recently labeled this Communism-for-the-tourists "Iron Curtain irony," noting that many who lived in the old East Berlin are actually, you know, kind of pissed off about it. For good reason: to reduce human misery to a theme park is not just to whitewash history but to glorify pain and suffering, to present long-term horrors as fleeting thrills and cheap entertainment.

Even for those to whom it's not a theme park, it can still be a living museum, more somber but still essentially a war monument rather than a functioning city. The tourist to-do list here includes a day trip to Sachsenhausen, one of the Nazis' first concentration camps (which Lee and I would visit a few days later); a tour of the infamous sites and grim living conditions of Soviet-era life in East Berlin; or the "Alternative City Tour" showcasing "streets, squats, subculture."

This type of tourism is nothing new. "Slum tours," for example, have been growing in popularity in the last twenty to thirty years. You can take a guided tour of Rio de Janeiro's infamous favelas or a *Slumdog Millionaire* tour in Mumbai or a day trip through impoverished areas in Los Angeles, Kenya, and elsewhere. In Cambodia the Killing Fields near Phnom Penh have joined Angkor Wat as one of the country's biggest tourist attractions. The rise of this sort of travel—"dark tourism" is the catchall term—is in large part, I think, a reaction against the sort of Grand Tour I was going on. It feels more authentic, less contrived. (The Anne Frank House, too, could be considered a stop on the "dark tourism" trail.)

Of course, "dark tourism" can still be a packaged, distorted view of reality. It's not an either-or proposition: theme-parky or gritty. The most disconcerting, I think, is when it's both, Nietzsche by way of Disney, when you feel like you're stuck on a ride called It's a Small, Sucky World After All (But Aren't You Entertained by It?).

That's what makes Berlin such a discordant place. The attitude seems to be "never forget, but don't spend too much time remembering, either." It makes for some serious cognitive dissonance,

Fusion cuisine at its finest: the famous German currywurst.

simultaneously overloading both the I-want-to-learn-about-the-world and the give-me-my-escapist-kitsch-fix parts of the brain.

I kept coming back, though, to what Ines XVI said: You can't make a museum out of an entire city. You can't *not* mention the war here, but you can't dwell on it, either. Go to one extreme and you cheapen the past; go to the other and you limit the present. You have to let the place evolve and be a functional home for its citizens—and visitors. To live is not just to remember.

In any case, I come back to this: in my day, taking an illicit photo of the guard at Checkpoint Charlie can get you a scowl from an actor. In Frommer's day, it could get you shot. If we're going to compare Berlin then and now, I'll take now.

. . .

Our tour ended in the former East Berlin. Ines XVI told the story of the night the wall fell. She reminded us how recent that was, how the city and the country were still trying to figure out their identity and piece themselves back together. The old wounds may not have closed, but they have at least superficially begun to heal, in what is, in the slow march of history, basically the blink of an eye.

If you were to drop me into a random Berlin neighborhood, I probably wouldn't be able to tell you if it was eastern or western. Aside from a few scattered dreary, blocky buildings, the side of town that was East Berlin looks exactly like the area that was West Berlin: same people, same landscape, same architecture, same tourist restaurants.

As we walked back toward the western part of the city, Lee and I paused for a moment to take in the scene. "Look down," I said to Lee. Without realizing it, he had stopped directly on top of the cobblestones marking the former route of the wall. We both instinctively followed the line with our gaze, seeing where it went from here. It ended a short distance away, running into the outer wall of a new Marriott.

Even in Frommer's day, the story of Berlin was about way more than *the* war, or war in general. Yes, there was that, but . . . Well, let's turn to Frommer, in fine form on the first page of his Berlin chapter:

> *Berlin possesses a kind of sophistication that will not be found in the rest of Europe. The city lives on the brink of danger; its citi-*

zens live from day to day. And yet, this insecurity has resulted in alertness rather than resignation.

The more Lee and I walked around Berlin, the more we, too, found charm and thrills to go with the heavy doses of history-induced unease. Beyond the monuments and *ostalgie* is normal life, and even the tourist passing through and seeing the sights has to realize that the city is more than a history lesson with residents.

The area in which we were staying, Charlottenburg, was surprisingly nontouristy. Now that the east side of town was open to visitors—and was still something of a novelty to them—the tourist center of gravity had shifted in that direction. For once, Frommer had led us to peace and quiet. Our neighborhood had no museums, no major landmarks, no flash; it was just a nice, calm place filled with shops and, *whaddyacallem*, Germans. We felt very much at home, particularly since we soon discovered that the spot-the-tourist game was impossible—in appearance, attire, and manner, everyone seemed thoroughly American (at least to our white, middle-class definition of the archetype). So it was downright baffling to hear them speak German; it felt like a put-on for our benefit.

In its own way, this was even more strikingly odd than the truly foreign aspects of European culture. The tourist trail was full of sights and people and moments that superficially fit within my frame of reference but on second glance were entirely different. This sense of the uncanny, of not-quite-right versions of familiar things, is one of the greatest delights and mindblowers of travel on the beaten path—it's the doppelgänger, not the complete stranger, who is most amusingly strange.

There were the teenagers on the U-Bahn performing an astonishing, soulful cover of the Cranberries' "Zombie" (a song about the horrors of armed conflict, I couldn't help but note), in German-accented mimicry of the Irish brogue of the original recording. The food carts selling not hot dogs but currywurst (*cultural confusion squared!*). The television sitcoms in an unfamiliar tongue but with all-too-familiar plot devices. Smaller details like the little glowing green and red men in the crosswalk signals—"Don't cross yet," Lee said as I stepped into the street. "We have to wait for the matador to turn into a leprechaun."

The discreet poetry of the everyday but unexpected.

It was time for some Frommering. Lee and I headed down the Kurfürstendamm, a wide street populated with both the impossibly ritzy and the astonishingly kitschy, and home to several of Frommer's recommended restaurants. Just one was still around, a big bistro called Berliner Kindl. You can't miss it: the name is on the bright red awning and spelled out in yellow neon letters that glow above the bar.

As we took our seats, Lee started laughing. He pointed to the top of the drink menu, which was lying on the table. The text read, "Alt-Berliner Biersalon." Below, in smaller type, was the name of the restaurant, heading a long list; there was a price after the words "Berliner Kindl."

"I think Arthur got the name of this place wrong," Lee said.

"Arthur wouldn't do that," I said.

"Well, he did. I'm pretty sure Berliner Kindl is the name of a beer, not the restaurant."

"What are you saying? That he just saw the beer sign and

assumed that was the name? Like thinking an American bar is called Miller Lite?"

Lee pointed to the drink list again and nodded. I didn't want to believe it. I pulled all the menus and daily-special lists and random promotional materials from the little rack on the table.

"Well . . . damn it, Arthur," I said. "You're letting us down."

I was less concerned about the name of the place than the fact that we were, finally, going to eat some real German food. For two days, we'd been avoiding it, since none of Frommer's other recommendations were open and since Lee and I shared a fondness for Thai curries and doner kebabs—the most European of all foods, I'd say, based on sheer ubiquity—a Continent-unifier in the form of veal, chicken, or lamb shaved from a massive, spit-roasted block of meat and tucked into a pita.

Here's the thing. My gut is not an iron one; indeed, given its fragility, it may be made of parchment paper. By this point, I may have gotten a bit more confident, but I sure as hell hadn't gotten over my single greatest phobia in life: German food. I understand they've been eating it for a few years. I realize that many of them—and perhaps one or two non-Germans—like the stuff. But it all seems intentionally calibrated for maximum lack of enjoyment: heavy, dense, not especially flavorful, and likely to contain animal parts that I'd actually rather not consume knowingly. Since I didn't speak the language, I was terrified of accidentally ordering the daily special of Boiled Sphincter Stuffed with Eyeballs *mit* Raw Onions.

Arthur Frommer, bless him, translates some of the expected menu items, like turtle soup (*Schildkrotensuppe*) or pig's knuckles (*Eisbein*) . . . or, yikes, *brains* (*Hirn*). He also apparently understands that not everyone enjoys weird foods. What's interesting, though, is how the concept of "weird" changed between then and now. Frommer notes the sense of dread many of us have when staring at a foreign menu and says, "Absent a translation of these exotic phrases, dinner becomes The Big Surprise. You stab blindly at the bill of fare, hope for the best, and usually end up with Octopus Soup or some similar delicacy."

Yes, that's his prime example of scary food: octopus! Eek! Sea monster! Today, when sushi is available at many grocery stores and calamari is on the menu even at dive bars, octopus just doesn't sound particularly odd. Brains, though? Yeah. Frickin' *terrifying*.

I settled on spaetzle. It seemed the most innocuous option—noodles, cheese. Even so, when the platter of food arrived, I sort of expected to find entrails and brain stems and who knows what else at the bottom of that steaming pile—they'd probably spring out at me like a slimy jack-in-the-box. I imagined the headline in the next day's *Der Spiegel*: "Tourist dies in spaetzle mishap." Subhead: "Last words: 'I should have stuck with pastries.'"

"Well, at least we're finally eating authentically," I said ruefully as I started to pick at my food. "I suppose Arthur would approve of that."

"Yeah, I'm sure this is exactly what Berliners eat every day," Lee said. "A huge meal in a tourist restaurant."

I'd been so nervous that I hadn't taken stock of our fellow patrons. Sure enough, though: all tourists.

"With a City Safari Tour bus letting people off out front," I noted. And a massive sandwich board on the sidewalk listing the menu in six languages, and sometimes multiple languages in one listing, as in *"Groker Baconburger mit Käse und Pommes Frites."*

"Totally authentic," Lee said. After a few moments, he added,

"This feels like some tourist version of *Cheers*. We could make a sitcom out of it."

"*Schnitzel, Spaetzle, and a Girl Named Gretel*," I said. "That could be the name."

"Yeah!" Lee laughed. "Okay, so it's a tourist bar, and our pilot episode opens with them hiring this new manager, Gretel. And she sort of shakes things up, brings a new attitude to this place."

"Maybe it's a Berlin *theme* bar," I said.

"With a wall." Lee nodded. "The decor and menu are different on the east and west sides. More bleak in the east."

"But also more heavily themed in the east," I said, "to give it some kitschy appeal. And the host stand is Checkpoint Charlie."

"Yes!"

We both laughed for a moment, then realized what we were laughing at.

My mother also had war on her mind—a different war.

"Got a bitter letter from Jo—2 pages of anti-Vietnam from my apolitical friend was quite a shock," she wrote from Florence on November 4, 1967. "Larry's brother is going over, as I guess you know." Left unsaid in that letter was her own apprehension about my father's impending air force enlistment, although it came through loud and clear in other correspondence, prompting my father to write, "Don't be so down on Air Force life even before you try it—to accept something as bad before proven so is sure to make it so." He went on to criticize the French antiwar talking points that Mom had been espousing, labeling French president Charles de Gaulle's foreign policy arrogant and "inane"—although, given his overall tone, Dad was merely resigned to air force life, not at all eager for it. He went on active duty a year later, in October 1968, and was sent to an air force base in Myrtle Beach, South Carolina, where he and Mom were the token Yanks and token hippies. Though Dad was never sent to Vietnam, there was always that unspoken, unnerving possibility.

American foreign policy, then as now, was a topic of much conversation. Like me, my mother felt compelled to keep a low profile as an American abroad in an age of tumult, although neither of us went as far as affixing a Canadian flag to our bags—a tactic used by some Americans-in-hiding both in the 1960s and today.

Among various other incidents during my trip, Drunk Girl in Amsterdam had complained bitterly about the U.S. war in Iraq and George W. Bush. I couldn't say I disagreed, but I felt obliged to point out, "Yeah, well, he's gone now. Back in Texas, puttering around the ranch—not in the White House."

"You know what I *do* like about America?" one of Drunk Girl's friends said. "Dixie cups—is that what you call them? I went to a party in New York, and they had these plastic cups—they were red and big. We don't have those. You can fit a lot of beer in there." She was completely earnest.

(So there you have it, diplomats. Start handing out the party cups.)

My mother waded into the foreign-relations fray, too, finding herself on the receiving end of some thought-provoking criticisms of U.S. policies. Some then-and-now parallels are especially striking. Ann's fiancé, Terry, got into a discussion with a student from South Africa about "the Arab-Israel bit," Mom reported, and I was depressed to realize that roughly the same conversation had probably taken place in the same hostel every day since then.

It's sometimes easy to forget that ours is not the only era of discord and fear. The world has always been a scary, violent place. It's just that we forget the full picture; memory edits history, erasing complexity as it sees fit. So on the one hand, we forget that the Berlin of the past was more than a place of war and tumult, and on the other, we forget that travel—*life*—in eras past was not truly more innocent. The truth is, we do not, in fact, live in particularly exceptional times.

When I was about eight or ten—right around the time the Eastern Bloc was crumbling and all those adults were telling me to remember this history in the making—my worldly mother took me to see the musical *Cabaret*. It is set in, well, a cabaret called the Kit Kat Klub in 1930s Berlin, against the backdrop of the Nazis' rise to power. Mom had seen it years before but had forgotten this key detail: it is unquestionably, empirically, emphatically *risqué* and dark. It was my first introduction to leather. And pasties. And, wow, *lack thereof.* As Mom would later say, "No wonder there were no other kids there." It left more of an impression on me than those grainy images of the wall did, I'll tell you that.

Frommer's 1963 descriptions of Berlin's bars and clubs make it sound like the musical got it right: the nightlife here, fueled by the city's fatalistic energy, is "highly esoteric and intense" and often "erotic and exotic." Consider:

The Resi: *The famous Berlin nightspot where telephones and pneumatic message tubes connect each of the 200 tables in its cavernous ballroom. Women outnumber males here three to one. If you're even slightly better looking than Yogi Berra, you'll no sooner sit down than the tubes will go pow! pow! pow! carrying* *messages from the scores of lonely Berlin femmes who spotted you the moment you entered.*

Der Goldene Hufeisin: *[G]uests can ride a horse (!) on the combination dance floor–riding rink (price for a trot is 50 pfennigs, a gallop is a stiff 150 marks).*

Eden's Saloon: *[P]acked not only with happy young people, but also with every conceivable type of whiz-bang invention and entertainment device.... In one room, for instance, the bar-maid delivers drinks by placing them in a wicker basket hung from a clothes line, which then transports the basket to waiting customers. In the same room, home-made movies—like the one containing surreptitious shots of babes on the beach in St. Tropez, are shown continuously on the bar-room wall, while an American-imitating folksinger bellows from a balcony.*

Lee's eyes bulged when he read the listings. "There's no way *any* of these places are still open."

And thank God, I added to myself. I was perfectly happy to be spared from riding a horse on a dance floor.

Our Frommering confirmed that, yes, they were all closed.

"What we should do," Lee said, "is see what kind of nightlife they *do* have today. You know, for research."

I stared him down. He was serious—and my pained expression seemed only to be fueling his enthusiasm.

"Adventure," he said, an impish grin spreading across his face, that devil-may-care glimmer lighting up his eyes once more.

My anticlubbing instinct kicked in. (Some might call it misanthropy or social anxiety. I call it reason.) A new death-in-Europe scenario flitted through my mind, this one involving a 'roided-up former East German bodybuilder, possibly known by the moniker Helmut der Hulk, with greenish skin and reddish eyes and a hobby of literally snapping scrawny tourists in two. Or, best-case scenario, it would be epically awkward, even by my standards, with Lee dancing with a gaggle of supermodels as I nursed a Sprite at a table in the back or retreated to the bathroom to check my hair and mope.

After a few moments, though, this subsided. In a weird way, I kind of, sort of *wanted* to check it out for myself. Frommer, I reasoned, would have demanded it.

"Spirit of adventure," Lee said.

"Spirit of adventure." I nodded, feeling my own eyes gleam.

The fatalistic energy that Frommer found so enthralling clearly had not subsided. If anything, it seemed to have new life in the unified city. Berlin the awkward teenager was also Berlin the partying teenager. The bar and club district of the former East Berlin was crowded with revelers when we arrived.

Thirty seconds after we sat down in the first bar, Vanilla Ice's nerdy Teutonic cousin sidled up. His blond hair was plowed into pseudocornrows that peeked out from beneath a baseball cap tilted at an impossible angle. He was a parody of a wannabe gangster.

"Whaddup, Americans!" he said, his voice jaunty but sinister. "What you want, homeboys? Weed? Coke? Refurbished East German military weapons?"

I'm not sure if that's actually what he said. We surmised. It was implied in his tone and his furtive head swivels. This was one time when we were happy to have a language barrier.

It was that kind of bar. Everything I'd feared. Between the clientele and the bizarre decor—hobbit hole meets steampunk meets landfill—it was seediness as accidental performance art. Even the intrepid Lee found it unsettling.

We moved on, dodging the masses thronging the sidewalks. One group of men wore matching black shirts reading "OLLIE'S STAG—BERLIN 2009," the screen-printed slogan giving their revelry a melancholy, conventioneer air.

"That's better, right?" Lee asked, pointing to another bar. It was sleek, sophisticated, calm.

"Yes," I said. "Much better."

We settled onto a pair of stools at the U-shaped bar that dominated the middle of the space. Lanternlike pendants traced the curve of the bar and cast an amber glow on the room. It felt like that rare place that tries to contrive hipness and actually succeeds.

"Have you ever had an Old Fashioned?" Lee asked as we looked over the lengthy drink menu.

I had not.

"I think you'd like it. And we definitely need to get you a cocktail—they clearly know what they're doing." He gestured to the bartenders' setup, pointing out the fresh fruit, the obscure bitters, the mad-scientist contraptions.

"Do you get mostly tourists or locals here?" Lee asked the bartender as we sipped our drinks—Old Fashioned for me, gin and tonic for him.

"Tourists. But it's cool," the bartender replied. His name was Tomas. He had an easygoing urbanity, with tousled hair and a tailored black shirt with rolled-up sleeves, which he absentmindedly adjusted every few minutes. He stepped over to the two women seated beside us, and we could hear them order in English.

"Americans?" Lee asked the women as Tomas made their drinks, each action meticulous but executed with a subtle flair.

"Yeah! You, too?" said the one seated next to Lee.

I noted with amusement that the farther we get from home, the broader the range of common ground we use to connect with strangers. In Minneapolis, seeing someone wearing a T-shirt of my high school *might* make me strike up conversation. If I go to New York, anyone wearing a Minnesota Twins hat is suddenly my friend. Abroad: *We're from the same huge country! What an amazing coincidence! Let's hang out together!* In the midst of unfamiliar surroundings, we instinctively, subconsciously seek out whatever reminders of home we can find.

Tara was in town for a work-related conference; her sister, Amy, was a graduate student savoring her last days of vacation before school started up again. As usual, we found it surprisingly easy to slip into banter about the city around us, the reasons that brought us here, and where we had come from. Our tourist status gave us common ground, and conversation, which had never come easily for me at home, suddenly felt like second nature. Tomas dropped in and out of the conversation as he worked, trading cocktail knowledge with Lee and slipping us all samples of concoctions he was making.

"What do you suggest next?" I asked him when I was done with my Old Fashioned. I had been sipping it, savoring it, for the better part of an hour. Lee, too, was still on his first drink.

"You liked it?" Tomas asked.

"Yes," I said. "Very much."

Tomas thought for a moment. "Have you had a Sazerac?"

"A classic cocktail—from New Orleans," Lee said approvingly.

"Never heard of it," I said. "Love to try it. I trust your judgment."

All of my anxieties had melted away without me even noticing.

We sat for another hour—maybe two, maybe three; I lost track of time—nursing our drinks, enjoying the conversation and the show, soaking up the scene.

I kept waiting for Lee to make his move, to start flirting with Tara or Amy or to seek out one of the many well-dressed—and English-speaking—women around us. He never did.

I can't believe it took me this long to figure it out, but the Lee of the page was not the Lee of real life. The one I was getting to know was a lot less of a roguish lothario than I'd expected.

Sure, Lee was still far more dashing and confident than I was. He was more than willing to push me out of my comfort zone—and thank goodness for that. But he had no more interest in the esoteric nightlife of Berlin than I did; his spirit of adventure was not all that adventurous. We weren't going to wind up in jail or face-down in the river. The reasons he liked to go barhopping, I finally understood, had nothing to do with excess or debauchery, nothing to do with getting smashed or scoring a hostel hookup. It was simply about hanging out with friends and maybe, if it happened, making some new friends. That was why he always wanted to sit at the bar, the social center, where he could chat with the bartender, get some local knowledge, and, in the true manner of a writer, just sit back and watch the minor dramas unfolding around him.

There's something that social theorists call a "third place," a place in life other than home or work, a space used purely for socialization, without the obligations and burdens of the first two places. Diners and coffee shops are prime examples, and so are bars. That was the appeal of nightlife to Lee: just hanging out, savoring the moments and the company like a finely crafted cocktail.

Of course, that's also a big reason why we tourists travel, even on the beaten path, even if we only have a few days, like Amy and Tara—to escape the burdens of the familiar, to enjoy the new, to savor the world. Lee's attitude toward bars was similar to mine about the tourist trail: if you approach it with the right mindset and eyes wide open, intent on soaking up the atmosphere and making those connections rather than simply doing the cliché, shallow things in the cliché, shallow way, you really can discover new places, meet interesting people, and feel a sense of wonder and delight.

I surveyed the scene, telling myself to remember this more than I remembered the wall coming down. It was what I'd come to think of as a Montmartre Moment, an unexpected but wonderous encounter, when my anxieties evaporated and all felt right with the world. The Goddess Serendipity had done it again.

"Two oh six a.m.," Lee said as we arrived back at the hostel. "By Berlin standards, we are pathetic."

There was no frustration in his voice, though. It was an observation, not a complaint.

Munich

If You Brew It, They Will Come

A light-hearted, fun-loving city whose residents look upon the pursuit of pleasure as a full-time occupation. If you want to imbibe something of the atmosphere of nineteenth-century Europe—go to Munich.

—Europe on Five Dollars a Day

"Cheers," I said to Lee, raising my mug, a veritable Big Gulp of beer.

"Cheers," Lee replied, clinking his glass to mine.

On the table in front of us were trays piled with food, including pretzels big enough to wear as necklaces. Moderation and Munich, as we would soon discover, are contradictory terms.

We had arrived in Munich just a few hours earlier, but we had already found our way to one of the city's oldest beer gardens, Augustiner Keller, which dates to 1812. Frommer doesn't mention it, but I hope he came here anyway, because it seems like his kind of place: plenty of people, barrels of beer. The sprawling grounds can seat five thousand patrons, and even with a paltry couple thousand here tonight, it had an electric, heady atmosphere. Of course, the liter-sized mugs of beer helped with that. But even before we started drinking, the place had the feel of an enchanted forest, with scores of towering chestnut trees forming an almost unbroken canopy soaring above a white-gravel carpeting. (We later learned that chestnut trees were chosen specifically because they don't have deep roots, thereby enabling a larger beer cellar. Score another point for German engineering.)

"The most brilliant part of this place is right behind you," Lee said, pointing with his fork.

I turned to see, in the middle of the sea of tables and committed drinkers, a little playground, with Teutonic tykes climbing on a jungle gym. Bacchanalia for the whole brood.

The garden was populated with an impressive cross section of humanity: tourists of all ages and nationalities, families having picnics with food they'd clearly brought in themselves, lederhosen-clad German men with ruddy cheeks bisected by sculptural mustaches. Servers delivered beer steins eight or ten at a time, grasping them in double handfuls.

"Maybe you should bring the Contessa here on a date," I suggested to Lee.

The Contessa was the woman working at the front desk when we checked into our hostel. She was beautiful, with an enchanting, oft-flashed smile bracketed by deep dimples. Lee was convinced that she was Italian, most likely a countess. Some obscure provision in her grandfather's will mandated that she come here to find a mate. A backpacker. An American. At least, that was the theory, and I was too amused to dispute it.

"Nah, she's probably already been here too many times," Lee said. "She probably *owns* the place, actually."

"It's hard to impress someone like that," I agreed.

I proposed another toast: "To the Contessa and your prospects for wooing her. Cheers." We clinked glasses again and settled back to enjoy this party in a forest.

On every tourist thoroughfare in Europe, you will find the following:

- A dreadlocked backpacker moaning into a didgeridoo, with a Buddhist prayer bowl serving as a change bucket.
- A classical string trio, hip in black shirts and dark jeans, playing Pachelbel's Canon.
- An opera singer belting out "Nessun dorma" or "O sole mio." Slightly frayed, rumpled formal attire.
- An aggressively bohemian (and possibly fedora-wearing) guitarist singing either "Mad World" or a Bob Marley mix that is not so much medley as stoned confusion about which song is which.
- A ponytailed guy of unknown South American extraction playing Simon and Garfunkel songs on the Peruvian pan flute.
- One person playing the local traditional music. This musician will have the smallest audience: zero.

By now, Lee and I were playing street musician bingo every time we were in a tourist area (that is to say, every day). And tonight, man, we were hitting the *jackpot* as we meandered down Neuhauserstrasse and then Kaufingerstrasse, the pedestrian malls that serve, collectively, as the main tourist drag in Munich.

For good measure here, there was also a group singing glee-club versions of Amy Winehouse songs (you have not lived until you've heard "Rehab" in chipper four-part harmony) and a couple of extra classical groups, including one that had hauled out an upright piano. The rest of the scene, too, was ideally clichéd: Gothic architecture; seemingly few locals aside from teenagers (although the spot-the-American game was difficult here, too); a living statue, this one dressed as the Tin Man from *The Wizard of Oz*; and assorted chain stores (after we'd walked a ways, I exclaimed, "I can't believe we haven't seen an H&M. Where is it?" No more than ten seconds later, Lee pointed: "There it is."). Most impressive, I thought, was that nearly every window display, even the chain stores', had an at least quasi-Bavarian theme. C&A, a hip clothing store, was selling designer lederhosen for ninety-nine euros; more upscale boutiques displayed lederhosen and dirndls for several times more.

There was a quiet energy pulsing through the streets, much as there had been at the beer garden. An anticipatory buzz. Oktoberfest, that famous carnival of carousing, was to begin in just over a week, and the preparations for the tourist onslaught were well under way, the hatches being battened down, the commemorative beer steins being placed in every shop window, the clichés being dusted off and polished up.

We started the next morning with a visit to an attraction that gave *Manneken-Pis*, the ribald little mascot of Brussels, a run for his money in the Silliness Sweepstakes. Let's check in with the Frommer guide—or rather, a correspondent quoted in the Readers' Suggestions section at the end of the chapter:

> *One of the best free sights in Europe is the Glockenspiel, the animated clock tower of the city Rathaus, which "performs" at 11*

a.m. each day, when its colorful figures dance the ancient steps of
the Beer Barrel Makers.

I'd like to think that this comment is a sign of a more innocent time, that it conclusively demonstrates that not so long ago, life was more full of wonder, and tourists were more easily amused and less jaded. Because my reaction to it—indeed, the only possible reaction for the twenty-first-century viewer—is: *Seriously? Thousands of people watch this every day?*

On the tourist trail, the difference between the tourist traps that are actually kind of interesting and those that are fairly awful—by which I mean awful-awful, not amusingly awful—is paper-thin. When it comes to tacky tourism, you just know it when you see it, as the saying goes about a certain other, more lurid form of spectacle and exploitation. The Eiffel Tower is unequivocally cool—that I say without hesitation. *Manneken-Pis* is absurd, clearly, although intriguing in its irreverence and broader symbolism. The Glockenspiel, though, is the beaten path at its most stereotypically crowded and inane. This is one cliché I could never embrace.

The whole show—think glorified windup toy and you pretty much have it—lasts some twelve to fifteen minutes, during which even the most committed Luddite will inevitably give thanks for living in an age of video games and other amusements a bit more whiz-bang than this. Even our tour guide openly mocked the Glockenspiel ("Here come the mechanical hip thrusts—he's a cheeky fellow, that one!") and gently chastised those who were taking photos: "Don't bother. Your arm will get sore now and your friends will be unimpressed later."

I took a Not-So-Flattering Photo of the scene, skipping the landmark entirely and focusing instead on all the people filming the spectacle. Several others also turned their viewfinders on the crowd. A few took photos of me taking photos of them: the tourist as attraction, the funhouse mirror of the beaten path. It was not the first time I'd seen this, nor would it be the last.

It made me wish, for a moment, that I had ditched Frommer and gone to a charming Mediterranean village—filled with eccentric, authentic locals—after all. But then I reminded myself to be happy, to embrace the cliché. I was in Munich. Life was good.

Even our tour guide couldn't kill my blissful buzz, though I have no doubt he accomplished the feat for others in our group. He was the opposite of Ines XVI. I won't use his real name; let's just call him Nigel. Here and there, he had some fleeting moments of serious-ness and stone-faced recollections of Nazi-era events and other painful chapters in the city's history—Kristallnacht, the terrorist attacks at the 1972 Olympics—but he recounted these in a hurry, eager to change the subject; his stories tended to take a ribald turn. And in Munich's culture and history, he had a bawdy enabler.

He told us about the "beer wenches" at the Hofbräuhaus (the city's most famous beer hall), a chuckle of dirty-old-man delight in his tone as he spoke of the women who historically served drinks in their "tight dirndls." As we passed a statue of Puck, he grabbed the hand of one of the women in our group—who had already rebuffed his advances—and cupped it over the figure's crotch. "Ooh! Eew!" Nigel crowed. "You touched his willy!" He snickered loudly. She shook her head and cast him a contemptuous smirk, not offended so much as sorry for him. A few moments later, he pointed out a gutter that was once an open sewer, then shoulder-checked another woman into it, laughing, "Eew! You just stepped in piss!"

Whenever someone kindly observed that he should, you know, cut that out, he just shrugged it off.

I couldn't help seeing this offensive behavior as a reminder of how far we've come. Comments that were commonplace or seemingly innocuous in the era of *Europe on Five Dollars a Day* would play quite differently now, give or take a Nigel or two.

Take the examples of certain guidebook writers. Neither Fielding, Fodor, nor Frommer was always what we might today call politically correct. Fielding's nightlife sections are often filled with borderline salacious commentary, as in his recommendation of a Paris club that is "one of the top bets for aficionados of the female torso." Arthur Frommer, for his part, suggests a visit to a swimming hole for "a view of Paris babes with a little less on" and a café notable for its "buxom waitress." (The café is still open. My waiter was a middle-aged guy who looked like Rodney Dangerfield.) His Stockholm chapter includes nearly two pages on "girl-watching," beginning with this: "In the area around Skansen, you'll soon discover why the girls of Sweden are that nation's chief export, best tourist attraction and most highly developed achievement." Here in Munich, he says, you can't miss the Hofbräuhaus, not only because of the beer but because "this is your choice for a terribly inexpensive evening, full of Teutonic hanky-panky." Each chapter has lines like that. It's not just the prices of the book that are anachronistic.

(I strongly suspect that the Frommer of today would wince at his earlier comments on "girl-watching" and, had he been on our tour in Munich, may well have rebuked Nigel for his boorish behavior.)

My mother encountered more than a few Nigels during her travels, most notably in Italy (like those lustful teenage boys who followed her back to her guesthouse in Florence) but elsewhere, too. In a postcard from Munich she told my father, "We are sick of 'dirty old men' as Ann calls them. Last night a Swiss student saved us from an Italian. We feel like skipping Italy at this point." Her letters and postcards are, alas, full of such comments and stories.

But times have changed. Sexist comments and caddish behavior are less tolerated in modern society and the tourist trail is safer for women.

I think. Maybe. Not being female, I can't say for sure.

As it happens, Elizabeth Gilbert makes similar observations in her 2006 blockbuster *Eat, Pray, Love*: "I ask around [Rome], and everybody here agrees that, yes, there's been a true shift in Italy in the last ten to fifteen years. Maybe it's a victory of feminism, or an evolution of culture, or the inevitable modernizing effects of having joined the European Union. Or maybe it's just simple embarrassment on the part of young men about the infamous lewdness of their fathers and grandfathers."

Guidebooks have also caught up with the times. *Europe on Five Dollars a Day*, as I've mentioned, didn't have much in the way of tips, tricks, and general travel advice, and it had no specific guidance for women travelers, solo or otherwise. (There were travel guides for women back then, though, including Fodor's *Woman's Guide to Europe*, first published in 1953.) The 2011 version of *Rick Steves' Europe Through the Back Door*, on the other hand, begins with 442 pages of "Travel Skills," followed by just 252 pages of where-to-go-what-to-do content. Steves offers chapters for travelers of color and gay travelers and nine pages for women traveling alone, including this priceless tip: "There's no need to tell men that you're traveling alone. . . . Lie unhesitatingly. You're traveling with your husband. He's waiting for you at the hotel. He's a professional wrestler who retired from the sport for psychological reasons." I can imagine my mother, in her breezy but assertive manner, using that line while glowering at countless dirty old men throughout the Continent.

All that said, I still rather hoped to see Lee woo the Contessa. In a discreet, debonair, nonsketchy kind of way, of course. But still. I was once again starting to think of my journey in terms of Sundance film plots and travel-memoir tropes and . . . well, they would have made a very cute, narrative-enhancing couple. It would have fit nicely with my new embrace-the-cliché attitude. Or maybe she would rebuff his advances, saying that she was more interested in his friend, the shy one with the funny old travel guide. That would also work.

But the Contessa had disappeared.

"I'm sure she's gone back to Italy to prepare for the lavish wedding," I assured Lee. "The aristocratic guest list alone takes a while to plan."

We hadn't seen her since that first evening, and now Lee even had a question for her: we needed directions to one of Frommer's favorite restaurants whose precise location was unclear.

The Contessa, however, was not playing along, and the guy who had replaced her, a punk rocker with a paunch, just didn't hold the same conversational appeal. So we headed off to find some other company. And drink.

We had no historically driven motivation for going on a beer hall tour. Oh, sure, I could point out that Frommer gives the Munich chapter a subtitle of "Beer and Wurst at Bargain Rates." I could note that when my mother was here, even she, who hates beer, felt obliged to sample the suds. But no. We—and I do mean both of us this time, not just Lee—mostly just wanted to meet people and gulp down Munich's biggest clichés. We would be missing Oktoberfest by just a few days, so this would have to suffice as a stand-in.

The hostel bar where we gathered was a good start, as clichés go. It was very much the archetypal backpacker hostel, the modern equivalent of the cut-rate accommodations (and alcohol-enabled socializing) that Frommer recommended in *Europe on Five Dollars a Day*. The bar got bonus cliché marks for its other highly typical features: the currency from around the world taped to the pillar in the middle of the bar, the nonnative bartenders (all British, in this case), the Jägermeister shot dispenser . . . and, alas, the many travelers ignoring the conversation and focused on their laptops, updating their blogs or Facebook statuses.

The key touch, though, was the guy holding court at the end of the bar. I didn't catch his name, but he seemed to have wandered off the set of the backpacker-dystopia movie *The Beach*; call him Random Backpacker #22. He wore a tattered black T-shirt and a look that was at once vacant and spiteful. "Twenty-five euros is the *maximum* I will pay for a place to crash," I heard him grumble, "but that's pushing it." He bragged about spending less, about spending nothing, and about the sketchy fleabags and shacks and ditches he'd slept in. He took Frommer's signature axiom—that the less you spend, the more genuine your experience—to its farthest, filthiest extreme, apparently mistaking adversity for authenticity. He'd done Paris; he'd done eastern Europe; he'd done Southeast Asia; he'd done everywhere; he was over it all.

I hoped that if I kept listening, I'd hear the phrase I'd been expecting for weeks but which had so far proved elusive. I strained to eavesdrop through the rising buzz of conversation and clinking glasses in the now-crowded room. I waited and waited . . . and there it was, with maximum haughtiness and impeccable timing, right as our guide began to round us up, in that Archetypal Hostel Bar a block from the Munich train station: "You gotta be a *traveler*, not a tourist."

Lee and I fell in with three other twenty-somethings doing solo tours of Europe. Annie from Johannesburg seemed aloof and bookish at first glance but quickly asserted herself with a cutting wit and an astonishing enthusiasm for beer. Jacob from Edmonton tried to keep pace with her, though it was quickly clear that his stomach was no match for his fervor. He was an engineer by occupation and a hockey player by passion, though in some cruel twist of fate, he had the brain of a hockey player and the brawn of an engineer. Sam from "a small village in northern England" provided the hipness—red glasses to go with her scarlet hair; yellow-and-white-striped sweater—and the pop culture commentary. It was she who brought up John Hughes, the director, who had recently died.

"The story of my youth: *Sixteen Candles*," she said.

"And *Breakfast Club*," said Annie.

"Yes!" the rest of us said in unison.

We all chattered: Wasn't that *just* like our high schools? Pretty much, we agreed, despite having grown up in four different countries, on three different continents. (Though, admittedly, all middle class and white.)

"To John Hughes," Sam said, raising her stein.

"To John Hughes!" we toasted.

"*Ferris Bueller's Day Off* was always my favorite," I said, confessing that I'd sort of wanted to be like Ferris.

"*Everyone* wants to be Ferris," Sam agreed, "but I rather prefer Cameron. He's more realistic—that's more like what we are most days, isn't it?"

Well, yes, I thought.

"He has a bit of neurotic charm to him," Annie said.

And that, I thought.

The five of us quickly became inseparable, not that the others in our group seemed to have much interest in socializing. Three guys from Los Angeles, traveling together, mostly kept to themselves, smoking nervously and apparently intimidated by their surroundings; one confided that he'd never even been on an airplane until a few days earlier. I empathized with them and realized, in a rare moment when we pulled them into our conversation, that they thought *I* was a badass, proper-noun Traveler. Meanwhile, Alejandro from Argentina and Miyu from Japan had apparently just met but were already inseparable, making for an incongruous couple, he gaunt and bearded, a stoner Jesus; she tiny but with a spunky, rock-star bearing. (Not surprisingly, Random Backpacker #22 had stayed behind. "Already done it," I'd heard him mutter as we headed out the door.)

At the second beer garden Lee jumped up on a picnic table, stein in hand. Our beleaguered tour guide had nearly given up on trying to explain history and culture to his increasingly inattentive charges but had made one last gallant effort, telling us about Bavarian drinking songs. Lee was eager to share his knowledge on the subject from his tabletop pulpit.

"I'm going to teach you a song called 'Jesus Can't Play Rugby,'" he said. "It's about the, um, reasons Jesus can't play rugby. Like, 'Jesus can't play rugby 'cause . . . his headgear is illegal.' And then we all sing, "Cause his headgear is illegal, 'cause his headgear is illegal.' "

Alejandro broke his tractor-beam gaze into Miyu's eyes and looked at Lee. "Yeah, that's funny, man," he said, his voice a blues-singer rasp. "I *like* this song."

"Okay, so . . . ," Lee began. He flashed that conniving smirk to our gathered group, and we all fell under his spell, even the guys from L.A. Lee swung his mug like a frothy metronome. "Jesus can't play rugby 'cause . . . *his dad fixed the game* . . ." He paused and gestured toward us, imploring, conducting. We laughed and sang along, "'Cause his dad fixed the game, 'cause his dad fixed the game."

"Again!" Lee crowed. "Jesus can't play rugby 'cause . . ." He pointed to one of the Californians.

"Uh . . . because . . ."

"His team's too big?" someone suggested. We were too far into the evening for quick thinking or creativity. We all laughed and Alejandro offered a few more raspy affirmations ("Yeah, man!") and Lee maneuvered himself down from the table.

"You were like Ferris Bueller up there," I said approvingly.

Sam and Annie agreed—and decided that I was Cameron. Given their earlier comments, I didn't mind. They, like Lee, decided that what I really needed was adventure and fun. And since there was no red Ferrari at hand for me to drive around with reckless abandon, drinking excessive quantities of German beer would have to suffice.

"C'mon, Cameron, *finish it*!" Sam cried, eyeing my stein, which I was thinking of, optimistically, as half empty.

"You can do it, Cameron!" Annie grinned as she examined her own nearly empty stein. Next to this was another mug, this one long drained.

I pointed at her accomplishment. "How is that possible at this point?" I asked.

"Johannesburg is high above sea level," she replied. "I'm used to drinking at altitude. So having a few beers here is nothing, *dude*." She said "dude" ironically, with an American accent. Then she downed the rest of her glass in one long gulp.

Jacob lowered his head and stared at his own nearly full stein. "I might be done," he moaned. "I have . . . failed."

Annie beamed.

It is at this point where my memories of the night are blurred to the point of wholly unreliable. I've read other travel books where authors comment, by way of indirectly indicating that they maybe possibly drank too much, that their notes for the evening become nonsensical or entirely illegible. I would like the record to show that I never reached this point. No, I had other people do my writing for me, as designated note takers. I don't recall this, but the handwriting in my notebook suddenly becomes unfamiliar. So I can tell you that we talked about South African vs. English accents. We discussed my declining motor skills, specifically my inability to spin my pen around my thumb. And then, on the last page of the notebook, there's this poem by Annie:

I wish I were sober
No, I don't
Then the story might be better
The second time around.

. . .

So maybe Lee liked to go a bit overboard sometimes after all. Maybe I did, too. Comfort zone successfully escaped—or rather, redefined. Cliché successfully embraced.

The next morning, the sunlight cut through the window with a laserlike intensity. I buried my head under my pillow and wondered why it seemed so bright and why there was a horrible throbbing sensation in my head—it felt like one of those street performers was blasting a didgeridoo in my frontal lobe. I peeked out from my cave and stared at Lee. He, somehow, looked worse.

Grumbling, I trudged to the bathroom and cranked the shower handle toward *C*. A blast of boiling lava poured out instead, and I swore I saw my melted skin circling down the drain as I frantically turned the handle the other direction. Either way, though, mission accomplished: I was awake.

Burned and then iced and washed and cleansed and freshly clothed, I stepped back into the room feeling . . . completely fine. Great, even. The didgeridoo was gone; the sunlight had dimmed. There were signs of life in the other bed, as well. "Do you have any Tylenol?" groaned the Lee-shaped object tangled in sheets. I dug the bottle from my bag and handed him two pills and a glass of water.

"Thanks," Lee mumbled. "If you want to head out on your own, that's fine. Otherwise you might be waiting all day. Wake me up again when it's time to get the train to Zurich."

I headed to the northern part of town, to a neighborhood called Schwabing. I was intrigued by Frommer's description of it as "the

Greenwich Village area of Munich . . . in some respects, it's zanier and more colorful than anything New York offers."

What I found was . . . well, pretty much just that, at least compared to the tourist center.

I walked for blocks and blocks, on side streets and the main drag, and didn't hear English spoken once. There were bistros and hip record stores, guys on skateboards, women on bikes (their scarves flowing behind them; I fell in love with every one), teenagers doing parkour stunts in a plaza by the U-Bahn station, and a cluster of old men playing chess on a massive board, with three-foot-tall pieces, in a convivially overgrown park. An orderly row of bicycles stood locked in a rack, and I noticed that balanced within the frame of one of the bikes was a Saran Wrap–covered bowl full of a freshly made salad topped with a careful arrangement of sliced tomatoes. You won't find that in a tourist hot spot. I pictured a German beatnik on the way to a potluck. I wondered if I could tag along.

On Occamstrasse, I searched for restaurants Frommer recommended in *E5D* and found none. But the street and the neighborhood were just as he'd promised: quiet and cheerily funky. (Though I was later told that the true bohemian, hip areas today are elsewhere, in the Glockenbach and Westend neighborhoods.) Even so, when I stopped at a bakery for a pastry, the woman behind the counter took me in stride, not at all surprised to see a tourist here.

The area fit a template that I'd noticed in Charlottenburg in Berlin, Jordaan in Amsterdam, and other just slightly outlying neighborhoods: a place where tourists were welcome but relatively scarce, the middle ground between the roads less traveled and most trampled. Call it the frontage road to the beaten path. This, I suspect, is what many tourists are actually after: the just-right combination of foreign and familiar, everyday local life and tourist amenities. A sense of place and community, plus easy access to the landmarks, but without tourism's most tawdry trappings, none of the crowds and souvenir vendors and musicians and touts that are as interchangeable as the chain stores lining a suburban American highway.

I sat on a bench in a lush pocket park, feeling very much at home. "This is great, Arthur," I caught myself saying aloud. "Thanks."

I pondered how it was that Schwabing had retained—or, perhaps, reclaimed—much of its charm since the 1960s, avoiding being overrun with tourists and the attendant kitsch.

My one-word answer: Oktoberfest.* Maybe you've heard of it. Little festival involving drinking songs and men in lederhosen and women in dirndls and pretzels and schnitzel and inadvisable amounts of beer. Major tourist bait. And, crucially, on the other side of the city from Schwabing.

Oktoberfest started in 1810 as a celebration for a royal wedding, continued as an agricultural fair the next year, and began to take its current form as a beer-themed carnival when rides were added in 1818 (because there's no better chaser for a liter of suds than a roller coaster). Frommer's '63 guide says not a word about it, which I find curious given that he subtitles the Munich chapter "Beer and Wurst at Bargain Rates" and writes at length about beer halls and the city's love of a good time. It was certainly popular enough back

---

* After I returned home, I got in touch via email with an American expat in Munich. Another key factor, he said, was rental prices: "In Munich, Schwabing is the most expensive [area] . . . so most of the touristy or hip cafés and restaurants just couldn't pay the rent and moved to less expensive parts of town."

then: in 1950, Oktoberfest visitors consumed 88,294 servings of chicken and 1.5 million liters of beer, according to official statistics. Seems like a pretty big deal to overlook, right? Perhaps. But those numbers are paltry compared to their 2010 counterparts: 488,137 servings of chicken, 7 million liters of beer. ("I've no idea why people drank that much," an Oktoberfest spokeswoman told *Spiegel Online* that year. "They were simply thirsty.")

Today, some 6 to 7 million visitors come here every year to eat, drink, be merry, and observe, at late hours, the correlation between the loping, giddy pulse of a polka song and the particular rhythmic swaying of the world when you're drunk. Such is the reputation of the festival and its consequences that the Australian government sets up a temporary consulate in Munich during Oktoberfest specifically to help all the Aussies who lose their passports or find themselves in beer-induced dire straits.

Even when Oktoberfest isn't going on—when Lee and I were there, for example—it imbues much of the central part (the tourist part) of the city with its spirit, exuding a certain magnetism, keeping visitors' attention focused squarely on the center of town, where the action, the stereotypes, and the beer abound.

That evening, Lee (who had eventually roused himself from bed) and I went to Frommer's top pick in Munich, a place called the Ratskeller. The menu was printed in English, French, Italian, and Spanish, although these translations weren't really necessary, because there was a photo of each dish, and if there was meat involved—and in Germany, there's *always* meat involved—the photo was accompanied by a little illustration of the animal in question. I had one of the lighter-sounding things on the menu: pork chop topped with bacon and fried pork rind.

It was a charming space, kinda sorta: arched ceilings, wood paneling, murals on the walls, a rambling layout filled with booths in nooks. But it also felt contrived for our benefit—authentic plus one, as I'd felt that first day in Florence—because of the tourist clientele, the photo-filled menu, and the over-the-top "*Ja*, we are so German" vibe.

I recalled Le Grand Colbert in Paris, the restaurant row section of Brussels, and the "Miller Lite Restaurant" in Berlin. Different cities, same phenomenon. The vast majority of Frommer's 1963 recommendations that have survived offer an exaggerated version of the culture. Stereotypes sell: an eternal truth.

The Ratskeller made for an odd comparison to Schwabing. Here, amid jovial tourist crowds and pork-festooned pork, you have the more superficially authentic scene and historic *aesthetic* character. And out there, up Leopoldstrasse, you have the actual Germans. The businesses may have changed, but the *spirit* of the place—the people, the general atmosphere—endures, at least more so than in the center of town, where the authentic, historic character is rather overwhelmed by all the people who have come to marvel at the authentic, historic character.

Nearly 60 percent of Munich's historic city center was reduced to rubble during World War II, but the Altstadt, as the area is known, still looks old, full of imposing Gothic buildings. How is that possible? Because they rebuilt it to appear pretty much as it had before the war. It's fake historic architecture. Nigel pointed out examples like the Old City Hall, which ostensibly dates to the fifteenth century, although—*shh*—the tower was destroyed during the war and rebuilt in the 1970s. (And is newer than the so-called

New City Hall.) Why would you do that? Tourists. The architects—both literal and figurative—of Munich's postwar reconstruction were well aware of the city's status as a hot spot of arts and tourism, and the role of the built environment in fostering that atmosphere. In 1930, according to Gavriel D. Rosenfeld's book *Munich and Memory*, a full 10 percent of the city's total revenue came from tourism. Munich's modern reputation for historic architecture, Rosenfeld says, "was largely the product of postwar reconstruction, which paradoxically made it more 'historic' than other German cities that were more heavily damaged [during World War II] and less thoroughly rebuilt."

When you compare Schwabing and the big beer halls, it's clear that at least here in Munich, tourism promotes a particular variety of preservation, an exaggerated, theme-park-ish, spectacle-heavy one, where amusement reigns supreme and where that destruction, that *war*, maybe didn't happen. It's a jarring contrast to Berlin: fewer souvenir stands but also fewer major monuments.

So here's the question: without tourists, would Munich's beer halls be replaced with modern buildings and eyesore malls or would they remain packed, per tradition, with old men wearing lederhosen and singing drinking songs without the slightest trace of irony or snickering in their voices?

I tried to answer that question—which, really, is one of the central ones of modern tourism in general, the tension between preservation and distortion—but couldn't. It all seemed a confusing haze; the whirlwind of my Not-So-Grand Tour catching up to me, fixing me in a state of travel vertigo and unease. I reminded myself of my goal to stop worrying and embrace the cliché. There was one big heaping serving of Bavarian stereotypes left to consume.

Come on, Cameron, finish it.

. . .

"Bavarian cocaine!" yelled the guy in the green felt hat with a little red feather as Lee and I found an open table.

"Wunderbar!" roared his friend.

This, finally, was the ultimate tourist cliché in this ultimate tourist cliché city: the Hofbräuhaus. It's the most famous of the Munich beer halls and one of Frommer's top picks. It also now has outlets in Las Vegas, Dubai, and elsewhere. Across the street, another of his recommendations has been usurped by a Hard Rock Cafe. The two make an interesting pair, two symbols of globalization and two reminders of the worldwide appeal of a theme party. My mother came here, on her one day in Munich. She was miserable: she doesn't like beer, and this isn't really the sort of place where you order wine. Still, then as now, if you were a tourist in Munich, you had to go to the Hofbräuhaus.

"Wunderbar!" yelled one of the Germans again. I had my back to them, so I was only able to see the goings-on with occasional glances over my shoulder.

"You should come sit on this side of the table," Lee said. "It's quite a show you're missing. Have you ever been to, like, a Lions Club or something similar? It's totally like that, but they're wearing lederhosen."

Sure enough. From my new seat, I could see that the "Bavarian coke" was actually snuff. The guy consuming it was a fiftyish, ruddy-cheeked fellow in suspenders, lederhosen, and that green felt alpine hat. And a mustache? Yes, of course: wide and well kept. Six of his tablemates were similarly attired.

"I wonder if they pay those guys to be here," Lee said, shaking his head in wonder. "They almost seem too perfect."

A waiter came to take our order. He had the classic Bavarian name of Nguyen. At the table on the other side of us, a family of Japanese tourists shared an apple strudel. A few feet away, another pair of tourists, clearly American—I could hear snatches of their conversation—but of Latino ancestry, examined a menu. It was, all told, a classic scene of the modern tourist trail, traditions and stereotypes both celebrated and subverted.

The eighth guy at the table of old German men looked just like Jimmy Buffett—he might have been Jimmy Buffett, actually. He had long gray hair and wore a bright, patterned shirt under a leather vest, a toucan amid more formal penguins. They were all exceptionally drunk and sang along boisterously whenever the oompah band struck up "Ein Prosit," which seemed to happen every thirty seconds or so (presumably because this is the only drinking song that most non-Germans know). Each man clutched an ornate beer stein, and we noticed that next to us was a massive wrought-iron rack with slots holding similar mugs, an ingenious convenience for the truly dedicated drinkers.

One of the lederhosen-attired men was exceptionally old, the Methuselah of Munich—or perhaps the Ponce de León, because his wrinkles and hunched posture belied his energy: he was as boisterous, as beaming, as drunk as anyone. There was nothing self-conscious about their fervor, nor was it tempered with any concern for the voyeuristic tourists. It was an unalloyed enjoyment of life and friends . . . and beer.

Nguyen placed two steins on the table, our first drinks since the tour.

I raised my glass. "Thank you for joining me here," I said to Lee. "I was sort of expecting that you'd ditch me for a date with the Contessa."

His response came out as one word: "Yeahshenevershowedup-again." He was resigned to his fate as a lowly commoner. We drank in silence for a few moments, and Lee's dispirited expression faded as we watched the German revelers.

"Wunderbar!" The cry went up and the band started playing "Ein Prosit" yet again.

We eyed the group from our front-row seats. They seemed friendly. They probably didn't speak any English, but they were certainly gregarious. Maybe this was our best chance to meet the locals and—

"Hey, guys!" Two backpackers—basically our Canadian clones—slid onto the bench across the table from us, blocking our view of the Bavarians. "Cool if we join you?"

We sighed and reminded ourselves that this, too, was part of embracing the cliché.

"Sure," I said. "Cheers."

Unfortunately, we had just met the only two genuinely boring tourists in all of Europe, all rosy cheeks and center-parted hair and zero stories to add to the communal stockpile. Their most grating characteristic, of course, was they were not lederhosen-wearing German men. This cliché sucked; *that* cliché, the one on glorious display at the other table, was interesting. Artificial, at least kind of? Sure. Kept intact partly through the artificial preservative of tourism? Yep. And sweetened with the synthetic sucrose of spectacle. But at least these were home-cooked stereotypes; Munich had evolved on its own terms.

We stopped talking with the Canadians and stared over their shoulders instead.

"Wunderbar!"

Zurich

Money Matters

[The city] enjoys all the better attributes of a Swiss tourist attraction: heartstopping scenery; the restful calm that comes from an atmosphere of cleanliness and honest dealing; [and] the variety and interest to be found in the multi-lingual, multi-national character of the country.

—Europe on Five Dollars a Day

The Russian couple stood ten or fifteen feet away from us trying to look nonchalant, but their cameras betrayed their attention: Lee and I were the local color in their snapshots. I like to imagine them pointing out the details to friends later: a background of a historic apartment building with eye-catching turquoise shutters and flower boxes overflowing with red petunias; a cobblestoned public square below; and in the center of the frame, two Swiss locals—*bookishly handsome* Swiss locals—lounging at an outdoor café, dipping baguette slices into a pot of fondue, their wrists moving with a fluid grace, like a Roger Federer forehand in slow motion. Just a typical Zurich street scene.

I gave the Russians a nod of acknowledgment and then turned my attention back to the task at hand: stuffing myself with bread and cheese. Elegantly.

My mother and Ann had finished their trip with a gourmet meal in Paris, courtesy of Dad's parents, so now, as I prepared to bid Lee farewell—he had to get back to his job—my own parents had offered us the same present.

The point of the gift, in both cases, was to live it up, to eschew frugality for once. I was particularly keen to have some fondue, because (a) it would be a nice change from the meat overdose of Germany; (b) it's considered somewhat highfalutin back home, so, I figured, it must be superexpensive over here, where it originated; and (c) Frommer touts it as a real whiz-bang novelty, right at the top of the chapter's meals section: " 'Fondu'—melted cheese with wine and Kirsch, lapped up with chunks of bread—is the food specialty of Switzerland, and you ought to head immediately for a place that serves it."

Lee and I had walked around the city for a while before settling here, taking in the bourgeois bustle, marveling at the lake and the fog-cloaked mountains beyond, and having a drink at what may have been a transvestite bar (though, this being Zurich, everyone was dressed conservatively). The neighborhood, filled with students and hip boutiques and cafés, was on the east bank of the Limmat River, just across from the historic city center. It was a warren of hilly, cobblestoned streets and tall, narrow buildings at once overbearing and twee with their gabled roofs and brightly colored shutters—storybook gone big city. We had selected our fondue spot in part because it had a detail that seemed befitting of the quirky but well-kept spirit of the neighborhood (and which was perhaps the real reason for the Russian tourists' photos): on the balcony above the café's front door, a blue fiberglass cow appeared to be walking through the railing. It wasn't charging, mind you; there was no intensity to its gaze, and it had been positioned so as not to disrupt a flower box filled with petunias. It seemed very Swiss, cordial in its contrariness.

"I need to get a fondue set and have parties," I said. "Or maybe I can just take my parents' pot." Mom and Ann had both had their first taste of fondue in Switzerland, and when my parents got married the following March, Ann gave them a set.

"Would you actually use it?" Lee asked.

I stopped to think about how often my parents use theirs.

"Once," I said. "Every few years, maybe."

"Yeah, exactly," Lee replied. "It's like a sushi kit—everyone has one in an unopened box. Get a grill instead. You'll use a grill."

"Okay, but in concept, you must admit, fondue is cool. Even those Russians thought so."

"Please. Just get a grill."

Our bowl of bread had a single token piece of wheat baguette— health food. I speared it with my fork, dredged it through the fondue, and popped it in my mouth, then quickly wiped the cheese goatee from my chin. And then I said the words I never thought I'd hear come out of my own mouth.

"So we're going to go out barhopping tonight, right?" I asked. "It's your last real night in Europe." Lee would be leaving two days later, but early in the morning. "Last call to live it up and stay out late."

"I think I'm up to the challenge," Lee replied. He paused and his smirk slumped into a grimace. "Though I have to say, I'm feeling kind of tired. I didn't sleep well last night. It's those damn European sheets—I was dying under them and freezing without them. Not sure how long I'll last."

"No!" I couldn't believe it. "You're the rascally sidekick! That's why you're here! To lead me to the parties, to get me into trouble, to help me find my own Contessa!"

"Ah, the Contessa . . ."

"Maybe she's out there, at the bars," I said. "Waiting for you. For us. C'mon. The drinks are on me. Let's go."

We were tired of hostels. Tired of the noise, the grime, the lumpy mattresses, the lack of top sheets and presence, instead, of duvets—"those damn sheets" that Lee despised—of such bulk that they surely would have suffocated us had we used them. Some of the duvets we'd encountered had suffered such wear and tear and aggressive staining that we could only assume that at some point they had, indeed, been used to transport a corpse or two. And the hostels and cut-rate hotels had been loud, packed with all manner of yellers and stereo-blasters and hyena-laughers. We kept track of our earplugs like they were family heirlooms.

So when we saw that the Zurich hotel that Frommer described as "restful and quiet, old-fashioned" was still around, we decided to go for it, even though it was in an outlying neighborhood and the rate was twice what we had been paying elsewhere. (In 1963, it cost $3, including breakfast. Adjusted for inflation, that's $19.61. Actual price for us: about $140. Breakfast not included, we learned the hard way when we were presented with a bill for $16 each.) No matter. The hotel was near the convention center, so presumably that meant it catered to businesspersons from around the world. Which meant top sheets and other elusive luxuries: Washcloths! Reliable hot water! *Sleep!*

Well . . . yes, it had those. Other than that, though, the best I can say is that the next time someone wants to make a movie about the existential angst of a globe-trotting executive, circa 1985, I have the *perfect* setting. All of the old-fashioned charm had been Sheet-rocked over—no molding, no trim, just flat white surfaces every-where. It almost made the teal carpeting and discount-bin acrylic landscapes on the wall look appealing. It boggled my mind that at some point, this was considered good interior design; truly, the 1980s have a lot to answer for.

"There is no such thing as a bad Swiss hotel," Frommer says. "This is the 'nation of hotelkeepers,' the training ground for aspiring hotel managers of every land.... The difference, therefore, between a low-cost and a deluxe Swiss hotel is in decoration, not in comfort, and not in service."

Okay. Yeah. Fine. But it turns out decor matters. No highly trained concierge could compensate for this soul-sucking bleakness.

It all made us feel very sorry for the businesspeople for whom this is the norm. It used to be that those who traveled the most were the explorers and conquerors. Today they're the globe-trotters like Ryan Bingham, protagonist of Walter Kirn's 2001 novel *Up in the Air*—better known as the George Clooney character in the 2009 film adaptation of the same title. People who travel the world without seeing much of it beyond settings like this hotel. People for whom, in fact, such settings are so familiar as to be comforting; people who find their identity in the most anonymous of places and feel grounded only when in transit. "Planes and airports are where I feel at home," says Bingham, an archetype of our age, in the opening chapter of *Up in the Air.*

Everything fellows like you dislike about them—the dry, recy-cled air alive with viruses; the salty food that seems drizzled

with warm mineral oil; the aura-sapping artificial lighting—
has grown dear to me over the years, familiar, sweet.
*   . . . I suppose I'm a sort of mutation, a new species, and though*
I keep an apartment for storage purposes . . . I live somewhere
else, in the margins of my itineraries.

The Ryan Binghams of the world are decidedly at ease on the road; they fit in everywhere and nowhere. But theirs is a Bland Tour, a journey to the most placeless parts of the world's great places, a sojourn without struggle, devoid of the necessity of figuring things out. It's travel, too, with *obligations*; it is not the road as "third place" but, instead, as both home and office. I thought of Jay back at Montmartre, Tara and Amy and Jian in Berlin, Terrance in Amsterdam, travelers all—initially on the road for purposes of study or work—but at their happiest, it seemed, when escaping the rigors of the everyday to revel in the sights of the beaten path.

In a sense, the joy of tourism is the return to youth and innocence. It's finding wonder in the unfamiliar, of not being afraid to say, *"Wow, that's so freaking cool!"* It's arriving in a place with the anticipation of a child on Christmas morning. Meanwhile, the Ryan Binghams and the Random Backpacker #22s are the adults, world-weary and wise, but missing out on the fun and the sense of discovery and delight.

Somewhere, Arthur Frommer was shaking his head. In the depths of my inner ear, I heard his voice: "Spending more does not mean enjoying more. Go back to the hostels."

"How strange," Frommer says in *E5D*, "to be in a country where (a) everything works, (b) everyone seems well-off, (c) all appliances, machinery, telephones and gadgets are more modern than ours."

Zurich is a Ryan Bingham city: successful, savvy, bustling, *bland*. So goes the stereotype, one that a stay in a business hotel out by the convention center does nothing to dispel. (Admittedly, this sort of place should not be anyone's first impression of anywhere.)

The view from here is this: Zurich is the better-off cousin of Brussels, a blur of cultures and official languages, a crossroads of businesspeople and bureaucrats. As in Brussels, much of its appeal is its very banality—it may not have much to attract tourists, but because it is such an international crossroads, the whole place feels agreeably neither here nor there. It was odd, after being surrounded in Germany by the monuments and still-fresh memories of war, to arrive in a famously neutral country, a place that by staying out of conflicts has also missed out on the historic sites they leave behind. It's crass to say it, but here's the truth: happiness and pragmatism can be pretty dull. In a blandness-defending essay titled "The Discreet Charm of the Zurich Bourgeoisie," native son Alain de Botton adds, "Zurich's distinctive lesson to the world lies in its ability to remind us how truly imaginative and humane it can be to ask of a city that it be nothing other than bourgeois."

There's a catch to the banal bourgeois bliss, though: *it's really freaking expensive*, apparently set up for those with expense accounts worthy of Ryan Bingham.

Lee and I had thought that our fondue meal, our big-time splurge, was high livin' at about sixty dollars total, including drinks. The next day, as we searched for some lunch, we discovered this had been a bargain. A Big Mac Value Meal (not that we had one) cost eleven francs, with the Swiss franc essentially even with the American dollar. At a café by the river, not a fancy place by any means, a chalkboard advertised the day's lunch specials: a hamburger for twenty-two francs and a club sandwich twenty-three. Even a Snickers bar from a vending machine would have set me back over two francs. Strolling through the commercial heart of town, we ogled all the tourists—speaking English, German, Russian, and languages we didn't recognize—who had apparently come here to shop in stores where the windows displayed four-thousand-dollar cuff links and twenty-three-thousand-dollar watches. It was difficult to fathom.

Frommer promised a city with "costs low enough to remove the fear of expense from your vacation thoughts," but this turns out, today, to feel like a cruel joke. A 2010 study by the financial services company UBS found that Zurich is the second most expensive city in the world (of seventy-three cities studied), after Oslo.

"The question is, how long will a family with an average income be able to afford a trip to Switzerland?" a Zurich hotelier asked *BusinessWeek* in 2010. The Swiss franc was gaining strength, but to the hospitality industry, it was cause for panic rather than celebration.

It's impossible not to think about cost when planning a trip. Travel has certainly come a long way since the days when my father's parents assumed that my mother was independently wealthy because she was traveling to Europe. Not really—she was just incredibly diligent about following Frommer's advice. The truth is, though, that the Frommerian ideal of travel as accessible to everyone is still nowhere near reality.

Take a look at the evolution of the titles of Frommer's signature guidebook series. The budgets started at $5 a day, then rose to $10 in 1972, $15 in 1979, and so on, but they rose faster than the overall cost of living—travel inflation outpaced everyday inflation.

(Although, as noted earlier, airfares today are substantially cheaper than they were in the 1960s.) For example, according to the U.S. government's inflation estimates, $5 in 1957 had the same buying power as $36.89 in 2007. The guidebook title that year, though, was *Europe from $95 a Day*. It was the last of the Frommer's "dollar a day" books; the series was retired before it could cross the $100 threshold.

Being in Zurich, where I felt broke, was a reminder that leisure travel is still not truly accessible to all—not to most of the world, not even to many people in my own prosperous homeland, where the poverty rate was basically the same as it had been during my mother's trip (14.5 percent in 2010 versus 14.2 percent in 1967).

The common wisdom among many travel bloggers and self-appointed travel experts today is that going abroad is less expensive than you think; you just have to know what you're doing. It's a talking point that Frommer helped create, and there's no denying that it's still valid: you can go farther than you'd think on a limited budget, especially in these DIY days of Internet research, Internet cost-comparisons, Internet booking. The point sometimes spins out of control, though, myopically dismissing the reality that international travel, however cheap, remains an inaccessible luxury for much of the world. When you get right down to it, no, the open road still really isn't all that open.

After much searching, we found an affordable lunch option the next day. A long line snaked from a shack of a restaurant out onto Limmatquai, a street along the river. The patrons seemed to come from all walks of life, at least by Zurich standards, meaning one or two wore jeans with the slightest of fraying around the cuffs. Lee and I exchanged looks and joined the queue, trusting in the frugal instincts of the masses and the Goddess Serendipity. When we got to the counter, we ordered what everyone else was having: half a rotisserie chicken, with a huge rustic roll on the side. Cost: 9.50 francs. That sounded about right, maybe even a bit cheap, given the quantity and quality—the chicken was succulent and delicious, street food at its best.

Afterward, we sat by the lake. The meal had boosted our moods and choice of adjectives, replacing "boring" with "placid." Boats and swans carved figures in the water, their listless gliding an odd counterpoint to the bustle of the people on the shore. Our gaze kept drifting to the mountain ranges in the distance, the mists somehow giving each peak its own hue, hazily delineating the forms and distances, sharpening rather than flattening the scene.

"It looks like they've got the fog machines fired up," I said.

"And carefully placed," Lee added. "It's pretty impressive." He thought for a moment. "Maybe that's why everything here costs so much. Their fog machine budget must be huge."

"Not worth it," I grumbled. "Not enough to make me want to linger here—I'm gonna go broke in the next twenty-four hours. And *I'm* only about halfway done with this trip." I paused, letting that thought linger in my brain. Wait: did I *want* to go home, impending brokeness aside?

I cleared my throat. "Uh. I mean . . . Not that I'm complaining about the fact that I'm staying here and you have to go home."

Lee chuckled. "Ah, no. You'd better not complain about that."

The fog machines reminded me of my favorite of my mother's postcards. It's from Switzerland. There's a picture of a bull on the front, all jowls and horns, with an enormous bell dangling from a leather collar around its neck. The photo is cropped to a heart-shaped frame; the rest of the front is bright red, lipstick red, with text printed in a jaunty handwriting script: *"A toi mon coeur!!!"* My heart belongs to you. Mom has crossed out *toi*, though, and scratched in the word *vous*. My heart belongs to you all. The postcard is addressed to my father and his housemates, "The Men of 1003 8th St. SE."

> *Dear guys—*
>
> *Ann and I saw this postcard today in Geneva, before we climbed all over the castle at Chillon (of Lord Byron fame)—and decided that someone ought to buy it and send it to a deserving soul far away so that it could be appreciated in more than one part of the world. In other words, I can't believe anyone would make anything like this, let alone buy it! The castle is fantastic. I took at* <u>*least*</u> *10 photos, slides, and bought multi postcards which you shall see. To Florence tonight by train—hate to leave Switzerland.*
>
> *Love (esp to Bob),*
> *Pat*

I love it because it's so silly: the cow, the bell, the heart, the Valentine declaration. I love it because it's such a classically tacky postcard, and because this is the precise reason Mom bought it—it's a nice reminder that self-awareness and irony are timeless, not a modern invention, and that Mom, too, delighted in embracing clichés and finding a certain joie de vivre in the absurdity of it all. I love it, too, because of that penultimate line: she took, gosh, at *least* ten photos.

Here in Zurich, I found that I was taking fewer pictures than usual—that is to say, in the low dozens rather than the low hundreds. Part of it was that aesthetic irony was in surprisingly short supply in this boring bourgeois city—I had few opportunities for my Not-So-Flattering Photos of Famous Places. There are only so many times you can take a picture of a historic clock tower, a cobblestoned street winding down a hill lined with ski lodges on steroids, and mountains cloaked in machine-made fog. Lee had been rolling his eyes throughout the trip as I took my photos, and now, as our journey together came to an end, I realized it was time to put the camera away and enjoy the moment.

It's a problem that my mom didn't have to worry about: addiction to overdocumentation. She had to put effort and forethought into her photos. Film was expensive. Processing was a chore. Today, thanks to the instant gratification of digital cameras, we can spend all day seeing the world only through the comforting, limiting shield of the lens. Too often, I felt like I'd forgotten about the big picture, quite literally—I was missing out on the scene outside the frame, the sounds, the smells, the particular sense of place, the full narrative. I noticed, to my chagrin, that my first instinct upon seeing something interesting or beautiful was often not to take it all in but to think, "Can't wait to post this on Facebook!" Then, when it wasn't perfect—and it never was—I'd scowl at the tiny screen and try again, a dozen times.

This is a big reason I'd started taking those Not-So-Flattering Photos: because I wanted to document the landmarks, but I didn't want to spend hours trying to get just the right angle, just the right light, just the right photogenic passersby in the frame. It hadn't taken long—about ten seconds into my gawking at the Duomo in

Florence, an immense cathedral surrounded by a piazza filled with crowds and souvenir kiosks—to realize that those vendors I was trying to keep out of my frame would sell me a much better photograph, on a postcard, for just a few (euro) cents. Or I could find them on Flickr for free. Why bother to replicate the views? More to the point, it was typically the story outside of the usual frame that was most interesting: the traffic at the Champs-Élysées, the gift shops near *Manneken-Pis*, Snackpoint Charlie, the swans pecking at our feet as we sat by Zürichsee (Lake Zurich) right now. (As it turns out, there's now software you can buy called the Tourist Remover app—it clears out the imperfections, such as, oh, other tourists.)

Well, enough of that, I told myself. Frommer, I suspected, would have agreed: to spend less time obsessing about impressing others later . . . is to enjoy more.

I refused to put the camera away entirely, mind you. I still appreciated its ability—its *occasional* ability, which I naively hoped for every time—to tell more than words ever could. Because, man, sometimes the world is too weird not to document it.

Case in point: the woman in the flowerpot hat.

"That's quite an outfit she has on," Lee said. "She seems a bit . . . eccentric."

"There's no way she's not a crazy cat lady," I said as I pulled out my camera. "I bet she has, like, twenty cats. At least."

Lee and I had trekked up Lindenhof Hill, in the center of town, where a Roman citadel once stood. The fort was razed in the Middle Ages and is now a public square (How Swiss, I thought when I heard that—down with the military, up with quality of life), though the historic houses that surround three sides have a buttressing effect, making the grounds feel like the courtyard of a castle. We sat on a wall overlooking the northern part of the city, watching kids chase leaves in the occasional gusts and a wizened old man in a newsboy cap take on a young hoodlum-looking guy—amusingly, also wearing a newsboy cap—in a game of chess on one of those oversized boards that is apparently obligatory in urban European parks.

Crazy Cat Lady appeared to be leading a tour or, more likely, was out on a day pass from the asylum, with an assortment of orderlies trailing behind her. She wore a fluffy pink bathrobe and that hat, a plush flowerpot with felt flowers drooping over its sides; she was Martha Stewart meets Medusa meets Ophelia.

And then, dear God, she looked right at us and started walking in our direction.

I glanced at the drop on the other side of the wall. It was about twenty feet. There were bushes at the bottom. We could probably make it with minimal harm, I thought. The Swiss had a superb health care system, right?

As she approached, Crazy Cat Lady gave us a smile—warm and disconcertingly normal. I was reminded of Norman Bates of *Psycho* fame. I surveyed the drop again and tried to remember the safe falling technique I'd learned in that aikido class I took in college.

She said something in German. We grinned helplessly.

She said something in French. We kept grinning, saved by the language barrier.

"English?" she asked.

"Yep, English," Lee said. "Sorry."

"How much do you wait?" she said.

Wait? Wait for what? I wasn't waiting for anything. I was going to pull my best Spider-Man moves and get the hell out of there.

"We are having a party," she said. "It is . . . How do you say?"

Crazy Cat Lady and her companions conferred for a moment in French. I still wasn't quite sure what was going on. My muscles tensed. I took a tentative sniff, checking for the telltale odor of feline urine.

"A bachelorette party?" asked Lee.

"Ah! *Oui.* I have gotten married, so now my friends are having a party for me."

Lee and I each breathed an audible sigh of relief. Her friends snickered as they watched our posture ease and the color return to our faces. Well done, I wanted to say to them. The hat and bathrobe had been just weird enough to be a plausible outfit—for a crazy cat lady, anyway—and were therefore arguably more embarrassing than a more outlandish getup.

"I need to kiss one ton of men," said the bride. "So how much do you wait?"

Ah, *weigh,* not *wait.* We told her, then offered, in the European manner, two cheek-pecks each.

"Thank you!" the group called as they marched on toward the men playing chess.

"That was . . . interesting," I said after a long moment of silence. I could tell that we were both thinking the same thing. We had been longing for our exotic Contessas, our Hollywood love stories come to life. We had been counting on my guidebook to be our talismanic wingman. And now, on our last day together, in a deeply off-kilter way, it had provided a skewed version of wish fulfillment.

In the strictest, most literal sense, we had both kissed a mysterious woman in the ruins of an Old World castle. This is true; we can pass the polygraph test.

And yet.

"Lee, man," I said. "That was *not* the Contessa I had in mind."

Lee and I spent our final night together eating inferior, overpriced Thai food and attempting to replicate a grainy print of four photos that Mom and Ann had taken in a train station photo booth in Innsbruck. Their expressions are partially obscured behind mustaches and bouffant hairdos that Ann drew in later—"had to disguise ourselves to avoid the dirty old men of all ages that abound here," she explained in her accompanying note—but there's no hiding their general delight. Mom's eyes have a coy gleam in one of the photos, transforming her expression from innocent to mischievous. As I glanced at the photo before Lee and I went off to take our own, I did a double take. I knew that look—not from her, but from someone else. I'd seen it recently. Where? Who? I stared, I puzzled . . . and I laughed: it was Lee's trademark, that knowing glance that placates and cajoles and urges ever onward in the spirit of adventure.

Which brings me back to the previous evening, after the fondue. I, too, had worn that expression for once.

There are no pirate bars in Zurich, at least none that we could find. It would have been the ideal send-off for Lee but, alas, this ain't that kind of city. Instead, we settled in for the evening in an ideal neighborhood bar: cozy, casual, but with a subdued elegance. The space was just slightly bigger than the bar itself, a curving oak slab with little ornamentation aside from the rough bevel worn by countless wrists and forearms brushing against it. A bowl of limes sat at one end and the bartender—a middle-aged woman who seemed to have come straight from a day job in middle management, her attire and manner all business—periodically plucked a few of the emerald spheres from the stack and made mojitos with all the precision of a proverbial Swiss watchmaker.

I noticed the rum she was using: it was a brand I didn't recognize. We may not have found a pirate bar, but the pirate within me suddenly perked up. I wanted rum. Mystery rum. Potentially *illicit* rum. Actually, I wanted the glowing Bolivian booze that Lee had tried one night in Amsterdam—I had whimpered at the sight then, but was more than ready for it now. But this would suffice.

"Ever had that?" I asked Lee, pointing to the bottle. The label read "Havana Rum—Añejo Reserva."

"Never seen it before," he replied.

I did the mental calculation: Havana meant Cuba meant embargo meant illegal back home.

"We're having it," I announced. "A round of shots of forbidden rum. You know you want it."

Lee demurred.

"Oh, come *on*, sidekick," I said. "It's *illegal*! We can't pass this up!"

My own impish, coercive grin made its full debut. Lee met it with a bemused squint and a half-suppressed snicker.

"Spirit of . . . ," I started.

"I thought you might go there. Let's do it."

Vienna

Mozart Didn't Blog

*The trappings of the old Austro-Hungarian
Empire are faded by now, and the great rococo
buildings of Vienna are weatherworn and chipped. . . .
The mood of the city is like an old Nelson Eddy film,
gracious and slow, courtly and polite. It can be the
relaxing mid-point in your European tour.*

—Europe on Five Dollars a Day

I boarded the train to Vienna the next day in a funk. Lee was gone. Who would I talk to without him? He'd dragged me out of my shell, and I was pleased to be here—but I wasn't sure how long I'd last before retreating to my cozy bubble of self-doubt. There was even a downside to all that confidence I'd built up: a weary, unsettled feeling from all that headlong travel. Grand Tour Fatigue Syndrome. Motion sickness of the soul.

The Eurail pass—sold only to non-Europeans and one of those early tourist-boom catalysts, created in 1959—helps facilitate both the ease of travel and camaraderie. Best feature: to use it, you just step onto a train. If you miss the one you wanted, get the next. If you make a new friend and decide to grab lunch in Innsbruck on your way to Vienna, you can; just get on another train later in the day. The pass is technically a first-class ticket, but I usually rode second class, heeding the wisdom of Arthur Frommer—and pretty much every travel writer ever—that this is where you'll find the conversation, the intrigue. Right now, though, I headed straight to the quiet plushness of first class. I wanted to sulk and steel myself for the wingman-free journey ahead.

The view, too, would cure me, or at least distract me. The landscape looked like a model train set wrought large: more fog-shrouded peaks and placid Alpine lakes with music-box churches on distant shores. Even the grittier tableaus had a certain charm: one cottage had a bright red decommissioned ski lift gondola in its backyard as a gazebo of sorts.

Yet these sights did nothing for me; the touristic wonder lay dormant, surfacing for a few brief moments but never fully roused. It was every bit as stereotypically picturesque as my arrival in Florence had been, but that felt like someone else's life—an awe-struck rube I didn't recognize.

The train attendant interrupted my brooding. "Ticket?" he said. I pulled my pass from my pocket and handed it over with barely a glance. By now, this was routine for me.

"Tickets?" the attendant asked the family sitting on the other side of the aisle. There were five of them, three generations of a family: grandparents, parents, and a daughter about my age. The daughter sat directly across the aisle from me; the other four were in two pairs of facing seats just behind her. They dug through their bags, fumbling and apologizing all the while. I knew the feeling. That had been me a few weeks earlier.

The attendant muttered again as he looked over the tickets. "You speak English?" he asked.

"Yes, of course," the mother said.

"You are in zer wrong car."

I knew this feeling, too—I'd also been there, seated in areas that turned out to be reserved. Lee and I had pinballed around trains, constantly being booted by attendants or passengers brandishing reserved-seat tickets and annoyed looks. This family's problem, though, was slightly different.

"Zer tickets are second class," the attendant said. "Zis is first class. You must move."

"No, we *have* first-class tickets," the mother replied. She appeared to be in her midfifties and wore a fiery flicker in her eyes and a loose scarf around her neck. The family was of Indian descent and the grandparents both had a lilting accent, but they all lived outside of Washington, DC, they later told me, and the parents and daughter were American through and through, a typical suburban middle-class family.

"No, zer tickets are first class in *Austria*," said the attendant, an R. Crumb character brought to life, with a droopy brow, a splotch of a mustache, and a too-small uniform hat perched atop his head. "But still we are in *Switzerland*."

"How long until we get to Austria?" the mother asked, her tone indignant.

"Perhaps one half hour," the attendant said. He fidgeted nervously. "Please, you cannot stay here."

"We have all our bags here." The father sighed, gesturing to the five enormous suitcases and assorted smaller bags bulging from the overhead bins and the compartment at the end of the car. "It'll take us"—he paused, doing the calculation—"a *while* to move. But all right."

"*No.* This is *stupid.*" The mother rose from her seat, her index finger jabbing the air. "We're not going. That's *stupid*. We're almost to Austria and we're not moving all of those heavy bags. The car's almost empty—look!" She gestured to the seats around us, nearly all vacant, then shoved her hands to her hips.

The attendant scowled and said, "I will find someone to help, since you do not speak English." He disappeared.

The mother looked at me, her expression pleading for confirmation that someone else had heard that. "I speak English just fine!" she said, her tone half laugh, half yell. She took a deep breath and shook her head in frustration. "So . . . ," she said. "You're also American?"

"Yep," I replied. "From Minneapolis."

"Oh! I lived there for three years!" She turned to her daughter. "He lives in Minneapolis! Isn't that amazing?"

"Small world," the daughter muttered. She looked like she wanted to jump out the window after the scene her mother had just made.

The attendant reappeared with another train employee, a guy who had pushed a snack cart through a few minutes earlier.

"You are coming from India?" asked the snack cart guy, a wiry man of about twenty-five. "I am, too." Then he launched into a plea in Hindi—or what I assumed was Hindi. The mother's knowledge of the language was only marginally better than my own; her parents translated quietly, and then she replied with about three words of halting Hindi before switching to English.

"I'm sorry to get you involved," she said to the snack cart guy. "But we're not moving. And if he wants to talk to us"—she flicked her hand toward the attendant, who had been watching the conversation with a sour look on his face—"I really do speak English, a lot better than him, and way more than I speak Hindi."

The snack cart guy sighed. "I have German and Hindi and little English." He shrugged to his colleague and they both walked away. A minute later, I looked out the window and saw a sign. We were in Austria.

The stereotype of the tourist follows two threads, based on age: the young version has dreadlocks, an iPhone, a backpack, a Che Guevara shirt, and a trust fund; the old version has cargo shorts, an enormous camera, white walking shoes, a rolling suitcase, and a 401(k). They are both white; they are both well funded. I have a mental image of the two facing off in an Old World square, their respective cameras—the sleek phone and the oversized DSLR—aimed at each other, a digital duel of mutual disgust. It could be a *New Yorker* cartoon, with a caption of the classic Evelyn Waugh quip: "The tourist is the other fellow."

More and more, though, the other fellow looks increasingly less like those stereotypes, not necessarily Caucasian or particularly well-off. My new friends were hardly cultural anomalies—what's interesting, I suppose, is how uninteresting they were, just a few more tourists who didn't look like me.

The original Grand Tourists may have been British—recall the ribald Thomas Coryate—but in the 1960s, the typical "far-ranging" international tourist was American, notes Maxine Feifer in her book *Tourism in History*. Not all Americans, it should be noted— *white* Americans. Appealing to Americans of varied economic backgrounds had been part of the Marshall Plan's goals in promoting tourism; ethnic diversity, though, was a different matter. "While aiming for a society free of class divisions," Christopher Endy writes in *Cold War Holidays*, "Marshall Planners did so

within the limits of an idealized America of native-born whites."
Travel ads of the day skewed the same way, as I found when I spent
a long day paging through 1950s *Life* magazines at the library, looking for travel advertisements—the only nonwhite faces were ser-
vants or "noble savage" types in ads for African safaris. Still, Endy
says, Europe held an almost sacred status among many middle-
class African Americans—over there, they could travel more safely
than in many areas of their own country.

Wanderlust knows no cultural boundaries, and as the budget-
travel boom continued into the 1970s, Americans abroad were
joined by other tourists, often British, Japanese, or German. Then,
as now, the key to understanding the next wave of tourists was to
follow the money, to look to the rising economies. These days, that
means China, India, and Russia. The Chinese government began
allowing tourist visas to Germany in 2003 and to the rest of Europe
the following year. By the end of the decade, some 2 million Chinese tourists were visiting the Continent annually. In 2008, the
UN World Tourism Organization, in collaboration with the European Travel Commission, drafted a special report titled *The Chinese Outbound Travel Market*. The next year, they issued similar
reports for two more rapidly growing sources of tourists, India and
Russia.

Many of the new travelers are drawn to specific places they've
seen or read about in the mass media. A familiar story. Southern
France is particularly popular with Chinese tour groups, the *Economist* recently noted, "thanks in part to widely available translations of Peter Mayle's book *A Year in Provence* [a recent catalyst for
American tourism as well] and in part to a slushy Chinese television miniseries, *Dreams Link*, which was filmed amid the lavender
fields and walled citadels of the Midi." And in 2010 Switzerland

Tourism began a campaign to draw Indians to the Alpine areas that had been backdrops in popular Bollywood films.

When you get right down to it, the formula for the rise in tourism is essentially the same across cultures, a single timeless and universally applicable equation:

Expanding middle class + pop culture influences + increasing ease of travel = tourist masses

I chatted with the family from Washington, DC, until they got off in Innsbruck. I was again all alone with my view and my moping. I arrived in Vienna, boarded a tram toward my hostel, and moped some more. As we passed a manicured urban park—all sculpted hedges and monumental fountains—and the glorious neoclassical parliament building, with its grand columns and statues of noblemen on horses, I had just one thought: "Man, all these damn cities look the same. I am *so over* columns and horse statues and oh-so-orderly parks."

In Florence and Paris, hiding out in my room had been my preferred treatment for any ailment—anxiety, fatigue, hangnail. I'd eat an energy bar and have a long, delirious chat with my old Frommer guidebook and call it a night around eight. But now I was past that, and staunchly determined not to turn back, especially since my hostel was the sort of grime-tastic place that only Random Backpacker #22 could have loved. Frommer put this hostel in his "starvation budget" category, noting that for much of the year it's a college dormitory. There's a slight shudder to his description, the subtext being that, well, you *can* stay there, and it's supercheap at eighty cents for a single room . . . but you'd have to be pretty desperate. Still true, that, although the price was also still fairly low, about twenty-eight euros.

I had a realization: misery loves company, but most of all, misery loves beer and nachos.

I was going to go native in the Tourist Culture. Yeah, Tourist Culture—there is one. Though tourists may be coming from ever more widespread places and walks of life, the truth is that once they're on the road, they start acting in remarkably similar ways, all seeking acceptance in this society of outsiders. They—er, we—tend to go to the same places (Eiffel Tower, Venice), eat the same foods (kebabs, pizza), have the same rituals (*"Scusi, could you mein photo take? Merci por favor?"*), the same native dress (khaki pants, practical shoes—white ones for the novices, black for the advanced). It is indeed a unique culture, but one to which we belong only temporarily. It's a culture of transience and halfway points, located somewhere between our actual, native cultures and those in which we have booked ourselves for a stay and a look-see.

So I went to the Tourist Culture native hangout: an Irish pub. They're a case study in contrived authenticity and theme-park culture. They can seem nearly as ubiquitous as McDonald's—I'd spotted them in every city so far—and every bit as formulaic, with the Chieftains on the jukebox, dark wood paneling on the walls, and Guinness in every glass. (There's a corporation largely responsible for this phenomenon; it's called, no kidding, the Irish Pub Company.) Contrived, sure, but the success of the formula lies in its coziness and comfort and intimacy, trading on the Irish reputation for hospitality. Done right, the Irish pub feels more authentic, more enchanting, more Old World than its beaten-path surroundings. It's the tourist's shelter from the tourist storm.

I sat at the bar, figuring Lee would have insisted. I chatted with the bartenders—they were English, but never mind that—and my fellow bargoers from all over the world. A small television in the far corner broadcast a soccer game. The bartenders and Aussies cheered for one team; a pair of Indian twenty-somethings rooted for the other; the Americans cheered whenever someone scored; and the two guys beside me at the bar alternated between chatting with me in Irish-accented English, talking to each other in German, and bellowing at the television in the universal language of referee hatred.

For my dinner, I ordered the dish that seemed most authentic and appropriate for the context: a pint of Guinness and a platter of nachos.

They weren't very good. Which was probably to be expected.

When you're feeling Old World–weary, it doesn't help when Mozart starts stalking you. I do not mean that I kept hearing his music. I mean that everywhere I went the next day, there were guys dressed as Mozart. *Many* of them. It was like *Amadeus* meets *West Side Story*.

The one by the Mozart statue was especially menacing. He had the manner of a back-alley drug dealer, all shifty glances and corner-of-the-mouth sales pitches, though his goods—like those of his clones—were symphony and opera tickets.

"I can get you in, but you must buy now," he said, one hand clutching a seating chart while the other adjusted his ill-fitting powdered wig.

I looked at the prices on his chart and thought of my languishing bank account. "Probably still too much for me," I said.

"You cannot come to Vienna and not go to the opera!" Mozart insisted. "Please, I will find you a seat. My prices you will like."

"Maybe I'll just go to the box office tomorrow," I said, rather suspecting that Mozart's "tickets" might involve a Sharpie and a piece of cardboard.

"No, tomorrow is sold out. Is a very special performance and the doctors have purchased the tickets already."

"The doctors?" I asked.

"*Ja.* A confederation meeting. Twenty thousand physicians— the ones of the breathing?—are in Vienna. They buy many tickets."

I burst out laughing and dug into my bag. Mozart offered a hopeful half smile and scratched under his wig. He was disappointed to see my hand pull out not a wallet but my trusty Frommer book. I pointed to the Readers' Suggestions section:

Tickets for the evening's performance at the Staatsoper are often unobtainable anywhere. Fortunately, there's nearly always a medical convention in Vienna, and where there are doctors, there are opera tickets. A well-dressed American can walk up to the registration desk at any of these conventions, urbanely say, "I did not order my tickets in advance, but do you have any?", and usually get the finest seats available, in all price ranges.

I turned to the cover and showed Mozart the date. "Many doctors even in 1963."

"Yes, it is true," he said. "Many doctors. Twenty-five thousand of cardiologists last week." His lips curled into a sly smirk. "Your— how do you say? Tactic? Saying you are a doctor, it will not work. If you want tickets, I will sell you. The show tonight is very good."

But I knew what I needed to do.

. . .

Later. I would find the doctors later. First things first: I wanted a
photo of the Mozart statue. I had taken one out on the street, my
favorite Not-So-Flattering Photo yet. It shows a sidewalk stand
selling "KASEKRAINER—HOT DOG—FRANKFURTER" and a
transit shelter with a large sign reading "FUCK IT! LET'S PARTY!"
Between them, you can see a genteel park surrounded by a tall
wrought-iron fence topped with spikes that look like pernicious
fleurs-de-lis. Behind the fence, framed between the two sidewalk
structures, is a majestic man carved of white marble. Wolfgang
Amadeus Mozart, composer of some repute.

I wanted a photo *with* him, though, not just of him in his discordant surroundings. Photos are the currency of the Tourist Culture,
but its most sacred rite is the Tourist Dance: hold out your camera,
smile sheepishly, point to yourself. Half the time the other person
is already performing the same gestures to you. Sometimes you
don't even speak a word to each other until the end, at which point
you both guess the other's language and say thank you. Occasion-
ally you find that you both guessed wrong—you said *grazie* in your
American accent; she said *merci beacoups* with a lilt that you took
to be . . . Turkish, maybe? And sometimes you say it in the same
language and you both laugh and have a conversation.

William and Jean were my fellow dancers this time. American
couple, sixtyish, he stocky and studied, she gamine and gleeful. I
brandished my book as Jean readied the camera.

"I remember that—that was my era!" William beamed after the
photo was done. "Five dollars. Yeah . . . you could do it back then. I
never did it, but I know people who did. Now five dollars will get
you . . . what?"

"In Vienna? A couple of pastries," I said. "Or a handful of post-cards."

I offered William my book and he paged through it, a perplexed grin on his face all the while.

"It's so funny that you use the book as a photo prop," Jean said. "Will you take a picture of me with *my* book?" She waved a new Fodor's guide.

I snickered at the warmth of her sarcasm, then realized that she was completely serious. She handed me her camera and struck her pose, the Mozart statue behind her, the book in her hands, her lips spreading in laughter.

After less than a day in Vienna, I already felt like I knew how to navigate the city, not just geographically but culturally. I ordered food without getting flustered. I had halting conversations in something similar to the German language. I instinctively knew which direction to head when I got off the tram in an unfamiliar part of town. I never got lost.

Turns out if you do things the hard way, relying on your wits and not much else, well, at some point the hard way becomes relatively easy. It was a sudden, amusing realization, one that I recorded in my notebook, in enormous letters: I HAVE FIGURED THIS OUT.

During the course of the day, I had several internal dialogues that went like this:

"Okay, so take the U3 three stops, then walk in the direction *away* from the park and go about two blocks, then take a right and walk until you just start to see the canal in the distance, then take

A quintessential tourist trail scene: historic architecture, whimsical fountain, didgeridoo-playing backpackers. As seen on just about every street in every major European city.

a left on the next major street . . . and the restaurant should be right around there."

Shouldn't you check the map a few more times? Or at least keep it out?

"Nope. Not necessary."

Are you sure you know what you're doing? Really?

"As a matter of fact, yes."

Oh. Well . . . all right, then. Carry on. You're starting to sound like those girls in Paris.

"I know. Pretty great, huh?"

Except I really wasn't feeling triumphant. I was too busy moping and battling an oncoming cold.

Let me tell you, there's nothing like being sick in a foreign country to make you feel like a traveler, not a tourist. It makes the world seem less different, somehow, the culture and sense of place reduced to a scrim, hazy and two-dimensional and undistinguished. The colors are desaturated, the music muted. You become myopic, your daily existence limited to an inward struggle just to get by—you are utterly yourself, not a character walking through a set. You don't care about checking off the sights. You just want to find a damn drugstore, maybe a doctor.

Between the cold and the jadedness, efficiency was my new priority. No gawking, no lingering, just get through my Frommering obligations:

Restaurant OK, Frommer's "best spot for basic low-cost meals (the hurried and unextraordinary ones)": gone. What's there now? Oh, either a bank or a coffee shop or a convenience store. Or possibly a club advertising "GIRLS" and "TRIBUTE TO MICHAEL JACKSON."

The Danube: not blue, despite my mother's gleeful postcards to the contrary.

Swimming area in the Danube: replaced by a riverfront amusement park with forty trampolines (I counted, grumpily).

One authentic café was now a Chinese restaurant.

Another was a tobacco shop.

Another was an S&M gear shop. Really.

There were churches. They were gray and stone and tall.

There were bakeries. They sold pastries. They were fine.

There were parks. They had trees and statues.

There were people. They wore clothes. Some smiled at me. Some frowned. Most didn't notice me.

I blended in. Everything made sense. It was easy. It was boring.

So what did I do? I blogged about it, of course.

The journey of a thousand miles now begins with setting up a travel blog—it's practically obligatory these days. My mother has one. So does my godmother. They're so ubiquitous that some of the titles comment on this very fact: Just Another Travel Blog, Another Damn Travel Blog. It's the new version of the living room slide show, except now you don't have to wait until you get back home to bore your friends.

I went into the center of town the next morning and found an Internet café.

"Do you have wireless Internet?" I asked the man behind the front desk.

"No, I'm sorry," he replied. "You have your own laptop?"

"Yes."

He leaned forward for a moment, thinking, then sprang from his seat, speaking in warm, exclamatory bursts: "Come! Easy solution! We will take a cord from another computer! And put it into your laptop! Like wireless but with a wire!"

Problem solved.

I opened my email with the shaky hands of an addict. William, the man I'd met at the Mozart statue, had already sent me a message.

The guy at the desk asked me my name. I told him as I logged on to Facebook.

"A pleasure to meet you," he said. "I am ——." But I wasn't listening—I was already pulled into my friends' online banter: comments on the latest news, who went to a party last night, who ate what for lunch. If the Internet café guy were American, he would be named Billy; I'm sure of it. So let's just call him that.

Let's be clear about this: Email is great. No denying that. It helps you keep in touch. Ditto blogs. Ditto social networks. Ditto cell phones. I doubt that I would have stayed in touch with William had we met a generation ago, our disparate ages and interests creating a chasm that neither of us would have particularly cared to cross if not for the easy bridge-building of email. Blogs bridge even more distant gaps, allowing friends of friends and even total strangers into your travels and travails.

That's all fine and good. What's jarring, as Billy might have noted just now, is when that outside community takes precedence over one's immediate surroundings, when we chat with friends back home and say that we're bored and not meeting any interesting, eccentric locals . . . while ignoring the guy sitting a few feet away from us, trying to strike up a conversation.

"If you have an opportunity, you can visit my brother's souvenir shop," Billy said.

"Maybe later," I said. To my Facebook friends, I typed, "Doug is in Vienna, being stalked by Mozart."

Of the people who would read that, I knew many even less well than I knew Billy. But they were *friends*, damn it—it said so right on the screen: "Friends." Friends whom I could sort into lists or tag in photos. Friends who could "like" my travel witticisms, giving a digital thumbs-up for all of our other friends to see, eliciting more digital approval. Billy, being in real life, lacked all of these features.

"The shop is close to here," Billy said. "The best prices in Vienna! Sharon Stone went there."

"Uh-huh." I opened Twitter and reported my Mozart stalkers there, too.

"It is not a pressure," Billy said. "It is just an offer, if you are looking."

"Okay." I saw that my sister was online, so I opened up Google Chat and told *her* about the Mozarts.

There is no off button on modern life, not really, not for many of us.

A wide body of recent research, articles, and books have tried to untangle the cognitive and cultural implications of our wired-in era, including Nicholas Carr's *The Shallows: What the Internet Is Doing to Our Brains*, which persuasively argues that the Internet scatters our attention and makes our thinking more superficial. More data points do not equal more knowledge. Multitasking is a great way to get many things done poorly.

For travel purposes, disconnection helps you appreciate the strangeness of a foreign land or the ineffable wonder of a Montmartre sunset, which has a tendency not to hang on for just a sec while you finish your important email. It's not just the remote or awe-inspiring places that deserve our full attention, though—it's also the beaten path, where finding those small moments of joy and lingering bits of beauty can take as much effort as tracking an elusive animal. You already have all kinds of overload and messages thrown at you here—why add to the discord with your own digital dissonance?

My mother surely had distractions when she wrote her letters, but they weren't on the paper. They were in her surroundings: traffic, birds, people, smells. They were of the place. They weren't drawing her out of her surroundings; they were pulling her back *in*. That's the key detail, the difference between writing a letter and writing an email or a blog post. We're disconnected from everything but the screen.

"You like Vienna?" Billy asked.

"It's nice," I said.

"Where are you from? America?"

"Yes, Minneapolis. In the middle."

I went back to Twitter to see if anyone had replied to my brilliant bon mot.

Some neuroscientists think that even the anticipation of email effectively rewires our brains and reduces our focus; we're never fully in the moment, in the place. We're so worried about what we might be missing on the screen that we miss out on our surroundings. Interestingly, my mother had her own version of this. Each day, she trekked to the local Thomas Cook or American Express travel office in anticipation of mail (and to get money—she didn't have a credit card, and there were no cash machines). If there was none, she'd be sure to include a complaint in her next note to my father. Frommer even includes "American Express Area" as a neighborhood in many cases, listing the nearby shops and restaurants in the expectation that you'll spend a decent amount of time there during your daily mail-and-money runs. (Incidentally, this is a good reminder not to get too worked up about how commercial travel has become. Already was: in the 1960s, much of the Grand Tour ran through *one* company, American Express, from your package tour to your traveler's checks to your communication back home.)

At least Mom knew that when the mail run was done, that was it for the day. There was no refresh button.

"Oh, I know Minneapolis!" Billy said. "It is near Chicago. I have a friend in Chicago! It is cold there."

Yeah, what was the weather like back home? Thanks for the reminder, Billy. I typed in www.weather.com....

"Yeah, it's cold in Minneapolis," I said to Billy. "Colder than Vienna."

"Yes, Vienna is nice right now. I like Vienna! If you want any information, I can tell you. I like to help the visitors!"

"Uh-huh." Good idea, Billy: I should do a search on "things to do in Vienna when you're bored and jaded." I could hear Frommer tut-tutting, though, so I resisted that particular temptation. I went back to Twitter and Facebook to see if anyone had commented on my comments. Not yet. What was *wrong* with people? *Refresh.*

One thing that technology hasn't changed, at least not as much as you might think, is the content of our communication back home. It may be more frequent and in a different medium, but that doesn't necessarily mean the thoughts themselves are more scattered or less articulate than they used to be.

It's easy to rant that in our modern era of text messages and email and blogs, we've lost our literary flair or even basic literacy; our correspondence has become ever more abbreviated, ever more vapid, devoid of the innate poetry and profundity that gilded every sentence we wrote just a few years ago. Ah, the delusions of nostalgia. As much as I'd like to pretend that everything my parents wrote was dramatic and intriguing and elegantly phrased (and written in iambic pentameter, with quills, on fine vellum), the truth is that they often scribbled quickly, without concern for spelling or capitalization—as with a text message, the goal was basic communication, not lyricism. The content followed suit. "Gee whiz, Sil, nothing out of the ordinary has been going on for the last couple of days" my father wrote in a letter to Vienna (they both called each other "Silly," or, shortened, "Sil"). "I know you've heard that all to [sic] often, which would sound like life is dull, which it is not at all. In fact, it is not even really routine. . . . Let me see. What was my point."

Notes like that were pretty common, actually. In fact, that's a bit more lyrical than some of the letters—some were pure stream-of-consciousness, pithy non sequiturs that read exactly like a modern Facebook or Twitter feed. Even more than travel or love, Mom and Dad wrote about the mundane minutiae of the day-to-day: missing library books, enrolling for classes, Dad's impending air force enlistment, a bus strike in Minneapolis, and Dad's current projects in architecture school. The foundations of everyday life but not much of broader intrigue; more small talk than storytelling.

No, it's not the pure content of our communication—per se—that has changed most. It's the audience and the immediacy and the nuance of the presentation.

Mom often drew little flowers next to her name or wrote tangential comments along the side of a card. She sketched sheep and churches. Her longer letters spanned several days, frequently with comments on how her mood had changed since the earlier part of the letter—without a delete key, she left everything in, allowing her mood shifts to unfold on the page. Her handwriting was shaky when she was on a bus, large and loopy when she was trying to express a particularly important idea (usually, "I LOVE YOU"). She wrote on postcards, on wine labels, on tickets, on paper bags, on toilet paper, all adding an extra element of foreignness. An email looks the same no matter where you send it from.

The doodles and surfaces and handwriting—sometimes including the intriguing addition of comments from a mystery companion; you won't find that in a blog post—tell the story beyond the words, adding intimacy and intricacy and sense of place. There's more texture, both literal and figurative, which gives them all the more resonance.

In a 2010 poll of travelers conducted by the website TripAdvisor, a mere 11 percent said they still wrote postcards. Aerograms are even more endangered: the U.S. Postal Service stopped issuing them a few years back, as did Germany's Deutsche Post and others. According to the U.S. Postal Service's annual survey of households, personal correspondence has been on a downward trend since the late 1980s—in 2009, the typical household received 0.9 pieces of personal correspondence each week, down from 1.6 in 1987.

Today, "Sent from my iPhone" is the postmark of our times.

. . .

I moved on to the *Minneapolis Star Tribune* website, skimming the headlines: political squabbles, sports scores, human interest stories. *Click.* I read things I would never give a second glance if I were back home, idly following one link after another. What else was I going to do? Sit in another park, look at another church, eat another kebab?

We've forgotten how to be bored. We've forgotten how to fill the idle moments by, well, wandering a park or looking at a church or eating a kebab or making idle chitchat with a stranger without wishing we were instead reading our favorite blogs or checking our email. We want information; we want contact; we want it now.

What's most striking about our modern connectivity, in terms of travel, is when it also makes us forget how to enjoy being confused and have some common sense and just make it up as we go along. We're never really out of our element if we don't want to be. People joke that social networks like Twitter and Facebook are just a bunch of people posting what they had for breakfast, but I'm more annoyed by all the people who ask, "What should I have for breakfast?"

Descartes 2.0: I crowd-source, therefore I am.

How about that place right there in front of you? How about asking someone on the street? How about realizing that you can wander into a dumpy restaurant and have a horrible meal . . . and still get something out of it, a story, a friend, a quiet moment to yourself?

Constant connection to the lifeline of friends and family and

Google Maps and TripAdvisor is the twenty-first-century version of Temple Fielding's two suitcases, briefcase, and raffia basket. The mentality is the same: there's no place like home, especially when I'm on the road. The burdens of baggage are not limited to suitcases and backpacks.

I understand the appeal. I understand that something—namely, security and comfort—is gained. But there's nothing wrong with not having all of the answers or with being a bit uncomfortable or lonely, completely unable to contact anyone you know. There's nothing wrong with returning home *still* confused—in fact, there's probably something wrong if you don't.

The point is this: the most important travel app is the off button. And the most important travel guides are some basic common sense and open-mindedness and willingness to go with the flow and trust the Goddess Serendipity.

I knew what I was supposed to do now: hit my own off button, talk to Billy, be charmed by the eccentric local. I popped a cough drop and told myself I'd do it in a few minutes.

After someone emailed me or commented on Facebook.

Refresh.

When I finally went back into the real world, I found that Mozart was still following me, but so were the doctors. It actually wasn't very hard to find them, because Mozart was correct: they were everywhere. Easy to spot, too, with bright blue messenger bags slung over their shoulders. The bags had a graphic of a Ferris wheel—the iconic feature of the historic Prater amusement park—and white type reading, "EUROPEAN RESPIRATORY SOCIETY."

I followed a group of about a dozen doctors—Maltese, German, Portuguese—onto a train, hoping we'd end up at convention headquarters. I could do this—the New Me, the Travel-Enhanced Me, could outfox some lowly convention center employee and score a ticket. Right? Of course! I pumped myself up, trying to recall every lung-related term and tidbit I could recall from ninth-grade biology class and pediatrician visits for my childhood asthma: pulmonary, cough, wheeze, trachea . . . those little things inside the lungs, what were they called? Aioli? No, that wasn't it. . . .

This train ride was taking a long time, but that was a good sign. Surely it meant we were heading toward a far-flung convention center or hotel. When we got off the train, I let the doctors get a good distance away before I started tailing them. We walked for a few minutes and then, there it was, looming in front of us.

The Ferris wheel. The iconic one emblazoned on their bags. Tickets cost 8.50 euros. I couldn't justify it, particularly given how wobbly and ancient the thing looked. My newfound adventurousness had its limits; this seemed like an especially ignoble and probable way of meeting my demise in Europe.

Question: Have you ever been to an amusement park in the off-season? I spent the whole time thinking of synonyms for "creepy": disturbing, menacing, nightmarish, ominous, eerie, frightening, hair-raising, shuddersome, direful, sinister. All appropriate. Half the rides were closed; the other half were either rickety or disturbingly forlorn.

The fun houses were open, with their elaborate facades—an array of fiberglass dinosaurs here; an army of the undead there—and their shifty-looking operators slouching in ticket booths,

ignoring the muffled screams that I sincerely hoped were record-
ings. A sad-looking father watched his sad-looking daughter ride a
sad-looking pony around in circles, led by a sad-looking handler.

Frommer had highly recommended a trip here: "At least one
evening should be spent at the famous . . . Prater, which is best
known for its ferris wheel, the largest in the world. . . . You'll get
quite a charge out of the Viennese touches that are added to the
normal carnival attractions."

The only distinctly Viennese touches I saw, alas, were the old-
timey graphics on the Coke machines. There was one old beer garden, the Gasthausgarten, but it appeared not to have been in
operation for years. Tall weeds had taken over the space, making
the vintage streetlamps scattered throughout look like metallic
flora. I have no doubt that if I'd stared for a few more moments, I
would have spotted ghosts waltzing through the weeds.

Back in the tourist center of town, I looked around for a restaurant
and found that one of Frommer's Berlin recommendations was
now here. It was called Wienerwald, though despite what one
might suspect from the name and the Germanic proclivity for
encased meats, it was not a sausage emporium. It's a small chain of
restaurants, Frommer says, which "you ought to try at least once:
they are one of the great success stories of post-war Germany,"
having made roast chicken, once an expensive delicacy, available
to the masses.

My chicken came with a red-pepper sauce that was spicy and
sweet, lively and sating, hitting all the right notes. I gobbled everything down in an embarrassingly short amount of time. Here,
finally, was a meal worth writing home about and a reason to

appreciate Vienna; my mood started to lift. The place was full and, judging by the voices, the customers seemed evenly split between locals and tourists. No wonder, I thought: it was the last holdout of a once-thriving chain of glamorous cafés. It deserved to be packed.

"That was really good," I told the waiter in all sincerity as he took my plate. I pulled out my book and showed him the description of the restaurant. "It was in Berlin in the 1960s, but I didn't see it when I was there. But now I found you here in Vienna."

"Ja," the waiter said.

"The food was very good," I continued. "But now this is the only one? The only bistro?"

The server gave a hollow laugh and walked two steps away, then turned back. "Bistro?! *Nein*. There are many, all over." As he rattled off a list of cities, his spiky hair seemed to droop in wary conde-scension. "It is nothing special," he said in a hushed voice. *"Really.* Just for normal people." As he turned and strode toward the kitchen, I heard an exasperated moan.

I grabbed a menu from the table next to me. I'd been so hungry that I hadn't really taken a look at all the details.

Yeah. My favorite meal in weeks. My triumphant find, a rare historic place still open and still patronized by locals and not overtly kitschy or overpriced . . . was basically the Teutonic Apple-bee's. *Of course* it tasted good—it had been focus-grouped and engi-neered and exquisitely formulated to hit all the right notes while keeping costs down.

But you know what? There were locals there. And it was a place that had interesting historic roots. In that sense, it was plenty authentic, at least as an emblem of modernity and the evolution of a place.

It made me laugh, once again, at the notion that, as Frommer says, authenticity is inversely related to price: the less you spend, the more genuine the experience. *Inherently.* I can't vouch for the truth of this in 1963, but it's manifestly absurd today. The cheapest readily available meal in most European capitals is a doner kebab. Or a pizza. Or a sandwich. Spend lots at a real bistro and you'll find plenty of fussiness, plenty of upper-crust cuisine—and also, presumably, some traditional and authentic, if pricey, meals. Smack in the middle, you may well find yourself in a place like Wienerwald. In any case, you'll find locals eating in all of these restaurants.

Authenticity has no price tag. I thought again of my imaginary dreadlocked traveler and cargo-shorted tourist having their face-off, both thinking the other shallow and silly and flat-out stupid— *inauthentic*—for spending too much or too little.

And then I sighed, paid my bill, and set out into the night to commune with the centipedes at the hostel.

"By this time, you've had enough of the Germanic countries," Frommer says to close the Vienna chapter. "The train for Italy leaves from the Sudbanhof."

I was counting the hours.

Venice

Brave New Old World

As you chug along, little clusters of candy-striped
mooring poles emerge from the dark; a gondola
approaches with a lighted lantern hung from its prow;
the reflection of a slate-gray church, bathed in a
blue spotlight, shimmers in the water as you pass by.
This is the sheerest beauty, and it is a moment
that no one should miss.

—Europe on Five Dollars a Day

The overnight train to Venice was an agonizing endurance test spent in a cramped compartment with two gargantuan Italians who took up most of the space—leaving me contorted in the corner—and were to snoring as Pavarotti was to opera. One of the most miserable, sleepless nights of my entire life.

And totally worth it.

Because I don't care who you are or how foul your mood, you cannot be anything less than awestruck and elated upon arriving in Venice in the long light of daybreak. In *E5D*, Frommer says the best time to arrive here is at night, "when the wonders of the city can steal upon you, piecemeal and slow," but I'd have to respectfully disagree. The best time is in the morning, when the soft rays of the rising sun paint the town a rich honeyed tone cut through with deep, dramatic shadows. The city was just waking up, the piazzas scattered with early risers reading newspapers, the cafés with bleary-eyed espresso drinkers. And all the tourists were still asleep.

The sense of arrival is without peer. Best in the world, for my money. You step out of the train station and you are on *the...Grand...Canal.* You stare, trying to take it all in. You gaze past the darting boats—not just gondolas but a whole ecosystem of skiffs and dinghies and delivery vessels. There's UPS; there's the grocer's supply boat; there's the barge piled with building materials. Steps away: the luminous white stone arch of the Scalzi Bridge. Beyond it: a classically Old World town in a wholly incongruous setting, as though a giant pulled up a city and casually tossed it into the sea, where it somehow landed fully intact, and its citizens just shrugged and said, "Yeah, we can make this work."

There are times on the tourist trail when you see something and think, "That's it?" (*Manneken-Pis,* Munich's Glockenspiel), and there are times when you think, "Whoa, that's *it!*" (Eiffel Tower, Berlin Wall), and then there are times when you just don't think. I'd had that feeling at the *David* in Florence. And now here.

And when your brain finally starts functioning again, the superlatives and incredulous thoughts flow like a faucet cranked open. You think what my mom thought, what she wrote on a postcard, words that countless tourists have surely repeated verbatim: "It's real! It looks like Venice is supposed to look!" You can be nowhere else on the planet.

. . .

Venice is famously composed of two interlocking islands, but it's actually a jigsaw puzzle of some 118 pieces, each its own discrete island. Canals everywhere. Bridges everywhere. In other words, amazing photo ops everywhere. The place begs to be overdocumented. I was happy to oblige. I basically kept my finger on the shutter-release button as I slowly made my way through the zigzagging chasms of buildings, history-steeped slot canyons where the sky was reduced to a brushstroke of blue above the encroaching walls. *Click. Click. Click.* Bridge: *click.* Clothesline: *click.* Interspersed through the crowded streetscape were Baroque, Renaissance, Arabic, and Byzantine architectural styles (*click, click, click, click*).

Eventually I found myself in an enormous plaza. I blinked at my sudden reintroduction to the sun, and my eyes took a few moments to reconcile the shapes sprawling in front of me.

Ah, yes. This must be it: the Piazza San Marco. There was Saint Mark's Basilica, Byzantine and opulent, its domes and mosaics like a carton of Brobdingnagian Fabergé eggs. There were the long loggias framing the other sides of the square. There was the famous *acqua alta*, the high water covering large portions of the piazza, though only half an inch deep right now. And the tourist crowds. The day was still young, but they were starting to gather.

They appeared to be most interested in the pigeons scattered in large clusters around the piazza. Specifically, the tourists were *stalking* the birds, tiptoeing into the middle of the flocks as though preparing to catch them. My sleep-deprived, Old World–addled brain slowly churned through the possible explanations. I knew the Venice Biennale was going on—was this some bizarre piece of performance art? Had I stumbled upon a nascent and awful tourist trend of capturing *living* souvenirs? I watched as two women stopped in the middle of one flock and raised up their arms as though impersonating scarecrows. Seriously: what was this? Forget *Sweatin' to the Oldies*; this was tai chi with *The Birds*. Several pigeons flew up, perching on the women's arms, shoulders, and—I couldn't help but shudder—*heads*. The women called out to their friends, who laughed in delight, then raised their cameras to their faces in unison.

Ah. It all made sense. To be a tourist is to pose for silly photos.

I heard a flutter of wings and felt a weight on my arms. A pigeon chortled in each ear. Anywhere else—*anywhere*—I would have yelped and gagged and flailed. But here . . . oh, all right. I cautiously handed my camera to a woman who was watching me with amusement. She took my picture and passed the camera back to me. On cue, the birds flew to her.

I walked back into the shadows. Exploring, meandering, taking too many photos, oohing and aahing at every new canal or street scene.

As the day wore on, the crowds started to build, first in fits and starts and then full-on. The quiet places became fewer. I got lost, yes—to be here, as a tourist, is to be forever lost, because the canals and streets conspire to confuse with their twists and turns and landmarkless uniformity. It turns out, though, that being lost is not so fun when the condition is perpetual and when every time you stop to ask for directions, the only people around you are fellow clueless tourists. It was as though we were all part of some collective effort, perhaps as part of the Venice Biennale, to create as many canals of humanity as there were of water.

Finally, after wandering for the better part of an hour, I found a tranquil piazza. Four kids kicked around a soccer ball; two old men chatted on a bench. *Ah, bliss,* I started to think, and at that precise moment I heard a pair of American voices echoing from the passageway behind me. Two women rounded the corner, then stopped a few feet from me.

"I need a beer," said one.

"Okay, well, let's go to the Hard Rock." The woman tapped on her cell phone screen. "But how do we get there?" More tapping, staccato and agitated. Then a frustrated grunt: "Ugh. I can't get a signal."

At least Venice was still pretty, I told myself. But even this couldn't last. Beauty has diminishing returns; familiarity breeds not contempt so much as fatigue. The canals were heartbreakingly lovely and picturesque for approximately six hours and forty-three minutes—and then, in an instant, I was over them. They had became mere nuisances, obstacles blocking my path, forcing me to walk two miles instead of twenty feet, when all I wanted to do was go to that restaurant *right over there, for goodness' sake.*

I thought back to Amsterdam, a few weeks earlier. I was happier then. The Old World was still new. Those canals were wide enough that you could actually appreciate the scene across the way—there was some breathing room. There were walkways along the sides, not just bridges over the water, as in Venice. Houseboats and trees created a layering effect. And there, the waterways were the spots of calm and respite, all the more enthralling because they were grace notes offering contrast to the rest of the city. Here, in Venice, they *are* the city.

Pity the claustrophobic, the agoraphobic, the aquaphobic: this must be their worst nightmare.

I thought back to the pigeons. They should have been my early-warning sign, a signal that my Grand Tour Fatigue Syndrome had not, in fact, been cured. Because though the gregarious birds were kind of neat at first glance, the more I thought about it, there was something just not quite right about a place where even the pigeons are willing to pose for tourist photos (and ask for a small fee, maybe some bread). When it comes to this point, which is the true pest: the corpulent, cooing creature . . . or the bird?

Enough, I thought. It was dank and crowded and now that I had seen the canals . . . now what? It was a case study in all the ways that tourism can really, seriously mess up a place. This wasn't a city; it was a tourist playground. It was sinking at an ever-faster rate (twenty centimeters in the last century) while the waters rose (and will likely keep rising, due to global warming). The smog from cruise ships was quickening the deterioration of the buildings. What once was a bustling hotbed of artistic expression had become a place of pure consumption, where everyday people doing every-day things were an elusive, endangered species. Perhaps Frommer and my mother and everyone who followed them really had ruined it all. Maybe the travel snobs, the tourist haters I loved to hate, actually had a point. This realization only upped my ire. *Seriously, screw this place.*

Oh, I know what you're thinking: you would love to be in Venice right now. And I'm going to whine about being there, in the charm capital of the world?

Damn straight.

Thing is, Venice is a one-trick town. Sure, it's a hell of a trick.

But really: six hours and forty-three minutes. I defy you to remain interested longer than that.

I had three more days.

I wanted to like Venice. I really did. The woman who rented me the apartment where I was staying—all of Arthur Frommer's recommendations from *E5D* were, once again, closed, booked solid, or far beyond my ever-dwindling budget—was simply one of the sweetest people I have ever met, and desperate to make sure I was enjoying her beloved hometown. She had the sorrowful eyes and earnest smile of someone who has been routinely let down by the world but who hopes that this time will be different. Every time I saw her, I offered my assurances that I was enjoying the apartment, which was true. And then I changed the subject if she asked about anything else.

"You took the boat tour?" she asked. She had helped me make arrangements.

"Carla, the apartment is *beautiful*," I said. The boat was small and crowded, with a tinny sound system and dirty windows. I had found that I could both see and hear only if I sat in a precarious position on the edge of the boat, leaning out over the water, praying I wouldn't get conked by a passing vaporetto.

"And the food is good?" Carla asked, adjusting the sunglasses perched atop her flowing, sandy mane. She was effortlessly glamorous in that Italian way.

"Carla, the view out the window—it's unbelievable!" I replied. I wasn't going to tell her about my lunch at a Frommer-approved place a few steps off the Piazza San Marco. Twenty euros, though

The acqua alta *and temporary boardwalks in the Piazza San Marco,*
which allow dry passage through the square and, most of all, provide
a spot to sit and rest and complain about all those other *tourists.*

that did include bread and calculatedly indifferent service, plus a
pasta sauce that could have done double duty as an adhesive.

But, yes, the apartment was wonderful. It was on a quiet side
street—a passageway, really. In the stone slab above the entrance
to the street was a carving of a man holding a coat of arms. All of its
icons and text had long since faded to oblivion, along with the
man's nose. I came to think of him as both the friendly face wel-

coming me home at the end of the day and a cheap but effective metaphor for the city itself, its enlivening details eroding into obscurity. He was a Venetian Dorian Gray.

Inside the apartment were terrazzo floors, antique furnishings, a canopy bed, and a wall of windows just a few feet above a canal—if my arms had been just a bit longer, I could have touched the water. It was everything I could ask of a Venetian apartment, elegant and vaguely mysterious. Outside, my mood was bitter and aggravated; in here, it was melancholy and wistful—unhappy, still, but in a more inward-looking way.

As darkness fell that first night and I'd already had my fill of the city, I headed back to the apartment to wallow in my unhappiness and read a few of my parents' letters.

My mother didn't go to Venice in 1967. But she and Ann embarked on a second Grand Tour in the summer of 1975, and this time they made it here, toward the end of their trip. My father—now out of the air force, working for the National Park Service in Washington, DC—had joined them for the first leg of their journey. They all went to Paris and Normandy together, and then Dad returned home.

Throughout the letters in 1967, my parents both spoke of seeing great "gleams"—their word for children. "I've decided that we'd make great parents—LATER!" Dad wrote in one letter. By 1975, "later" had come. In the weeks after my father left Europe, my mother started to feel a bit sick—especially in the mornings. Mom wrote a postcard to Dad from Trieste, Italy: "Today was the first time without nausea. . . . Please get info on pregnancy tests. You'll love Venezia." My sister, Elisabeth, was born in April 1976.

My parents scrimped and saved, determined to travel together as a family as soon as possible. In 1980, the three of them—Mom, Dad, and four-year-old Elisabeth (note the French spelling)—went to Europe together. It was my parents' first step in indoctrinating their children in the joys of travel, and though I wasn't there, I certainly appreciate the broader significance of the trip. Nine months later, I was born. You do the math.

If my goal in looking at the letters had been to distract myself from the frustrations of Venice, I'd succeeded. Sort of. I was now world-weary *and* lonely. And this, it turns out, is an even more miserable feeling than the lost and lonely sensation I'd felt in Florence a year earlier. It didn't help that I had grouped the letters from Venice and Vienna together and was now realizing that these were apparently the gooshiest, most heartbreaking ones. Like this, from one of Dad's letters to Mom in Vienna in 1967:

> *Dear Patricia,*
> *Just a very short note to tell you that I love you very much and want to marry you when circumstances permit. Was up late last nite studying for hist. exam and then woke up at five for no reason at all and just wished that you were there so I could reach out and pull you close to me and kiss you . . .*

I did laundry in the sink and hung my clothesline between two chairs. I opened a window and pulled back the sheers to let the canal breezes aid the drying. A shaft of light fell on my queen-size canopy bed, casting a spotlight perfectly on my nonexistent companion. I popped a couple of Tylenol PM and fell asleep hugging the light and listening to the drip-drip-drip of my clothes on the Venetian terrazzo floor.

. . .

While I'm complaining, I might as well bring out the lineup of other complainers.

Arthur Frommer may have become a cultural phenomenon worthy of a place on a presidential commission by 1968, but with popularity comes disdain, and the critics had uncapped their poison pens. There were accusations that Frommer himself had changed, his concerns turning from helping others travel cheaply to focusing on his own bottom line, in the form of an expanding guidebook company; partnership with (and sponsorship by) SAS Airlines and later KLM Royal Dutch Airlines; Arthur Frommer hotels in Amsterdam and Copenhagen; and—ironically, for someone who built his burgeoning empire on the joys of independent travel—a package tour company. In Stanley Elkin's 1972 profile in *Harper's*, Frommer predicted that in the coming year, some fifty thousand Americans would go on his tours of Europe.

Much of the backlash was driven by some observers' sense that as the pied piper of low prices, he had created the beaten path, conjuring crowds, obliterating authenticity. Nora Ephron, in her 1967 *New York Times* profile of Frommer, accused his followers of borderline cultish adherence to his recommendations: "Today's Frommerite carries his big red book like a banner, daring natives to cheat him, challenging fellow tourists to underspend him. He worries as much about losing his book as he does his passport."

It wasn't just the multiplying masses that bothered Ephron and others. There was also the very tone and style of Frommer's prose. "The writing, with few exceptions, is humorless, uninteresting and given to rhetorical questions and exclamation points," wrote

Ephron, and Elkin made a similar criticism: "exclamation points dagger the pages until they bleed."

There's no denying that Frommer's writing often blurs the line between enthusiasm and hyperbole, though humorless and uninteresting it is most certainly not. And if you consider the context, his enthusiasm and credulousness make sense; indeed, I'd wager they were entirely intentional. A book that's intended to start a movement demands an infectious, populist voice. There's no introductory paean to the joys and mind-opening wonders of travel; instead, Frommer's very tone—he himself would later call it "young and naïve, full of purple prose, and overly awed by the pleasures of that continent"—achieves the same effect. It does what good writing is supposed to do: show, don't tell. The exclamation points are the point.

Inevitably, though, the freshness of Frommer's voice and message had begun to fade; the cultural mood had shifted again.

By the early 1970s, the baby boomers had come of age, and the European Grand Tour had become a rite of passage for many of them—so many as to become a cliché. The Continent was crowded, but with the wrong crowd; the backpacker's quest for authenticity is always, *always* away from the other backpackers. With the counterculture movement in full flourish, the youthful travel trail now led to Asia.

Just as Frommer had piggybacked on Fielding and Fodor, offering a new way to travel their territory, a new crop of travel guides built on Frommer's methods, including Lonely Planet, Moon Guides, and Insight Guides, all of which began in the early 1970s. The upstart guidebooks pared down Frommer's shoestring-budget approach even further and also applied it to other parts of the world.

Some of the broader travel attitudes, the essential motivations for going abroad at all, shifted along with the backpacker routes. For Frommer and other travelers of the early and mid-twentieth century, travel was its own pursuit, its own end. You went to Paris to go to Paris; you went to Rome to go to Rome. There was nothing wrong with that, just as there was no shame in considering oneself a tourist. This was the foundation of the leisure-travel boom: it wasn't about immigration or education or commerce or power but essentially aimless wanderlust.

In the 1970s, though, as the mass-tourism backlash began and the ascendant counterculture movement started to become more mainstream, the pendulum began to swing in the other direction, a trend that has largely continued to this day. Among a certain portion of today's travel cognoscenti, it is necessary to have some deeper motivation—to find one's roots, to learn to make authentic Tuscan peasant cuisine, to escape the rat race and live the good life in Provence. A friend of mine, upon hearing that I was going to Paris, informed me that I should try to go the whole five days without ever seeing the Eiffel Tower, even for a moment, even as a speck on the horizon. In fact, in certain quarters, you're deemed an Ugly American if you head to Paris rather than spending your trip trekking through the Alps, herding goats, or, even better, hitchhiking across Mongolia or hanging with Maoist rebels in some war-torn republic.

But of course I went to the Eiffel Tower. Because the Eiffel Tower is cool. Just as the Hofbräuhaus or pretty much any oft-scoffed "tourist trap" is, in its own unique way, cool. Interesting. Worth the visit.

They're cool because of their intrinsic merits—symbols of ingenuity, invested with stories and showcases of a culture's self-worth, once you begin to understand why anyone erected them in the first place. They're also cool and intriguing specifically because they have, over time, acquired a totemic status in society—there's a shared meaning that goes beyond the original stories and context. This is a wholly unoriginal observation, but to be a tourist is to be part of something collective—these places are the crossroads of the world for a reason. The crowds are not the drawback; they're actually kind of the point.

I have to say, though: in Venice, I sometimes had a hard time remembering that.

A very hard time.

At dinner the next night, I found another one of Frommer's 1963 picks, this one on the Lista di Spagna, near the train station. I'd been trying to follow the advice in *ED5* that you should always order from the *prezzo fisso* menu in Venice—but as far as I could tell, that was now an openly understood synonym for "half-assed tourist menu." The same applied to any sign—in English— advertising "Typical Venetian Cuisine." This restaurant had both, which should have been a warning. My lasagne bore the distinctive pockmarks of microwave reheating. They didn't even bother to remove it from the Pyrex dish before serving it. As for the roast chicken, I strongly suspect it was neither roast nor chicken but one of the semidomesticated pigeons from the Piazza San Marco, boiled in fetid canal water.

I was starting to think that if I wanted to improve my mood, I might need to start cheating on Arthur. After all, this was Italy. Why eat lousy food?

I wondered if the information overload and crowd-sourcing of the Internet would be any better at guiding me to the good stuff. Perhaps it was time to test out those twenty-first-century tools I'd intentionally been shunning. So I went to an Internet café and put out a call on my blog, on Twitter, on Facebook. For one day—and one day only—I would rely on tips from the masses.

Sorry, Arthur. Just a trial separation.

Of course, it would take a few days for the tips to come in. By then, I would be in Rome. For now, I still had to get through Venice.

Two more days.

Nothing snowballs like unhappiness. Day three passed in a haze of frustration, playing out like a tourism blooper reel:

Here were the gondoliers whistling "O sole mio," that most famous of Venetian love songs (which is actually from Naples).

Here was the Bridge of Sighs, the view toward it framed by massive billboards, on the surrounding buildings, for diamond jewelry.

Here were the bridges and landmarks where, desperate for interaction, I did the Tourist Dance with anyone who would follow my lead. Here were my uncooperative dance partners, scowling and begrudgingly taking my photo, then turning on their heels and walking away.

Ah, but now the scene changes. Here were the two radiant Indian women—drop-dead gorgeous, I kid you not—in copper-hued sundresses who approached *me* on the Accademia Bridge to initiate the Tourist Dance. Here they were, the tourist starlets, beaming as their handpicked paparazzo took their picture; here

Ah, Venice. The canals. The grand architecture. The ... billboards obscuring some of the most prominent views of said architecture.

they were, laughing when I posed with *Europe on Five Dollars a Day*; here they were, peppering me with questions about my project, grinning in wonder when I told them about Le Grand Colbert in Paris.

Here I was: triumphant! Because here were all my points about the joys of tourism coming together perfectly, as though scripted: Tourist Dance, Crossroads of the World, Diversity, Tourists Are Smart and Interesting, and There's Plenty of Lingering Old World Magic—cut, perfect, fade to black, applause! Here I was, putting all my hard-won confidence and citizen-of-the-world savviness to good use by ... droning on and on about how many countries I'd been to and all the profound things I'd learned and, God, all those tourists are ruining this city. Here were their smiles fading by about the third minute of my soliloquy, and here was me thinking, *Oh, no. I have become everything I hate.*

Though they were typically upbeat, both my mother and Arthur Frommer also had the occasional lament about the ubiquity of their fellow tourists.

Take Harry's Bar in Venice, still one of the iconic touristic institutions of the city. Here's what *ED5* advises in the Readers' Suggestions section:

> *You should mention Harry's Bar as a place to avoid like poison, unless you want to come to Venice to spend time in a cocktail lounge like any at home, hear screams of "how are you, dear?!" from all the rich American tourists (nobody but Americans seems to go there) and pay an outrageous price for a Tom Collins.*

I feared that a visit to Harry's would finally push me past the brink of despair—I just might swan-dive into the path of a tour boat. I gave the Tom Collins a pass.

I was also in good, grumpy company with, among others, one Virginia Woolf, who wrote to Vanessa Bell in 1913, "I'm glad to find that you dislike Venice because I thought it detestable when we were there, both times."

Venice is a muse, famously, but not a very creative one: people tend to say the same things about it, over and over. One particularly common sentiment: Venice as tragic heroine, Ophelia of the Adriatic, glamorous, mysterious, doomed, drowning.

Some Venetians are sick of the hand-wringing and metaphor-slinging of outsiders: "The hackneyed image of Venice as a drowning city isn't entirely accurate," novelist Andrea di Robilant told the *New York Times* in 2006. "Lately, there's been a resurgence, a great influx of artists, actors and creative people." Carla, my majestic and melancholy host, likely would have agreed: Venice may have seen hard times, but don't write that obituary yet. A city built on water is a city built on world-class stubbornness and determination; if they could do *that*, my God . . . surely some high water and a few more visitors won't make them give up on this insane experiment of a town.

But there's no denying some essential truths: namely, that the increasingly *alta* water is threatening the city, and so, too, are the tourist masses. Some 20 million come here every year (most of them day-trippers). The vast, *vast* majority of them are heading to the *centro storico*, the historic city center, which is about one-twelfth the size of Manhattan. And they're not spread out; they mostly come between April and October. Have I mentioned it's crowded?

The permanent population, meanwhile, is heading the other way. One hundred seventy thousand people called Venice home in 1951. In 1993: seventy-four thousand. In 2009, shortly after I was there, the population dropped below sixty thousand. To mark the occasion, Venice residents held a mock funeral, ferrying a hot-pink coffin down the Grand Canal.

Back in the Piazza San Marco, I noticed that the temporary boardwalk above the flooded ground had become an attraction in its own right, a snapshot scene nearly as popular as the pigeons. I could only imagine how this photo would be described to the friends back home or online: "Check out this water! Look at what all those tourists are doing to this place! Terrible!"

I joined the crowds seated on the boardwalk and pulled *Europe on Five Dollars a Day* from my bag, mildly tempted to chuck Frommer into the *acqua alta*. Around the piazza, string quintets and larger bands played in front of several sidewalk cafés. It was a humid afternoon, the air languid and uncomfortable, and all the people around me looked exhausted and addled from the heat, the walking, the eternal crowds.

"Check it out—that's what I need," I heard an American-accented voice say. "*Europe on Five Dollars a Day*." A group of four American college students—three women and one man—was sitting on the other side of the riser, looking at my book. I smiled weakly.

"Kind of a joke. You can't really do it," I said. "Especially here."

"Yeah, no kidding," said the man. He had close-cropped hair, a black shirt, and a snide smirk. He said he was from Ohio. He filled a plastic cup with red wine and took a quick, pained gulp, like a child downing cough syrup. "Good thing we brought this with us on the train." He held up the bottle for inspection. A bright orange sticker gave the price: six euros.

"This is the only fun part of being in Venice," one of his companions said. "Sitting here, drinking." She took a swig from her cup. She was attired in what I was coming to think of as the uniform of young American women abroad: white skirt, loose black blouse, flip-flops. Trying to blend in among the Italians, but not quite succeeding, the footwear and slightly baggy cut of the clothes betraying the tourist truth. All four of the students had glazed, unsmiling expressions. I looked at their bottle, but it was only half empty. Either they'd already gone through another and discarded it or there was something else fueling their dour, unsteady manner.

"How long are *you* here?" Ohio asked.

"Four days," I said.

"That's too long, bro. Way too long. One day is enough."

"Are you here for the semester?" I asked.

"Heeelll no," one of the women said. "Just here a couple of nights. Piled into a hostel room on the mainland, you know? It seemed like a fun idea . . ." Her voice trailed off.

"*I'm* on the late train back to Naples tonight," Ohio said. Smirk. Swig. We were quiet for a moment. Finally he added ruefully, "This city is like that Disney place, with the pavilions for the different countries."

"Epcot?" one of the women asked.

"Yeah. It's like Epcot."

If there's one especially common insult for the beaten path, it's this one: it's so *Disney*. At the mock funeral for the city, one of the mourners told the *New York Times*: "The real question is the future: will Venice become a Disneyland or no?" Actually, the Mouse has already made inroads: when I asked Carla how to get to an Internet café, the two major landmarks in her directions were the Rialto Bridge and the Disney Store.

Here's one solution: let Disney take over Venice for real. That's what British economist John Kay suggested in 2006. The logic: If the city has effectively become a theme park, why not let the experts run it as such? Mickey Mouse as benevolent dictator will do a better job than the ineffectual hand-wringing that currently

passes for a solution. Put up a visitors' center. Make it easier for the
day-trippers to get in, get their landmark snapshots, and get out.
Charge a fee to enter. Put proceeds into building restoration and
flood prevention. Kay's proposal earned him the expected eye rolls
and rebuttals but also five thousand euros from the Istituto Veneto
for his "thought-provoking critique."

Kay's suggestion dovetails with a broader and equally counter-
intuitive argument that goes like this: The most ethical way to
travel is, in fact, on the beaten path. These places are already overrun; they can handle the visitors. So please don't go beating new
paths. An ecotourist lodge in the middle of an otherwise-untouched
beach or jungle may do its best to educate visitors about the place
and be light on the land, but many of these places would be better
off left alone. Each new travel boom results not just in more tourists from more places venturing abroad, but also in more tourists
from more places going to more *new* places.

In his 1972 *Harper's* profile, Stanley Elkin credited—well,
blamed—Arthur Frommer for inventing the notion of "Europe for
everybody"; by the 1970s, though, that was spreading to "Asia for
everybody, too." Today it's more like "everything and everywhere
for everyone—and not just to see those places but to feel them in
some mystical way."

As much as I like the notion that travel is becoming more egalitarian, I can't help but recoil at the perception that it's everyone's
birthright to see everything, do everything. It's manifest destiny
for the masses, this sense of laying a personal claim to a culture or
place before other outsiders "spoil" it.

In a sense, Venice and other cities on the beaten path play
the same role that Oktoberfest plays in Munich, but on a broader
scale. They keep the invading masses concentrated in specific

places—places that are accustomed to tourists and have the where-withal to deal with them. Personally, I think there's still value to seeing these places, hearing these languages, eating these foods, experiencing these cultures in their original and ever-evolving context—please don't just go to Epcot or Las Vegas and call it good. But is staying here on the beaten path, trampling it to death, still more ethical than blazing previously uncharted paths and making them the new Venice? I fear the answer is yes.

My last night, I finally figured out my cure. *You're going to do this,* I told myself. *You're going to get over this dark mood. Stop moping. Be a tourist, not a traveler.* I recalled Frommer's lyrical scene-setting at the start of his Venice chapter:

> *At the foot of the Venice railway station, there is a landing from which a city launch embarks for the trip up the Grand Canal. As you chug along, little clusters of candy-striped mooring poles emerge from the dark; a gondola approaches with a lighted lantern hung from its prow; the reflection of a slate-gray church, bathed in a blue spotlight, shimmers in the water as you pass by.*

I hatched a simple plan for happiness: find that scene.

I walked to the big gondola station by the Hard Rock Cafe. Nothing. No lanterns. In fact, there were no gondoliers at all.

I kept going. To the Accademia Bridge. Still nothing. Rialto Bridge. *Nope.* I strode quickly, confidently, never lost, always purposeful: *find a damn lantern-lit gondola.* Finally, to the train station, where Frommer had told me to go all along. I could hear him scolding me for grumbling at him earlier, and reminding me, with a sage chuckle, to just trust me, *trust me.*

So here I was, at the train station, scanning the canals, staring hard past the Scalzi Bridge, looking for a lantern, but lowering my standards with each passing moment. Any floating point of light would do. Hell, I thought, I'd even settle for a claptrap of a boat paddled by a gondolier sending a text message.

Niente.

I skulked back across the bridge. To my haven, the one place where I could be happy, or at least agreeably melancholy. I wearily nodded at the worn stone man as I passed beneath him.

I kicked off my shoes and sank into a chair, closing my eyes and letting the lapping water outside the window soothe me. *Come on, water: hurry up with the calming. Hurry up with the enlightenment and the love.* A distant pulsing noise formed the bass line below the lapping. Muffled yells joined the chorus. *This was not what I had in mind.*

The pulse became a roar; the voices became bellows of Dionysian delight. A party boat passed by my window—and the canal was just fifteen or twenty feet wide, so when I say "just outside," I mean that I could have reached out and smacked one of the revelers. It was awfully tempting.

My last bastion: officially ruined. A minute later, the boat went by again in the other direction. And this time, the loud, drunken revelers were singing—ruining—one of my favorite songs of all time. "Volare." Gipsy Kings.

Charm capital of the world, my tourist ass, I grumbled to myself. *Get me out of here already.*

Words I never thought I'd say: I kind of missed my nine-to-five grind back home.

Rome

Eternal City of Tourism

*Whenever 6 p.m. approached last summer, Hope and I
felt a genuine urge to rush back to the [Hotel] "Texas,"
to hear the exciting conversation that fills the cocktail-
lounge of the pension (our fellow guests, among others:
a member of the Minneapolis Philharmonic, and
his wife; a professor from the Free China
University on [sic] Formosa).*

—Europe on Five Dollars a Day

There's nothing like having your life flash in front of your eyes to reboot your spirit and remove any sense of jadedness. I was happy to be away from the City of Canals, but had forgotten one of its few perks: a refreshing lack of cars. I had become accustomed to walking straight down the middle of every road without a single cautionary glance. I left Rome's Termini Station, bouncing in jubilation—*I'm not in Venice anymore!*—and into traffic.

Beeeeeep!! A Fiat scorched past me. A millimeter closer and I would now be known as the Noseless Wonder.

Braaaap!! A tour bus took a corner on two wheels and gunned for me.

I scrambled back to the curb. *Oh, right.* They have cars here. Famously. Ubiquitously. Dementedly. I waited for a gap and then made a run for it, crossing in furtive bursts and getting religion for perhaps the first time in my life, wondering who the patron saint of pedestrians might be.

Perhaps the nuns on the other side of the street knew. They stared at me as I caught my breath. They looked every bit as overwhelmed as I was by the automotive mayhem. Another "Oh, right" moment: this is the cradle of Catholicism, where the nuns are tourists and the tourists overrun the holy sites, worshipping with their flashbulbs and seeking the holy trinity: meaning, happiness, gelato.

I felt like a panicked, ignorant, amazed tourist again, no longer weary but invigorated—I was out of my element and therefore, in a strange way, entirely back in it. I practically skipped all the way to my hotel.

A few words about the Pensione Texas, courtesy of Arthur Frommer circa 1963:

The Big Splurge: *A bright, young Italian named Guido Agnolucci, and an American named Marvin Hare, teamed up three years ago to open a pensione in Rome that would cater to the thoughtful tourist—people anxious to absorb the highest cultural lessons of the city. To give their establishment a name no one would ever forget, they called it the Pensione Texas. You'll realize how perfectly inappropriate that moniker is when you enter this glamorously-decorated, duplex apartment.*

Pensione Texas occupies the fourth and fifth floors of a historic but nondescript building. Walking by, you might guess it was apartments or offices or, more likely, you wouldn't notice it at all. The downstairs restaurant is now Chinese. The elevator—an elaborate wrought-iron cage of the "they don't make 'em like they used to" variety—was out of order, so I took the stairs.

After finishing the check-in formalities, I pulled out my book and showed the above passage to the desk clerk, Dario, a tall, middle-aged man with a long face framed by dark curls of hair. Like my Venetian host, Carla, he wore a perpetually wistful expression on his face, as though forever recalling some long-lost, bittersweet memory. It grew more pronounced as he examined the book.

"Yes," he said. "I remember this."

Fireworks went off in my brain. *Wait, really? Finally!* The words I'd been waiting for! After all these weeks, I'd become accustomed to blank looks or, worse, concerned stares from people trying to figure out if I was the dangerous or the benign kind of crazy.

But Dario understood. Dario *remembered*.

"We were in many books," he continued. "And the *New York Times. Esquire.* The president of the Diners Club credit card came here with his wife and two children. Elizabeth Taylor—do you know Elizabeth Taylor?"

I did.

"She stayed here. She was at another hotel, more famous, but they all found out and were bothering her, the . . . press, the . . ."

"The paparazzi? She came here to hide from the paparazzi?"

"Exactly."

"Elizabeth Taylor?" I said, slightly stunned. "Stayed *here*?"

"Exactly. With Richard Burton."

He held up a finger, remembering something. He opened a desk drawer and pulled out a brochure from the 1960s. "I show people this sometimes, so they can see what it was like."

The brochure was a treasure of midcentury graphic design, all clean fonts and glorious Technicolor photos. The scenes followed suit: grand to the point of borderline camp, rooms overstuffed with rococo furnishings and enormous artwork, the textiles and surfaces a cornucopia of textures and patterns. The photo on the back of the brochure was especially stunning: a room with black-and-white checkerboard flooring, one wall painted cardinal red, two others covered with a wallpaper of interlocking swirls, and in the center of it all, a matching set of two chairs and a sofa, all whiter than white and squat but hulking and very, very *mod*.

Double take: I looked at the room we were in—same size, same door openings, same inset arched shelves. Had to be the same space. But now the surfaces were drab, the furnishings a few simple wooden tables and chairs. The aesthetic had gone from Liberace to library.

Dario pointed out more praise listed in the brochure: there was the quote from *Europe on Five Dollars a Day*, right at the top. And *Fielding's Guide to Europe* ("Texas sized values at Rhode Island prices . . . What martinis!"). *Holiday* magazine. The *Los Angeles Times. Dollar Wise Guide to Italy. Rome Daily American. Esquire.* The general sentiment was that this pensione was glamorous but inexpensive, with, as Frommer had noted, an eclectic clientele. *Esquire* added: "One's table companions range from a British nobleman to a Brooklyn cab-driver, such is the range of personalities who come to content themselves before the homey hearth."

"May I take a photo of this?" I asked, pointing to the brochure.

Dario shrugged. "You may have it, if you like."

"I . . . are you *sure*?"

"Yes, of course. I rarely show it to people anymore—I don't think it would be right to distribute it. The rooms . . ." He paused and looked down, a far-off glimmer in his eyes. "The rooms no longer look like they once did."

He shook his head almost imperceptibly and then looked back to meet my captivated gaze. Smiling, he handed me the brochure. I held it gingerly.

"Ah, but I'm sorry for going on. I will show you to your room."

"No, no," I said. "I'm happy to hear the stories. I'd *love* to hear more." I was digging my notebook out of my pocket, frantic to start writing this all down.

But Dario was already striding down the hall, key in hand.

"Your room has a bathroom," he said. He opened the door to reveal a small space, decorated in the same manner as the lobby, spare but homey, with a twin bed tight up against one wall. "This is why Elizabeth Taylor came here—it was one of the only hotels where some rooms had private baths. Now everyone has them."

"Really, I'd love to hear more about all of that," I said, trying not to beg.

"Yes, of course," Dario said. He turned and headed back to the lobby, leaving me mystified for now. But it was a good confusion. My glee and energy were replenishing. I was a happy tourist.

The evolution of private bathrooms is a telling detail. These were one of the amenities that Arthur Frommer typically viewed as superfluous and decidedly not budget-traveler friendly. He says it right up front, in the Rules of the Game chapter at the start of *Europe on Five Dollars a Day*: "Rule 1 of your European travels is, therefore,

never to ask for a private bath with your hotel room. It is impossible
to travel cheaply in Europe otherwise." He lists no Rule 2.

European hotel owners could be forgiven for thinking the
American tourists were sending mixed messages—it was only a few
years earlier that the Marshall Planners had been encouraging
them to install private bathrooms, to attract the tourists of Fielding's and Fodors's ilk. (It's a reasonable guess that the owners of
the Pensione Texas, which opened in the mid-1950s and catered to
Americans, knowingly heeded this advice.) Frommer ushered in a
new type of traveler, one of aspirational thriftiness, replacing conspicuous consumption with conspicuous cost-cutting.

Private baths represent one area where Frommer's legacy has
not endured—witness Dario's comments that this amenity was no
longer notable or the fact that of the few recently built hostels I
stayed in, most had not only private rooms (not the rowdy, bunk-
filled quarters that the term "hostel" often conjures) but private
baths. And I have to say: this is one aspect of modernity for which
I am exceedingly grateful.

"It's so cool," my mother told me when I first started interrogating
her about her trip. "There's stuff *everywhere* in Rome: the Colosseum, the Trevi Fountain—and, oh, look, the Spanish Steps!"

The place she remembers most clearly, though, is a restaurant.
She couldn't recall its name or where it was, but the meal was
indelible: "We're sitting there eating lunch, and this little girl
walks up—three, maybe four years old. The owner's daughter. She's
holding something in her hands, and we think, 'Oh, that's nice, she
has a gift for us.' She's grinning. And then she opens her hands"—
I've heard this story many times, and Mom always leans forward

at this point, making eye contact before the kicker catapults from her mouth—*"and it's a bird! A* dead *bird! A very dead starling!"*

I was a bit on guard as I ate my dinner that first night under a grapevine-covered arbor at an outdoor café. But I relaxed as I sipped my second glass of wine and tucked into a plate of ravioli far better than anything I'd had in Venice. An accordion moaned softly from the shadows, its player unseen. And despite my fears, there were no children bearing unwanted corpses. (Thankfully, I missed out on the dead birds altogether in Rome.)

The other stuff, though—the cool stuff, the historic stuff—was still ever present and ever impressive. Rome really does have more than its fair share of historic bounties, and you really do just sort of stumble on one after another: *Whoa, there's the Colosseum! And right next door, isn't that . . . yep, that's the Roman Forum!* Walking around Rome was like an inadvertent scavenger hunt with genuinely epic treasures at each turn. *Oh, hey, the Pantheon. Well, since I'm here . . .* And then, a few minutes later, I spotted a sign for the Trevi Fountain. All right then, I thought. Don't mind if I do.

It was getting late by now, approaching midnight, but the area around the fountain was packed with giddy gawkers from all over the world: Russians over here, Koreans over there, a church group from Kentucky a few feet away. Perhaps a hundred people total. The Trevi Fountain's beauty is a grandiose variety, not the fragile, tragic kind I'd found in Venice—this is vigor and might and potency; it wants, *demands* some fellow revelers. There was even dancing— the Tourist Dance, of course, with the added step of an over-the- shoulder coin toss for the camera, in keeping with the tradition that said coin toss will ensure a return trip to Rome. (The coins add up to an estimated three thousand euros *every day*.) I joined in, get- ting my own photo. *Veni, vidi, proieci*: I came, I saw, I tossed.

The various groups were intermingling casually like a cocktail party gone right. If anything, the tourist crowds enhanced the spectacle of the fountain and its marble figurines, creating a festive air. I took a Not-So-Flattering Photo of the scene, noting to myself that, really, the surrounding spectacle was every bit as alluring as the grand fountain itself. Every landmark and street scene I'd stumbled upon in Rome had been like that, each one buzzing with a lively mix of locals and tourists, of sweeping history and the messy, quirky present.

This was my kind of city.

The next morning, the time had come for the breakup with Arthur Frommer, my Roman Holiday from the old guidebook and my brief experiment in modern-day crowd-sourcing.

It's worth noting that even when I was relying on *Europe on Five Dollars a Day*, I was still crowd-sourcing, albeit using the crowds of the 1960s. The Readers' Suggestions sections that Frommer included throughout the book were effectively the same thing as modern-day blog comments or reviews on travel websites like TripAdvisor. Then as now, the comments ranged from truly insightful and practical to self-serving, questionable, and downright spammy. By the mid-1980s, Frommer had become so exasperated by the number of duplicitous recommendations he was receiving that he dropped the Readers' Suggestions section altogether.

Most of the dozen or so suggestions I received through my blog and online social networks came from friends or friends of friends, so I trusted there wasn't any underhanded manipulation going on. My bigger worry was that a large portion of the recommendations would just be total duds, well-intentioned but not well-informed, based on hearsay, speculation, or hazy memories heavily filtered by nostalgia. I wasn't sure whom to trust, or who would be offended if I didn't like—or worse, even try—their generously offered recommendations. So I selected based on random whim and gut reaction, supplemented by some quick research on user-generated websites like TripAdvisor.

As I stood outside my first Internet-selected stop of the day, I looked at the signs by the door. This was one of the top-rated gelaterias in Rome on TripAdvisor, but apparently the guidebooks shared the love, judging by the laminated, blown-up pages from Lonely Planet and others. The shop was a tiny place called Gelateria del Teatro, on a dead-end nook of a street near the Piazza Navona. It sure didn't look like much worth mentioning—no long line, no fancy interior. I got a scoop of the *torta al limon* (lemon pie) and a scoop of chocolate with wine, the swirled flavors packing a one-two, upper-downer, bright-heady punch. It was glorious.

So score one for the Internet. Knowledge has its benefits, I reminded myself. And then I looked at my watch and got a fresh reminder of the perils of too much information. I didn't have time to linger and savor—I had too many other things to see and do.

"There's the real story," our tour guide said, "and it's a pretty good one. But it's not as good as the mythological version—that's the *fist-pumping* story." He flexed one biceps and contorted his face into an exaggerated glower. We laughed and his posture relaxed, his face entirely deadpan.

When I had posted my request for suggestions, I'd sort of assumed that the only people who would respond would be friends and family. I was elated when a total stranger, who just happened to read my blog on the right day, recommended this tour. So here I

was, sweating in the blazing midday sun at the Circus Maximus—
which the guide described, after a lengthy, erudite description of
its cultural significance, as "basically a NASCAR oval for chariots."

The guide was Jason, a thirtyish Canadian with a brain like an
encyclopedia and the mouth of a sailor; he was leading us on what
was officially billed as the "Rome(ing) Walking Tour," but which
might as well have been called "The Rise and Fall of the F-ing
Roman Empire." His manner was understated and stoic—as we
had all stood around chatting before the tour started, I hadn't realized this random dude in cutoff khakis and flip-flops was the
guide—which made his gratuitous swearing and bombastic storytelling all the more amusing.

"So first I'll give you the good version of the city's origins, the
mythology . . . and then how that shit actually went down," he continued, and with that he began a forty-minute narrative composed of
mythology, history, and jokes. Power struggles, weirdness, profanity.

Rome is built on that mix of the profane and the majestic, high
culture and low. So, too, is the Tourist Culture. As I'd learned from
reading *Europe on Five Dollars a Day*, none of this is really new. But
I hadn't realized how truly old this heady mix was until Jason sat
us down on a low wall along the Via dei Fori Imperiali and told us
about the Colosseum.

"Basically, nothing's changed in the world of entertainment,"
Jason said. "Ancient Romans wanted the same thing we want
today: big, loud, crazy shit. Epic spectacles. They'd flood the place
and have naval battles. And in the first one hundred days of the
Colosseum, they killed five thousand animals and ten thousand
people—all for entertainment."

We stared, jaws agape. I mean, presumably we'd all seen *Gladiator*, but still . . .

"That's messed up," the guy sitting next to me muttered.

"They'd bring a giraffe into the ring with a gladiator," Jason continued. "A giraffe has no chance against a gladiator, of course—what's it gonna do? But imagine you've never seen a giraffe, right? You're like, 'What the fuck is this alien-looking thing?!' Now, the gladiator knows that there are two big arteries for this long-ass neck and that if you slice those, the whole thing's gonna go back and forth like an unmanned hose. The crowds are going, 'Hell yes, this is *sweet*.' No People for the Ethical Treatment of Animals back then, I tell you that."

The results of the crowd-sourced day were mixed. Yes, there was that gelato. And, yes, there was that walking tour.

But I definitely didn't save money—the tour alone set me back twenty euros, and I still felt obligated to follow as many of my leads as possible. There was a second gelateria recommendation, which turned out to be much more crowded and much less sublime. There was also a decent pizzeria, an acceptable trattoria, a Bavarian-style beer hall with a nice, malty lager and the soundtrack of the iPod playlist from hell (one word: "Macarena"). On balance, it was a mix of hits and misses not so different from a normal day guided by Frommer and the Goddess Serendipity. Yet it all felt a bit too easy. Less excitement, less intrigue. Less fun.

I couldn't wait for my reunion with Arthur.

Rome's riches are such that even Frommer, who is generally averse to sightseeing, feels compelled to offer a top-ten list of things to see. Number one: the Vatican.

All I really wanted to see was the Sistine Chapel. But, as at many museums and landmarks, you don't open the door and go straight to the main attraction; first there are other things to amuse and distract. In this case, there was an endless series of rooms and halls and galleries, each more elaborate than the next, with vaulted ceilings and marble columns and mosaic floors and gold leaf and trompe l'oeil and more Marys than even the Uffizi Gallery, to say nothing of the parades of chubby-cheeked cherubs. And so many people: nuns in habits, church groups in matching shirts, and others like me who were here for no other reason than, well, *when in Rome* . . . Some of the tourist types wore loose scarves I'd seen for sale by the entrance, bare shoulders being forbidden in this holy place. They all mixed as one, clutching guidebooks and bags from the Hard Rock Cafe and doing the Tourist Dance. Even the nuns.

Soon enough, I was getting restless, ready for the main event, the Sistine Chapel. As the rooms got bigger and the decor got crazier, I kept thinking, "Is this it? There's a big, painted ceiling. This might be it. Right?"

I should note, perhaps, that I was raised Mennonite. Urban hippie Mennonite, not buggies-and-barn-raisings Mennonite. Still, the core values remain the same: humility, pacifism, simple living— the last especially important, my parents seemed to believe, for purposes of saving up for the next big trip. The Mennonite version of grandeur in church design is to paint the walls a color other than white, meaning I'm always a bit out of my element in more opulent sacred spaces, what with their vaulted ceilings and gold leaf galore and those cherubs leering from above.

So take that and factor in that I'm on the record as being easily bored by Renaissance paintings, especially by the third hour of them . . . and perhaps you'll forgive me when I say that when I got to the Sistine Chapel it was more relief than revelation. Yup, a lot of good brushwork, Michelangelo.

I was much more interested in the living, breathing, three-dimensional humans around me. Like the professional shushers. People whose job it was to keep us quiet. Every few seconds, this one guy would call out in a stern, stage-whisper yell, *"Silenzio!* No photos!" And then someone's phone would ring or a flash would go off and we'd all look around with looks of bemused denial—*It wasn't me*—and then the professional shusher would shush us again. I sort of wanted that job, actually, not just so I could put "professional shusher" on my business card but because the people-watching was even better than at most tourist landmarks.

The pilgrims and tourists didn't always fall into their assigned roles. One of the nuns looked bored out of her mind, clearly fidgeting beneath her navy blue dress. A few of the church group tried to herd their friends to the door, their expressions ones of fatigue, hunger, and full bladders. And a pair of women cloaked in gift-store scarves stared at the ceiling stock-still, necks craned, eyes wide, breathing shallowly.

I left them with their wonder and went off to find the gift shop— I owed my parents a postcard. As I browsed, I noticed one of the church-group men trying to get the attention of the shop clerk.

"Excuse me," he said. "Do you sell action figures of the Pope? Ones that move?"

The clerk was aghast. "No! Not here!"

"Do you know where I could get one?"

Long pause. Double blink. Sigh. "Try a shop by Saint Peter's Square."

. . .

I went back to the Pensione Texas to see if Dario was in a talkative mood.

He was.

"It was very different," he said when I asked him to tell me more about the hotel back in its heyday. "Things change very much. This city has changed very much since 1963. People here are not so kind and friendly as before. Now, George Clooney has a house on a lake in the north. I think he goes there for the quiet. It is the country—if you go there and ask someone where is the church, they will take you there, walk with you. Here in Roma, it was like that, but not anymore."

"Now that there are lots of tourists?" I asked.

"No, there were always lots of tourists. That is not new. But the people—the people have changed. Each time is different." Dario opened the old brochure and pointed to one of the pictures. There was a bar on the fifth floor, directly above us, he told me. The photo showed a chic lounge. He paused to gaze with a small, bittersweet smile. "It's closed now. For the restoration."

I got the sense that the restoration was ongoing—*very* ongoing.

"It is difficult to make changes to the building," he said. "Lots of money, lots of time. In Roma, they are very protective of the history. This is how it should be, but . . ." His voice trailed off, as though he had said too much. "The process of improving things is sometimes difficult. Especially if the building is important or had a famous person who was here. This building was designed by a famous architect who also designed the Victor Emmanuel monument on the Piazza Venezia.

"Because the building had a famous architect, any changes must be approved by the city, which takes a long time—often years," Dario said. "Both outside and inside of the building. Most of the other hotels now have air-conditioning, but we cannot, because it would cause too many alterations and there would be pipes and mechanical work on the exterior. They have become more strict in the past ten to twenty years. And the city has a very small staff to monitor and approve all of these things."

"So you just have to wait and hope?" I asked.

"Exactly. It is a long process." Dario paused. "But I do think it's better this way; it is necessary. It is important to keep the history—it is better."

After a long, awkward pause, he asked, "Do you know of Alfredo's? It is probably in your book. It was very famous, popular with Americans."

The restaurant's eponymous owner, Dario said, had invented the dish fettuccine Alfredo, and the flourish with which he served it was part of the attraction. (I later learned that the restaurant was such an iconic Roman place in the minds of Americans that it was part of the original Italy Pavilion when Epcot opened in 1982. That outlet of the restaurant closed in 2007, though one remains in New York City.)

"That sounds expensive," I said. "It probably wasn't in my book."

"Now, yes, it is expensive. I ate there once, many years ago. It was fine. My family—my mother—cooks in a more traditional way. I prefer that. Americans, maybe, are not so familiar with the traditional foods, but they like this. However, as you say, a place becomes famous, and then it becomes expensive."

Right, I thought. Except when it doesn't. Except when its history becomes a trap and the changing times pass it by and it becomes a symbol of fleeting fame and deteriorated grandeur. Like

the Pensione Texas. Dario didn't sound jealous of Alfredo's continued good fortune—not in the least. Things change, he said once
more. It made me hope, if only for him, that times will change
again, and the Pensione Texas will reclaim the glory that for now
exists only in memory and a brochure tucked into a desk drawer in
Minneapolis.

I couldn't help but think of fettuccine Alfredo as I dug into my des-
sert that night. "As my final send-off to Rome, I'd go to the Restaurant Tre Scalini on the Piazza Navona," says Arthur Frommer in
E5D, "and I'd have its specialty—a 'Tartuffo' (ice cream covered
with cherries and bitter chocolate chips)."

Like Alfredo's fettuccine, the Tartuffo had clearly become a star
with tourists, given its prominent place on the menu. (I couldn't
help but wonder how much of this came straight back to the prominent mention in *Europe on Five Dollars a Day*.) And like the pasta,
its fame had spawned a substantial price tag: nine euros. The serving was generous—baseball sized—but the ice cream had clearly
been prescooped and then dug out of a freezer; it was also baseball
hard. I was crushed. In Rome, I had finally gotten my traveling
mojo back, and this felt like quite the wrong send-off.

I recalled that Gelateria del Teatro was just a short walk away. I
hurried off to reboot my palate and give Rome a more fitting
final act.

It was just as good the second time.

Madrid

Better Living Through Tourism

*The amazingly low prices of this nation ... are not the
product of progress, but of decline. While we are the
lucky beneficiaries of those prices, it is nonetheless the
fervent wish of this book that the Spanish people will
have a better future, and that Spain, in the years to
come, won't be so darn easy to visit on $5 a day.*

—Europe on Five Dollars a Day

When I told people I was headed to Europe, or had just come
back, the subject of Barcelona inevitably arose—"Did you
check out the food scene?" "Did you see the Gaudí buildings?" or,
most often, a straight-to-the point "Isn't Barcelona *awesome*?"
And I'd have to say, "Actually, I didn't go there; it wasn't in my
guidebook"—it really wasn't on the tourist trail at all in the 1960s.
Today, Barcelona is one of the most popular cities in Europe for
travelers, trailing only London, Paris, and Rome, and ranking well
ahead of some of the places that did make the *Europe on Five Dollars a Day* cut, such as Nice, Athens, and Oslo.

And Madrid. Spain's capital did make it into *E5D*, but the

moment I arrived here, I realized that Frommer's comments about the place might as well have been about Mars or fifteenth-century Mongolia, for all the similarities it had to the city before me. In perhaps no place I visited other than Berlin were the differences between then and now more profound.

I bounded up the subway station steps at Puerta del Sol—basically the Times Square of Madrid—eager to poke my head above ground like a prairie dog and take in the scene. On one side of the square, a billboard for Nike soccer shoes towered above me; I winced and turned around to find long rows of Renaissance revival buildings—a tiny balcony at each window, terra-cotta tile topping each roof—stretching into the distance, along the streets that radiate out from the square. That was more like it. The buildings were just the right scale (four and five stories) to give a sense of officiousness and urbanity without being imposing. A bagpiper played at one corner of the square; on the other side, a duo of hammer dulcimer players of mesmerizing dexterity and virtuosity put on a show for the crowds streaming by, an even mix of gawking tourists and commuting locals. The street was all bustle and high spirits—even more so than Rome or Berlin or any of the other cities I'd just visited—a genial cacophony, more friendly than frenzied.

It would be incorrect to say that Spain was truly thriving. The recent collapse of the worldwide economy had hit the nation especially hard—by April 2010, unemployment would reach 20 percent and the burgeoning deficits here and in other countries (including Greece and Italy) would cause widespread concerns about the long-term fate of the common euro currency. As I walked up a pedestrian mall called Calle de la Montera, headed toward my hostel, I saw several people—each with a haunted, hard-luck expression—wearing sandwich boards that read, "COMPRO ORO."

I buy gold. They were handing out cards for a pawnshop. When I ventured back into the city after a few hours' respite in the hostel, I got propositioned three times in the span of one block. (Well, I thought, Frommer was right when he said the Spanish people are friendly and helpful. . . .)

Still, Madrid's exuberance was impossible to deny. That night I feasted on impossibly cheap and delicious tapas and hung out at a side-street bar, sipping beer and chatting with the bartenders— what a joy to be, finally, in a city where I spoke the language, albeit crappily!—and when I ambled back to my hostel after midnight, sated and giddy, the streets were still alive. There was even a book-store open.

Seventeen cities get the full treatment in *Europe on Five Dollars a Day*; Madrid is the final chapter and also the shortest. I would have more than enough time for Frommering, I knew, so I spent the next day biding my time, enjoying myself, tracking down places and sites listed in my *E5D* only if I happened to be in the neighbor-hood. My navigational instincts were in fine form, and the few times I did get lost, I discovered I was no longer the least bit con-cerned about making a fool of myself when asking for directions. "I'm getting quite brave about asking 'stupid' questions," my mother wrote from Rome—being a happy tourist is in part about acknowledging and accepting your own ineptitude, but being keen to improve.

In the morning, I took a bike tour. Our leader was a man in his early twenties named Ramón, tall but lean, and with a soft voice that belied the giddy delight he took in showing off his city. The bustle had not abated. Sometimes it felt like every other block had a festival going on or about to start—groups gathering, music blaring. When I asked Ramón about it, he shrugged. "Just regular life."

We stopped at Mercado San Miguel, a big Beaux Arts building with a decidedly modern interior. As a public market, it had historically been a community fixture, Ramón said, but in recent decades had fallen on hard times, becoming a forlorn, dismal place. A few months earlier, it had reopened as a showcase of regional foods. There were produce and fish stands as well as a chic little wine bar and a small tapas restaurant—modern and traditional, urban and pastoral, all rolled into one packed market. It, too, felt like a festival—but, no, just regular life, tourists mingling with locals, everyone beaming.

We got back on our bikes, reluctantly, and moved on. At a sprawling intersection where two major roads met at a roundabout—it reminded me of the Arc de Triomphe, albeit with slightly fewer cars and a massive fountain in the middle rather than a monumental arch—Ramón called us to a stop. The fountain was covered with an immense white tent, and a stage was being set up on one side of the intersection, just in front of the Palacio de Comunicaciones, the city's iconic structure, a Gothic-inspired edifice that was part wedding cake, part cathedral, but altogether stately.

"We are one of the finalists for the 2016 Olympics," Ramón said. "The vote is in a few days, so they are setting up for an event to maybe get the attention of the International Olympic Committee."

Spain's tourism boom traces its roots to the rebuilding of the country after the dictator Francisco Franco—the man most responsible for the "economic backwardness of Spain and the poverty of its people" that Frommer observed—fell from power in 1975. But the Barcelona Olympics are widely credited with being

Spain's big coming-out party, the catalyst that launched the country into the upper echelons of tourist destinations. (Frank Gehry's iconic Guggenheim Museum in Bilbao, opened in 1997, helped the trend along.) By 2007, Spain drew more tourists than any nation in the world other than France, although it has since fallen to fourth place, with the United States and fast-rising China rounding out the top three in 2010.

So now, Madrid wanted to claim some of that charm for itself, to reclaim its spot as Spain's cultural capital.

Ramón's brown eyes brightened as he explained, "We are trying to show the world we want this—we want them to come here."

As we pedaled off to see the rest of his beloved, reawakened city, I recalled Frommer's comments about the country's impoverished "quaintness" and his wish for a better, more prosperous future for the Spanish people. And I thought, happily, Mission accomplished.

Like Spain, the broader travel landscape has changed as well since the mid-1970s. Mass tourism has started to follow what was once the hippie trail into Asia and parts of Central and South America, and then, with the fall of the Iron Curtain, parts of eastern Europe have seen tourist influxes (Prague is a notable example). Some of the counterculture travel attitudes and methods have also become mainstream—the United Nations designated 2002 the International Year of Ecotourism. In 1988, Frommer released a new guidebook appropriate for the times, *Arthur Frommer's New World of Travel*, written with his daughter, Pauline. With a focus on ethical and offbeat travel—anticipating the rise of ecotourism—the book's suggestions are the anti–Grand Tour: homestays, voluntourism, yoga retreats, and "cerebral camping."

By the mid-1990s, the next big shift in travel would occur, but this time it wasn't about where to go or any particular attitude toward travel but how you planned and how you kept in touch. The new tool was, of course, the Internet. And one of the travel sites at the forefront was Arthur Frommer's Outspoken Encyclopedia of Travel, launched in 1997. This became Frommers.com, which remains one of the most prominent travel sites on the Internet. And, yes, the company now has a smartphone app, too.

On the agenda for the next day: the Prado, which Frommer lauds as "smaller and better arranged than the Louvre." It's one of the few museums or landmarks in Madrid that he talks about at length—allocating it about half a page—and I figured I was ready to get one last art overdose before I left Europe.

As I walked down the broad, thrumming Gran Via, I saw a mass of people clogging the street—tens of thousands, surely, maybe more.

"¿Qué está pasando allí?" I asked a woman. What's happening over there?

She cast me a confused look. *"Para los Olímpicos, ¿no?"* She pointed above my head and I glanced up to see a small banner hanging from the light pole—from every pole, actually, on both sides of the street. It had the Madrid 2016 "Ciudad Candidata" logo—a multicolored hand—and official slogan, *Tengo una corazonada* (roughly, "I've got a feeling"). The crowds were heading toward the intersection Ramón had pointed out the day before; this was Madrid's last big push to win its Olympic bid.

You know what? I thought. The Prado will be here forever. Let's party.

A smiling volunteer with a satchel full of white baseball caps and green sheets of paper handed me one of each and explained what was going on: we were going to create an immense version of the logo, a living mosaic. I could stand anywhere I liked, but I had to have the proper color of paper for the section. *"Muy importante,"* she said. We needed to impress.

I pulled on my hat and clutched my green placard and went to the appointed spot. In the next half hour, the crowd grew tight, tighter, tighter—news reports had a final count of four hundred thousand people, forming the largest mosaic in the world—with the mood never anything less than ecstatic. Here was their chance; here was their moment.

An emcee took the stage and riled us up with some party tunes. We sang along at the top of our lungs, about how we were the champions and about how tonight was gonna be a good, good night. We tried to do some sort of quasi-choreographed dance that everyone else seemed to know, but we were so tightly packed that we could only bump into each other and grin goofily and apologize and shout to each other that, yes, I love Madrid, and yes, this city's time has come, and yes, we will—we *will*—be the champions! *Tengo una corazonada*...

The emcee yelled for silence and the whir of a helicopter cut the air like a drumroll. We're gonna do this, the emcee said. Hands in the air, placards to the sky!

I couldn't help myself: I reached into my bag, grabbed *Europe on Five Dollars a Day*, and placed it on top of my sheet. I glanced around, seeing if anyone had noticed. An elderly woman a few feet away had; she stared, confused. I gave her an apologetic wince-shrug-smile. She laughed and looked up and danced in place for the camera, and I did the same, yelling, hoping that if I wanted it badly enough, this dream, my dreams, our dreams, would come true.

*Setting up for the Olympic
bid rally in front of the
Palacio de Comunicaciones.
Four hundred thousand
people showed up—Madrid
knows how to party.*

I made it to the Prado, by the way. Sprinting. With twenty minutes
to spare before it closed. I walked straight to the Goya section,
finally catching my breath—and then feeling it pulled out of me as
I surveyed the paintings and their haunting, ghastly, disturbingly
beautiful depictions of war and tyranny. It struck me again—as it
had in Berlin and, well, everywhere—that for all the faults of
modernity, I'll take it. Still plenty of conflict and discord in Europe
to go around—indeed, whispers of uncertainty about the very sur-
vival of the EU followed me everywhere—and yet I couldn't help
but feel won over by that Spanish optimism. In spite of everything,
the future's bright. The past really wasn't so great. No going back.

Back at the hostel, I sat in the lounge, reading *E5D* and realizing that I had precisely one place left to investigate. One. And then my experiment was complete. There was time to do it tonight . . . but a very cute woman had just sat down in the chair next to me. Arthur Frommer would have to get in line.

"Is that your guidebook?" she asked, flashing an incredulous smile. She fidgeted with her long hair, a shade lighter than her auburn blouse. Late twenties, I guessed.

"Yeah, I am," I said. "Following the footsteps of my mom. Lots of things have changed, of course, but some haven't at all. . . ."

By now, I was accustomed to using the book as an icebreaker; I had my introductory spiel down pat.

"So where have you gone with it, then?" she asked.

"Oh, Paris, Amsterdam, Brussels, Berlin, Vienna, Rome . . . all over western Europe. Ten or so cities."

"You've been to all those places?" She sounded genuinely impressed. She kept playing with her hair absentmindedly, wrapping and then unwrapping her finger, her bearing a jittery incandescence. "I've always been a bit reluctant to travel. I taught for a while in Australia—just got back from there—but mostly I've only been in the English-speaking countries."

"So what brought you to Spain?"

"I heard I could get a job teaching English and thought maybe it was time to get out of my comfort zone."

I told her I knew the feeling, then added, "I'm Doug, by the way."

"Ah, a good Scottish name!" I could tell from her accent that she was English.

"Don't hold it against me," I said, grinning.

"No, no, not at all!" she chuckled. For the first time, she stopped fidgeting with her hair. "My father's Scottish. Got lots of family up there. I'm Sarah McKay—another good Scottish name."

We kept at it for twenty, thirty, forty minutes, the conversation dipping through travel and European history and our mutual Scottish ancestral roots and our favorite authors and our lives back home. It was the longest, best conversation I'd had in weeks, far-ranging and easygoing, both of us recognizing in each other a kindred wanderlust-stricken spirit beginning to emerge from a shell and eager to see more of what the world had to offer.

The hostel lounge was starting to get busy. I wanted to keep chatting, but we were both straining to hear. I discreetly rubbed the cover of *E5D* for good luck and put on my best I-know-we-just-met-but-I-promise-I'm-not-an-ax-murderer smile. I asked, "Do you want to go somewhere and get a drink and keep talking?"

Time stopped.

I'd read enough travel memoirs, seen enough Sundance movies, to know how this ended, but I wanted to enjoy the moment. It was all I could do not to erupt in an enormous, cheesy, *I do, I do* grin.

Sarah's hand went back to her head. "Oof, no, I really need to go take a shower just now."

Wait! No! Wrong script!

Time stopped again, and I willed it to go back, back to two minutes ago, let me rewrite this; it's not what was supposed to happen. . . .

Now she was looking down at the ground, a grimace on her face, practically pulling out her hair.

"Okay!" I squeaked. "Well, it was really nice chatting with you!"

I rushed to the door as suavely as I could, trying to outrun the sound of my heart breaking.

Really?! After all that?!

But, yes. Really. The Sundance crowds began filing to the exit.

My last, best chance for a clichéd Hollywood ending was dashed by the clichéd brush-off excuse. She had to wash her hair.

And now I needed a drink.

I went to commiserate with Frommer one more time. The last place on my list was Casa Botín, *E5D*'s "big splurge" in Madrid. Frommer notes that it's the setting of the final scene in *The Sun Also Rises* and adds, "It's a pilgrimage spot for Papa [Hemingway's] admirers, and yet it continues, almost unaware of its fame, to cook magnificently Spanish meals, unaccompanied by most of the tourist touches you would expect at such a shrine."

I trust I do not need to say that this has changed—Don Ernesto is very much in the spotlight now. He is painted on the glass in the front window, seated at his typewriter, one hand grasping a piece of paper, the other a libation. Just inside the window is a framed certificate from the *Guinness Book of World Records* recognizing Botín—established 1725—as the oldest restaurant in the world.

It is, to coin a phrase, touristy. As I waited for a table, I heard a constant stream of American voices—including the "How are you, dear?!" exclamations that *E5D* warned about at Harry's Bar in Venice—as well as various dialects of tourist English from across the globe. Very little Spanish. The host led me through the kitchen to a back room, where a table for four had been set for one, the silverware like tiny sticks floating on a white-linen ocean.

My mind raced back to Le Grand Colbert, the most uncomfortable meal of my life. Here was the sequel.

I thought about how, in a better-scripted world, Sarah would be sitting here with me.

And then I laughed. Because of course life doesn't work out how you expect. Even funnier, though—and now the other tourists around me were staring at me, as I tried to stifle my snickering with my menu—was that I didn't care about the brush-off. Truly. What the hell was I thinking, trying to shoehorn a sappy ending into this Not-So-Grand Tour? I couldn't pretend that I'd had any profound, life-changing epiphanies these past few weeks, but if nothing else, I had learned to find amusement—even enjoyment— in those moments of being lost, both literally and figuratively. And the big reason I'd finally gotten to this point was that I had learned to fend for myself, both in awe of each new place and confident in my own ability to navigate it.

I'd noticed the confidence back in Vienna, but now there was something more, a jolting sense of ease with the world and, yeah, even myself. My posture had loosened. The thousand thoughts and anxieties clamoring for attention in my mind had not quite disappeared but had at least diminished from a fire hose of worry to a mere IV drip. The sense of always searching, without even knowing for what, had begun to vanish—not because I had any answers or had found anything but because I'd made my peace with confusion, with being a tourist in life.

My menu, I noted, was in Spanish. A quick glance around the room revealed that everyone else had an English version. At a tourist restaurant, they'd taken me for a local—funny, I thought, that at my moment of complete acceptance of my tourist status, I'd finally started to blend in.

And the food, my God, *the food*. A half carafe of sangria and *cuchinillo asado*, roast suckling pig—what Frommer ate, what Hemingway ate, what all the other happy eaters around me were eating. It felt like a dish of history, simple to prepare but rich in flavor—I could see why everyone came here, for this, and why they kept serving it just so, no fussy modern accompaniments or fusion remixes. I savored every bite.

On my way back to the hostel, I stopped at a quiet bar for a nightcap and to toast Frommer for our journey together. The bartender was scruffy but friendly, like Clint Eastwood trying to play a kindergarten teacher. He, too, greeted me as a local, in Spanish without a touch of wariness. But this soon became a problem, as it had throughout my time in Madrid. Because while my vocabulary is only middling, my accent is, apparently, pretty good. Everyone assumed I spoke fluently or was, in fact, a Spaniard—and then, once the conversation got going beyond the introductory salutations, they'd start talking at an astonishing rate, like an auctioneer on amphetamines, and my comprehension dropped to zero.

"*Lo siento, no comprendo,*" I said. I thought that the bartender had just said his name was José and then told his entire life story in ten seconds . . . but I wasn't quite sure.

Better to explain my status, I thought.

"*Yo soy un turista.*"

José laughed and slowed down, and the conversation kept going, our roles established, my admission the balm that put us both at ease.

So now I was done with *Europe on Five Dollars a Day*. For good. The next day, I bought a few *jamón ibérico* sandwiches at a shop I'd stumbled across in the preceding days—thank you again, Goddess Serendipity—and made my way to Parque del Buen Retiro, the city's sprawling, manicured central park, to soak up the lingering rays of Iberian sunshine before heading back to the frigid autumn in Minnesota.

In a week, I would be on a cruise ship with my parents, my sister, her husband, and their one-year-old twin boys—a family vacation with the express intent of exposing the next generation to travel at an early age. Compared to solo backpacking in Europe, a cruise with the family would be, you might say, a slightly different travel experience, and I was already starting to brace myself for the jarring transition. Between now and then, life would be a rush of unpacking and readjusting and then repacking—in a roller bag, not a backpack—and heading back out. (Also within a week, the 2016 Olympics would be awarded . . . to Rio de Janeiro.) This would be my only time to think.

If you read more than a handful of books and articles about tourism, especially those that take a critical angle, there's one quote you'll find over and over. It's this, from Daniel J. Boorstin's 1961 book *The Image*:

> *The traveler, then, was working at something; the tourist was a pleasure-seeker. The traveler was active; he went strenuously in search of people, of adventure, of experience. The tourist is passive; he expects interesting things to happen to him. He goes "sight-seeing."*

It's a common sentiment: proper travel is active, while shallow/inferior/clichéd travel is passive.

Now, I do think that passive travel has its place, that cruises and Walt Disney World and time-shares provide a much-needed escape for many overworked people who want to use their hard-earned two weeks of vacation time relaxing. All work and no play make Jack a dull traveler, and what's so wrong with that?

But what interested me more, as I sat on that bench watching the world—well, Madrid—pass by, was this: if you go by the active/passive definition, then the destination is irrelevant. If mindset is all that matters, you can go to Walt Disney World as a traveler and to the most remote parts of the globe as a tourist.

By that definition, what I had just done was to be a traveler on the beaten path. In every city, I had wandered until I got lost, and then I wandered some more. Once I overcame my early fears, I chatted with souvenir vendors and bartenders and others who saw the tourist experience from the other side. I was a tourist, no doubt, but active, always searching for what was beneath the surface. And I'll note again that I was hardly unique in this regard.

And that, I think, is the most important legacy of *Europe on Five Dollars a Day*: it's not about where you travel—on the beaten path, along a frontage road, or where no tourist has been before—but about what you make of it. Find your own way.

Arthur Frommer, after all, was the one who said to the masses, *You can do this.* You don't need a lot of instruction, really. Just get out there and make it up as you go along, guided not by rules or numbers but by an insatiable curiosity. No matter where you go or what your budget, you're bound to meet interesting people, learn about other cultures, see some cool things (and some not-so-cool things—but that's part of the experience), and come back alive and invigorated and slightly-but-in-a-good-way confused.

Tourism has always been, to some degree, an act of status, a statement that you have the time, money, and ability to go abroad. With the budget travel boom of the 1960s, though, it exploded and fragmented, open to more people and more ways of showing off, including not just conspicuous consumption but conspicuous frugality. Today, specific travel attitudes and methodologies are as carefully calibrated as attire worn on a first date.

Which is absurd. It's absurd when it means visiting only the most famous cities and landmarks, strictly hewing to the instructions of the latest Frommer's or Lonely Planet. It's equally absurd when it means *avoiding* cities or landmarks for the sole reason that they're popular. The net effect is the same, an attitude that views travel as a collection of merit badges to be earned, then flaunted: Saw This, Did That, Stayed at the Four Seasons, Slept in a Ditch. In some ways, both viewpoints are the legacy of Frommer and his generation of budget traveler, but each attitude completely misses Frommer's essential underlying point: what matters is not finding something your friends haven't found but appreciating and understanding that thing—that culture, that place, that food—on your own terms.

And though the task of finding the unexpected delights in Europe may have gotten more difficult since *Europe on Five Dollars a Day*, it's by no means impossible. You might need to put in some extra effort to find them, but therein lies the pleasure. There's still plenty of delight and wonder, both of the old-fashioned and the completely modern varieties, to be found.

Sometimes it is right there in front of you, in those tourist traps, the places that have stood the test of time, equally intriguing in Frommer's era and today. The Hofbräuhaus in Munich, Casa Botín in Madrid, landmarks like the Eiffel Tower or the Colosseum. These are places with stories and history—there's a reason they're iconic, there's a reason ancient Romans, seventeenth-century Grand Tourists, 1960s backpackers, and modern-day tourists all go there. They're part of the fabric of culture and spirit of place, and if you're paying attention, you can hear the echoes of history whispering, telling stories, tales that—as with *David* or the Anne Frank House for me—just might have their own unique resonance for you.

You'll find it, too, in the remixed culture—because, like the rest of the world, the beaten path is constantly evolving in interesting and unexpected ways. Of course it is. And to come here is to hear the discussions of how we live now and to see, firsthand, the modern world in the making, the past and the future manifest in the present.

One essential truth will never change: the tourist trail is the crossroads of the world, and not just for travelers. You meet people from the Official Local Culture but also immigrants who live there now and visitors from across the globe. You often can't tell who's who, at least not at first glance. In Brussels, you can eat *frites* and doner kebabs with EU officials, Malaysian tourists, and Algerian-immigrant locals (to be sure, this particular scene is possibly an idealistic pipe dream . . . but then, so are most of the touristic visions of Provence or India). It's a New Old World even more complex and wonderful than the long-gone version of collective memory . . . which never really existed at all.

I retired to the hostel bar for one last sangria while I checked my flight information online. I made the mistake of opening my email, where there was a message from my boss. There had been a semi-crisis in the office while I was away. I was supposed to be back at work in two days, on Thursday . . . but this couldn't wait. Could I meet with him on Wednesday?

I looked around the room at the happy travelers chatting and drinking. I glanced outside to the view of Madrid parading by.

Sure, I wrote. I can meet on Wednesday. *Fine, whatever.* A throb of corporate angst pulsed through my head; an unsteady weight settled into my gut. I stared at the screen for a long moment and remembered a quote from one of my mother's letters: "Do you understand that Minnesota . . . seems very insignificant?"

But it wasn't worth worrying about right now, I reminded myself. For the moment, I was still in Madrid, and the hum of friendly travelers beckoned. My gaze came to rest on a group at a nearby table. They smiled at me warmly.

I closed my laptop and tucked it in my bag, along with my dog-eared copy of *Europe on Five Dollars a Day*—I no longer needed it as an icebreaker. I ordered another sangria and went over to make some new friends.

FIVE LISTS FROM MY TRAVEL NOTEBOOKS

Five Things You *Can* Get for Five Dollars in Europe Today

1. A lollipop in the shape of the Eiffel Tower
2. A pregnancy test from a vending machine at the Oktoberfest grounds in Munich
3. A ticket in the nosebleed section at a *novillada con picadores* bullfight in Madrid
4. A medium-sized gelato in Rome
5. Two East Berlin stamps in your passport from a vendor at Checkpoint Charlie

Four Expressions I Really Wish Had Been in My Phrasebook

1. *Nee, dank je, ik ben niet op de markt voor verdovende middelen.* (Dutch: "No, thanks, I'm not in the market for any narcotics.")

2. *Mi scusi, ma non ricordo in che lingua parli qui a Bruxelles—è questo quello giusto?* (Italian: "Excuse me, but I can't recall what language you speak here in Brussels—is this the right one?")

3. *Je meurs d'envie de privation pain au chocolat. S'il vous plaît aider!* (French: "I'm dying of chocolate croissant deprivation. Please help!")

4. *Was ist das eindringliches Mahnmal Übernahme durch die hässliche Plakatwand?* (German: "What is that haunting memorial over by that ugly billboard?")

Five Things I Ate in Berlin While Attempting to Avoid German Food

1. Sushi
2. Tacos
3. Currywurst
4. Large quantities of pastries
5. Doner kebabs

The Five Stages of Learning to Cross the Street in Rome

1. *Virgin:* Stare slack-jawed at the automotive mayhem, then decide to take a different route or maybe, you know, just stay on this block.

2. *Amateur:* Wait for a group of Italians—nuns, preferably—to cross, then let them block for you . . . until one Vespa driver singles you out for Tourist Bowling.

3. *Intermediate:* Wait to cross when there's a gap and then feel smug about how you crossed alone, confidently, suavely, just like an Italian. Do not mention to your friends that it was 3 a.m. and said gap was roughly the size of the Colosseum.

4. *Advanced:* Have faith. Stride confidently into traffic, trusting that the cars will buzz around you and giving a small prayer to the patron saint of pedestrians. (Is there one? There should be. Let's call him Mort.)

5. *Black belt:* Same as above, but with *you* blocking for Italians/nuns. I'm proud to say I reached this level my final morning, on my way to the train station.

Five Unexpected Gift-Shop Finds

1. Condoms at the Eiffel Tower

2. Expedition-weight parkas at the Heineken Experience in Amsterdam

3. Clog-shaped plush slippers at any given souvenir stand on Damrak in Amsterdam

4. Reproduction of a letter from Galileo at the Vatican Secret Archives shop

5. Chocolates in the shape of *Manneken-Pis* throughout Brussels

FURTHER READING

In addition to following the path of Arthur Frommer and my mother, I've relied on a number of other travelers, writers, and scholars to tell the story of European tourism in the last generation. I've mentioned these works—including books, newspaper and magazine articles, and government documents (useful but decidedly less enthralling than the other research materials)—throughout the text, but a few merit special mention.

For a big-picture view of American tourism in the mid-twentieth century, I highly recommended Christopher Endy's *Cold War Holidays: American Tourism in France*, which focuses on de Gaulle–era France but touches on many broader themes relating to the Grand Tour experience in that period. Maxine Feifer's *Tourism in History: From Imperial Rome to the Present* was also a key resource, outlining the cultural basis for and implications of mass tourism in different places and eras. And Dean MacCannell's book *The Tourist: A New Theory of the Leisure Class* is simply the seminal work on the sociology of travel and tourism, thought-provoking but with a light, engaging touch. Pico Iyer is my go-to guide on the topic of travel in our era of hyperconnectivity and globalization—see, in particular, his books *The Global Soul* and *Video Night in Kathmandu*.

Among the many volumes that examine the evolution of European culture in the twentieth century—including the role of tourists in shaping that culture—two particularly lively and insightful books are *In Europe: Travels Through the Twentieth Century* by Geert Mak and *Not Like Us: How Europeans Have Loved, Hated, and Transformed American Culture Since World War II* by Richard Pells.

Looking a bit further back in time, *The Grand Tour* by Tim Moore and *Route 66 A.D.* by Tony Perrottet trace the routes of long-forgotten European travelers; in their comparisons between those earlier eras and our own, these books also helped guide my own approach.

And there were the vintage guidebooks, of course—*Europe on Five Dollars a Day* plus assorted other guides by Arthur Frommer, Temple Fielding, Eugene Fodor, and their contemporaries. If you want to learn more about tourism and broader culture in an earlier era, start there, with the guidebooks. Find a copy and open it up at random. Enjoy.

ABOUT THE AUTHOR

Doug Mack has written for the *Minneapolis Star Tribune*, *San Francisco Chronicle*, WorldHum.com, and other publications. He is based in Minneapolis with a digital home at www.douglasmack.net.